Social Nature

KU-176-245

SY

University of Liverpool

Social Nature

Theory, Practice, and Politics

Edited by

Noel Castree

University of Manchester

and

Bruce Braun

University of Minnesota

Copyright © Blackwell Publishers Ltd 2001
Editorial matter and arrangement copyright © Noel Castree and Bruce Braun 2001

First published 2001

2 4 6 8 10 9 7 5 3 1

Blackwell Publishers Inc.
350 Main Street
Malden, Massachusetts 02148
USA

Blackwell Publishers Ltd
108 Cowley Road
Oxford OX4 1JF
UK

British Library Cataloguing in Publication Data
A CIP catalogue record for this book is available from the British Library.

Library of Congress Cataloging-in-Publication Data
Social nature : theory, practice, and politics / edited by Noel Castree and Bruce Braun.
    p. cm.
    Includes bibliographical references and index.
    ISBN 0-631-21567-0 (hbk : acid-free paper)—ISBN 0-631-21568-9 (pbk : acid-free paper)
    1. Culture. 2. Social sciences—Philosophy. 3. Social choice. I. Castree, Noel, 1968–
II. Braun, Bruce, 1964–

HM621.S63 2001
306—dc21

2001025970

Typeset in 10.5 on 12pt Garamond
by SetSystems Ltd, Saffron Walden, Essex
Printed in Great Britain by TJ International Ltd, Padstow, Cornwall

This book is printed on acid-free paper.

Contents

List of Figures

List of Contributors

Kay Anderson is Professor of Geography at Durham University. She is a cultural geographer with long-standing interests in the issue of 'race' in Western societies, a theme she has recently been exploring through the lens of culture/nature/colonialism.

Piers Blaikie is a Professor in the School of Development Studies at the University of East Anglia. He is well known for his pioneering work as a political ecologist and is an expert on environmental policy in the developing world.

Bruce Braun is Assistant Professor of Geography at the University of Minnesota. He has published articles on cultural politics; environmentalism and colonialism; and science, culture, and power. He is the co-editor with Noel Castree of *Remaking Reality: Nature at the Millennium* and author of *The Intemperate Rainforest: Nature, Culture and Power on Canada's West Coast*.

Raymond Bryant has taught Geography at King's College London since 1993. He is the author of *The Political Ecology of Forestry in Burma, 1824–1994* (1997) and co-author of *Third World Political Ecology* (1997), as well as many articles and chapters on political ecology and environmental struggles in south-east Asia. He is presently completing a book on the empowerment of environmental NGOs in the Philippines.

Noel Castree is a Reader in Human Geography at the University of Manchester. He has published numerous articles about Marxist perspectives on nature–society relations. His current research critically examines the privatization of genes through 'life patents' and other mechanisms. He is co-editor with Bruce Braun of *Remaking Reality: Nature at the Millennium*.

David Demeritt is a Lecturer in Geography at King's College, London. His published work has focused on the politics of science and, more generally, the social construction of nature.

Derek Gregory is Professor of Geography at the University of British Columbia. He is author of *Geographical Imaginations* and co-editor of *The Dictionary of Human Geography*. In two forthcoming books he explores the intersections between colonialism, productions of space, and productions of nature. In *The Colonial Present* (Blackwell) he pays particular attention to Orientalism and the cultural politics of nature, and in *Dancing on the Pyramids* he examines the ways in which European and American travelers through nineteenth-century Egypt sought to come to terms with other "cultures" and other "natures."

Tom MacMillan is a geographer at the University of Manchester with interests in business–science–state relations as seen from a post-Marxist perspective. He is currently researching the regulation of rBST, a commercially manufactured growth hormone used in dairy farming, in the USA.

Jane Moeckli is currently completing doctoral studies at the University of Iowa. Her interests are in how "race," gender, class, and "nature" are remade in and through the international cosmetics industry.

Mark Pelling is a Lecturer in Geography at the University of Liverpool. He previously taught at the University of Guyana. His research interests include natural hazards, community development, and urbanization. He is currently writing a book entitled *Urbanization and Disaster*.

James D. Proctor is Associate Professor in the Department of Geography at the University of California, Santa Barbara. Co-editor of *Geography and Ethics: Journeys in a Moral Terrain* (1999), he is interested in the ethical and epistemological dimensions of environmental conflicts.

Joel Wainwright is in the department of Geography and the MacArthur Program for Studies of Social Change at the University of Minnesota.

Preface

Not so long ago, the idea that nature is social seemed contradictory, even perverse. In Anglophone geography, as in much of the wider world, the assumption was that the natural and the social were two different domains, related but distinct. Indeed, institutionalized as it was in the division between 'human' and 'physical' geography, the nature–society dichotomy was so funda- mental as to be disciplinary common sense. Who, then, would have thought that in a few short years the claim that "nature is nothing if it is not social" (Smith, 1984: 30) would not only become de rigeur, but even "passé, and . . . anything but shocking" for many geographers (Smith, 1998, p. 273)? Hardly anyone, to be sure. But this is precisely what has happened since Margaret Fitzsimmons (1989, p. 106) lamented the "peculiar silence on the question of . . . nature" within much of the human geographic community. In a little over a decade, there's been a veritable explosion of geographical research that seeks to denaturalize nature and thereby "challenge . . . the categorical cordon that has marked off the 'non-human world' and the grounds for understanding it" (Whatmore, 1999: 23). Though it has not been well received in all corners of the discipline (and largely ignored by physical geographers), this new work on 'social nature' has been sufficiently voluminous and incisive to call into question received ways of thinking about, and doing research on, everything from national parks to global warming to the 'nature' of sexuality and 'race.' Among other things, it's allowed geographers to move away from asking worthy, if limited, questions about what society 'does' to nature (and vice versa), towards more fundamental questions such as 'who constructs what kinds of nature(s) to what ends and with what social and ecological effects?'

Nonetheless, if, as Smith avers, the idea that nature is social is now axiomatic for many geographers, why further contribute to deforestation by publishing a book on the topic? It's a good question. Our answer is threefold. Firstly, there is currently no single volume that seeks to summarize, and critically review, the diverse geographical research on social nature. In saying this, we're not trying to imply that work on social nature is the preserve of geographers. One can look to insightful texts on the topic penned by anthropologists, cultural analysts, ethnographers of science, philosophers, and sociologists as part of what is now a genuinely interdisciplinary concern with how societies recraft the natural. Three good examples are Cronon's (1996) *Uncommon Ground*, Macnaghten and Urry's (1998) *Contested Natures*, and Soper's (1995) *What Is Nature?*, all of which resonate with the ideas and arguments presented in this volume. However, it remains the case that there is currently no one book that attempts to draw together over a decade of new geographical thinking on the society–nature nexus. Secondly, geography teachers offering upper-level undergraduate and postgraduate courses on the social redefinition and remaking of nature currently have to refer students to a disparate array of journal articles and books. In itself, this is no bad thing of course. But it seems to us that many of these papers, collections, and monographs are, for the most part, not written with teachers and students in mind. Finally, while the idea that nature is social is now 'anything but shocking' for those who teach courses on the topic, many geography students still, understandably, find it a genuinely arresting and counter-intuitive notion. We therefore wanted to produce a volume that would make some of the theoretical, empirical, and political insights emerging out of the research literature on social nature accessible and engaging.

For these three reasons, *Social Nature* is intended to serve as a key text for geography undergraduates, postgraduates, and teachers taking/offering university-level courses on the social constitution of nature and environment. That said, this is not a textbook. It is both less and more than that. On the one hand, because it's an edited collection, *Social Nature* necessarily lacks the narrative coherence of a single- or co-authored introductory text. On the other hand, though, *Social Nature* endeavors not merely to summarize new ideas about the society–nature nexus, but to critically evaluate them. It's therefore intended as an intervention into, as much as a representation of, ongoing debates over nature's social fabrication. This is true at two levels. First, this volume's title speaks to a desire to critique certain uses of the term 'the social construction of nature.' This term is both loaded and ambiguous. In Castree's introduction and the chapter by David Demeritt in particular, it is argued that work on social nature should not be conflated with, or reduced to, some of the more outlandish constructionist claims to emerge over the last decade. Questions concerning how far, and in what ways, nature is 'social' demand complex, plural answers not formulaic, one-dimensional responses. Second, in each chapter our contributors argue a case rather than offering a dry, agnostic recitation of specific work on nature's social character. Consequently, we hope that readers will find *Social Nature* to be a book that stimulates and provokes as much as it informs and educates.

Though many of our readers will be geographers, we also hope that students and teachers in related subject areas – like environmental anthropology and environmental sociology – might find *Social Nature* a useful resource. This is not a narrowly 'disciplinary' book, even though it's contributors are all professional geographers. The ideas and arguments presented here transgress subject boundaries, and each chapter draws upon research and thinking generated as much outside geography as within it. As editors, we've sought to bring together a mixture of new and established researchers in order to give a comprehensive – though not exhaustive – coverage of geographical and cognate work on nature's socialization. Each contributor was asked to write about their own topic area with a view to engaging, informing, and challenging readers. The result, we hope, is a collection of lively essays that students and teachers can turn to as incisive introductions to the central concepts, findings, and normative implications of geographical research on social nature.

This last comment bring us to the book's subtitle. In planning and editing this volume, we had three particular goals in mind. First, it seemed to us important to make accessible for our intended readership some of the key – and often competing – theoretical positions on the social constitution of nature. Though still considered an essentially empirical discipline by many nongeographers, recent work on social nature has given the lie to this idea about geography, for it's proven especially fertile in the theoretical sense. At its best, this work has developed and deployed theory to make the familiar seem genuinely strange, thereby calling into question conventional ideas and practices regarding what's taken to be 'natural.' Secondly, however, theory can seem abstract and ethereal when divorced from the complexities of everyday life – especially to those geography students who may be unaccustomed to thinking theoretically. The chapters in *Social Nature* therefore attempt to show readers how theory can explain, in practice, the ways nature is (re)constituted and with what social and ecological outcomes. Finally, it seems to us that the implications of recent and current geographical research on social nature are intensely worldly and political. As those who teach courses on the social construction of nature know, the bulk of the geographical research in this area is associated with so-called 'critical geographers.' In order that the normative force of this research is not diluted for student readers of this book, we asked the contributors to make explicit how seeing nature as social alters conventional understandings of what a 'politics of nature' is all about. In the final chapter of the book this becomes the focus of attention in its own right, but the other chapters, we hope, convey to student readers the sense that geographical knowledge about nature is ineluctably value-laden. At its best, the argument that nature is intrinsically social should encourage us to ask of our world: who is currently empowered to define what counts as 'nature' – discursively and materially – and what implications do accepted or hegemonic definitions have? In turn, asking such a pointed question leads to another: namely, what counterhegemonic definitions are currently available to us (in geography and beyond) and what kind of a world – socially, economically, politically, and culturally – do they allow us to envisage? This question is saturated with political promise. As each of the contributors shows, 'de-naturalizing nature' allows us to glimpse not just a different ecological future but a future where class, gender, 'race,' and interplace relations might be configured along more just and equitable lines.

Bruce Braun and Noel Castree

References

Cronon, W. (ed.) (1996). *Uncommon Ground.* New York: W. W. Norton.

Fitzsimmons, M. (1989). The Matter of Nature. *Antipode* 21: 106–20.

Macnaghten, P. and Urry, J. (1998). *Contested Natures.* London: Sage.

Smith, N. (1984). *Uneven Development.* Oxford: Blackwell.

Smith, N. (1998). Nature at the Millennium. In B. Braun and N. Castree (eds.) *Remaking Reality.* London: Routledge, 271–85.

Soper, K. (1995). *What Is Nature?* Oxford: Blackwell.

Whatmore, S. (1999). Hybrid Geographies. In D. Massey et al. (eds.), *Human Geography Today.* Cambridge: Polity, 22–40.

Acknowledgments

We'd like to thank Jill Landeryou, formerly of Blackwell, for commissioning *Social Nature*, and Sarah Falkus for seeing it through to completion. Katherine Warren has been very helpful along the way, while Cameron Laux did some sterling editing. Finally, as with any edited book, many thanks go to the contributors for writing their chapters more or less on time (!) and for being receptive to editorial suggestions.

Noel Castree and Bruce Braun

Chapter 1

Socializing Nature:
Theory, Practice, and Politics

Noel Castree

For over a century, geographers have sought to describe and explain the society–nature interface. When, James Bryce (1886, p. 426) – one of geography's early advocates – characterized the discipline as "a meeting point between the sciences of Nature and the sciences of Man [*sic*]" he sought to create a distinctive place for it within the academic division of labor. As we enter the twenty-first century, geography remains one of the few subjects dedicated to exploring the relations between humanity and nature. To be sure, the geographical project extends beyond the study of these relations. But many geographers remain convinced that the society–nature nexus should be a central disciplinary preoccupation. It's easy to understand why. The world has changed enormously since Bryce penned his words in the genteel surroundings of Victorian Oxford, where he was a university professor. In the twenty-first century, society–nature relations seem to be marked by a new breadth, depth, and consequentiality. By breadth, I simply mean that few areas and aspects of nature today remain untouched by human hands; by depth, I mean that many society–nature relations extend 'all the way down,' even to the level of genetic modification; and by consequentiality, I mean that what happens to nature today may be of world-changing importance, both for ourselves and other species. In short, Bryce could scarcely have anticipated a future in which mass deforestation, global warming, the collapse of commercial fisheries, chronic species extinction, transgenic organisms, a growing ozone 'hole,' and desertification would be just a few of the problems arising from human transformations of nature. And he could hardly have imagined that such problems would spawn a global environmental movement, or that governments worldwide would put the question of nature near the top of their political agendas.

So where does contemporary geography figure in this maelstrom of socio-natural change? Like most other academics, geographers respond to forces external to their discipline, in terms of what they study, how they study it, and the use to which the resulting knowledge is put. Arguably, there are three broad approaches to the society–nature problematic that are current in the discipline, one mainstream, two more radical. This book is the first devoted to presenting and evaluating the third, and most recent, of these approaches: namely the 'social' approach. This new perspective, as I hope to show in the pages that follow, is both innovative and exciting. In reality, it's less a unified worldview than a plurality of related positions and arguments. Before outlining these arguments, though, we need to relate the social view of nature to the other two approaches to society–nature relations current in geography: for it poses a provocative challenge to both of them.

The 'Nature' of Contemporary Geography: Three Approaches

The first, and arguably dominant, approach is a revivified 'people and environment' perspective. For many geographers, the early twenty-first century represents a timely opportunity to 'reclaim the high ground': that is, to refocus disciplinary research and teaching on the 'big' questions of our era concerning the problems and possibilities resulting from the human alteration of natural resources, environments, and organisms. I say refocus, because for commentators like David Stoddart (1986) geography has in recent decades become a divided discipline, with human and physical geographers drifting further apart as they pursue their own specialist interests. This is why he and others (e.g. Cooke, 1992), echoing Bryce's original prospectus for geography, argue for greater disciplinary coherence founded on the study of contemporary society–environment relations.

This injunction to 'unify' a currently schizoid geography is, at first sight, appealing. It promises to renew the discipline's distinctiveness as a 'bridge' between the social sciences, humanities, and natural sciences. As importantly, it also promises to make geography intensely relevant to some of the most pressing and profound issues of our age. Consequently, we are now seeing many geography departments refocus their research and teaching so as to ride the wave of contemporary concern about nature. For example, the University of Oxford – where Halford Mackinder, supported by Bryce, established one of Britain's first geography degrees in the 1880s – now has a high-profile Environmental Change Unit affiliated to the School of Geography. Meanwhile, across the Atlantic, the USA has in recent years instituted a major Global Change Program which, under the auspices of the National Oceanic and Atmospheric Administration, funds environmental research by geographers and fellow-travelers.[1]

However, while many geographers agree that this is a vital time for the discipline to anatomize the society–nature problematic, not all them concur with the Stoddartian vision of how such anatomization should proceed. This brings us to the two other approaches to society–nature now advocated in geography: the 'ecocentric' and 'social' approaches. Both are relatively new to the discipline, and both are associated with so-called 'critical geographers.' I'll explain the differences between them momentarily, but first it's useful to explain what they have in common. For critical geographers of an ecocentric and social persuasion, Stoddart's brand of 'human–environment relations' geography – far from being objective and neutral – is intellectually limited and politically biased. It's intellectually limited, the argument goes, because it equates nature with 'environmental problems', so ignoring other important human–environment relations (like commercial agriculture or forestry) and non-environmental natures (like the human body). And it's politically biased, so several critical geographers claim, because the knowledge it produces tends to be 'technocratic.' Articulated in the subdisciplines of 'resource-' and 'environmental management' and claiming the mantle of 'science,' what makes this knowledge technocratic is that it rarely discusses the fundamental socioeconomic processes transforming twenty-first century nature. Instead, it is knowledge that leads to policy geared to ameliorating environmental problems without ever addressing the deeper causes responsible for those problems in the first place. It is, in other words, knowledge by and for those with a vested interest in not having to pay the price for eradicating environmental problems altogether. For several critical geographers, the most prominent example of this kind of knowledge is that articulated in the concept of 'sustainable development,' an appealing but ultimately amorphous idea that can easily serve as a rhetorical cover for business-as-usual (see Redclift, 1996).

In light of this, a fast-growing cohort of human geographers have argued for approaches to the society–nature interface that are broader and deeper than that offered by the 'people and environment' tradition. The 'ecocentric' or nature-first approach urges a fundamental respect for, and need to get back to, nature. This is to be achieved through a profound critique and dismantling of existing systems of production and consumption. This way of thinking has grown out of the now popular 'green movement,' whose influence in many Western and several non-Western nation-states has grown enormously since the early 1970s. It's a way of thinking that can be contrasted with the third approach to society–nature relations currently extant in geography, the one that is the subject of this book. This approach – which is increasingly popular and influential among critical human geographers – sees nature as *inescapably social*. Here the argument is that nature is defined, delimited, and even physically reconstituted by different societies, often in order to serve specific, and usually dominant, social interests. In other words, the social and the natural are seen to intertwine in ways that make their separation – in either thought or practice – impossible.

Their differences notwithstanding, the ecocentric and social approaches regard the 'people and environment' style of geography as a hindrance to adequately understanding and altering society–nature relations. For ecocentrists, the technocratic knowledge it produces is unable to treat nature as anything other than a 'resource' to be used, destroyed, or regulated for mainly human benefit. For advocates of a social approach to understanding the natural, the technocratic mentality wrongly assumes that it's possible know nature 'as it really is,' such that when people physically interact with nature they are dealing with things that are, *inter alia*, nonsocial.[2] If, together, the ecocentric and social approaches dissent from conventional geographical understandings of society–nature relations, they are also radical in their political commitments. This radicalism has two connected moments: critical diagnosis and normative prognosis. The former entails a deep analysis of conventional understandings of, and interactions with, nature, with a view to eradicating relations of power and domination. The latter entails envisaging a future world in which principles of social and ecological justice organize the society–nature nexus at both the local and global levels. In short, from the ecocentric and social perspectives, taken-for-granted conceptions of nature among geographers and actors in the wider world – policy-makers, businesses, and ordinary people – are seen as part of the problem, not the solution, if societies are to build survivable futures.

Geography has always been a contested enterprise: it has no 'essence.' The discipline, like all others, has constantly changed its spots in response to external pressures and internal debates. Rather than asking what the true 'nature' of geography is, we therefore need to ask: 'who defines geography for what purposes and in whose interests?' This, in effect, is the provocative question that the ecocentric and social approaches ask about the way society–nature relations are currently understood and organized. These approaches should therefore be understood as part of the ongoing struggle to define what the geographical project is – and should be – about in the new millennium.

Despite the elective affinity between the ecocentric and social perspectives on nature, this book, as mentioned earlier, focuses exclusively on the latter. There are several good reasons why. Firstly, there are now several excellent introductions to ecocentric thinking.[3] Secondly, despite the recent explosion of geographical research on 'social nature,' there is currently no one text that describes, explains, and evaluates this work for the benefit of university students (undergraduate and postgraduate) and their teachers. For many geographers, the idea that nature is social still seems odd, even absurd. This is why *Social Nature* gathers together an international group of experts on the topic to explain both how nature is socialized and why it matters – theoretically, practically, and politically. Finally, there's a more substantive and pointed reason why this book examines the social, rather than ecocentric, approach as an alternative to conventional understandings of nature in geography and beyond. For, from the social perspective, ecocentrism has a crucial and problematic similarity to the technocratic approach it otherwise opposes: that is, it posits a foundational *distinction* between the social and the natural and assumes that the latter is, at some level, *fixed and/or universal*. Thus, where ecocentrists urge us to 'save,' 'live in harmony with,' or even 'get back to' nature, technocratic geographers propose to 'manage,' 'control,' or 'dominate' nature as if were a domain different to, and separate from, society. Deeply ingrained in Western thought since the Enlightenment, the society–nature dichotomy and the assumption that natural entities are unalterable 'givens' remain 'common sense' – even at a time when developments like gene-splicing have challenged them in dramatic new ways.

In light of this, *Social Nature* takes two things to be axiomatic. The first is that nature has never been simply 'natural' – whether it's 'wilderness,' resources, 'natural hazards,' or even the human body. Rather, it is *intrinsically* social, in different ways, at different levels, and with a multitude of serious implications. Second, the all-too-common habit of talking of nature 'in itself,' as a domain which is by definition nonsocial and unchanging, can lead not only to confusion but also the perpetuation of power and inequality in the wider world. From this perspective, then, geographers adopting *both* a 'people and environ-ment' and an ecocentric approach misleadingly abstract nature from its inextri-cable social integument.

Without pre-empting too much the essays that follow, I want, in the remainder of this chapter, to outline the different ways that critical geographers currently regard nature as a social artefact. My starting-point is to ask: what is nature? So far, I've used this term as if it were clear-cut and unproblematic. However, as we'll see below, my seemingly simple question demands a complex answer. It's an answer, moreover, that reveals how conventional, but very specific, understandings of the natural have functioned in geography – and indeed society at large – to discipline both people and other species.

The Nature of Nature

Nature is both a concept and all those physical things to which the concept refers. It's a complex concept, not just because it refers to many different entities – from the weather through animals to human 'nature' and beyond – but because it also has multiple meanings. As the philosopher Kate Soper puts in her book *What Is Nature?*, the concept "is at once . . . very familiar and extremely elusive" (1995, p. 1). It is, moreover, a promiscuous concept, in the sense that it is used daily in a multitude of situations by a diverse array of individuals, groups, and organizations. Geographers are only one of several constituencies who routinely invoke the idea of nature in what they do. Others include 'natural scientists', governments (who have the legal power to control and regulate society–nature interactions at home and abroad), businesses (who may, for example, pollute nature or exploit natural resources), the media (who report stories about such things as environmental problems or new developments like animal cloning), and the public (think about how often people say things like 'he's naturally intelligent' or 'her illness is genetically inherited'). In this sense, since the founding of geography as an academic discipline, it has both been influenced by, and influenced, wider societal conceptions of nature in Western countries. Despite its complexity, elusiveness, and promiscuity, the idea of nature can arguably be resolved into three chief definitions. Let's take each in turn.

1 External nature

The familiar distinction between society and nature indicates a long-standing assumption that nature is external to, and different from, society. Indeed, this assumption seems to be indisputable 'common-sense.' As geographer Neil Smith (1984, p. 2) puts it, "external nature is pristine, God-given, autonomous; it is the raw material from which society is built." Here, then, nature is seen as that which is inherently nonsocial and nonhuman, as captured in the term 'the environment.' This ontological separation of the natural and the social has, since at least the European Enlightenment, been associated with other dualisms organizing our thought, such as rural–urban, country–city, and wilderness–civilization. In geography, it's a separation that has organized teaching and research since Bryce, Mackinder, and others first sought to define the discipline. In the early part of the twentieth century, geographers were especially interested in how the environment determines the shape of human societies and cultures (see, for example, Huntingdon, 1925). By mid-century, they eschewed this simplistic 'environmental determinism' and looked at how an increasingly industrialized West was impacting upon local and international resources (Thomas, 1956). Indeed, the postwar division between human and physical geography led geographers to specialize on one or other 'side' of an increasingly asymmetrical society–nature relation. Today, as noted above, a renewed humans-and-environment form of geography has sought to focus center-stage on how societies worldwide are decisively and destructively altering nature. Yet for all the differences between the environmental determinism of a century ago and contemporary research into 'human impacts on the environment,' both share a common assumption that society and nature are related but ultimately distinct. Interestingly, although ecocentrists are critical of the mainstream 'human-impact' type of geography currently advocated by Stoddart and others, many of them also posit a society–nature separation themselves. For the ecocentric lament that societies are 'destroying' a 'first nature' that needs to be protected in 'biosphere reserves,' 'habitat areas,' and 'wilderness zones,' trades on the distinction between a predatory humanity and a fast-disappearing nonhuman world (see, for example, McKibben, 1989).

2 Intrinsic nature

A second, and related, concept is that of nature as "an inherent and essential quality" of something (Williams, 1980, p. 68). Here nature is seen as (i) fixed and unchanging and (ii) defined by one or other 'essential' quality or attribute. In geography, as in Western society at large, this idea of intrinsic nature has a long history, and has been applied both to 'external nature' and to 'human nature.' Here, then, nature equates with more than simply 'the environment.' Consider, for example, the words of environmental determinist Ellen Semple, writing back in 1911: "The northern peoples of Europe are energetic, provident, serious, thoughtful ... [whereas] the negroes of the equatorial belt degenerate into grave racial faults" (1911, p. 620). Though such racist ideas would not be countenanced today, ideas of nature as a fixed domain definable by one or other key attribute lives on into the present. For instance, pessimists among the 'humans and environment' tradition of geography take the Malthusian line that natural resources are fixed in quantity, such that sooner or later population levels will outstrip them with disastrous consequences (see Lowe and Bowlby, 1996). Similarly, there's still a good deal of research on hazards – like floods and earthquakes – that sees them as, essentially, 'natural events' governed by physical laws and processes (see Blaikie et al., 1994, for a critique). Again, ecocentrists too draw upon a repertoire of ideas about nature as an unmalleable, intransigent entity. For instance, for many geographers interested in animals and animal rights, a key part of their argument is that practices like hunting and vivisection are cruel insofar as they inevitably lead to physical pain and even death (for a review of work on 'animal geographies' see Wolch and Emel, 1998).

3 Universal nature

Thirdly, and finally, in contradiction to the idea of an external nature, nature is frequently seen as a universal dimension. This has two aspects. One is to see natural characteristics as general rather than particular. For instance, a hydrologist studying how pesticides leak from fields of a certain soil type into rivers might use a general theory of soil water movement. The assumption, here, is that *all* fields with this soil type – regardless of location – behave in similar ways *vis-à-vis* water percolation. Secondly, nature is sometimes seen as universal in the sense of encompassing everything there is – humans included insofar as they too, being biological entities, are part of a wider, global, ecological system. This second idea of a universal nature finds its most common expression in so-called 'Gaianist' versions of ecocentrism, where modern, industrialized societies are seen to have disturbed the 'natural order.' In the view of James Lovelock

(1995) – who has famously popularized this type of ecocentrism (Gaia means 'Earth goddess') – humanity must be seen as part of a holistic, living, integrated earth, one that will exact 'revenge' if humans (especially in the hyperindustrialized West) continue to disrupt the ecosphere.

At once overlapping and different, these three definitions of nature have been – and continue to be – commonplace in both geography and the wider world. Most readers of this book will, I suspect, be very familiar with them – either explicitly or implicitly. Before going on to show why, according to certain critical geographers, "the one thing that is not 'natural' is nature . . . [it]self" (Soper, 1995: p. 7), it's worth pausing to consider what the three definitions mentioned have in common and what their strengths and weaknesses are.

In terms of commonalities, several things stand out. The first is the belief that nature can be known 'in itself.' In all three definitions, there's a presumption that the 'facts' of nature 'speak for themselves' once geographers have adopted the 'correct' perspective. For mainstream 'human impact' researchers, the 'scientific' methods of physical geography are routinely invoked to yield singular 'truths' about how natural systems operate. In the ecocentric case, things are slightly more complex. In some instances, ecocentrists embrace field science in order to point-up facts about fast-disappearing environments. In others, nonscientific assertions are made about how societies, especially Western societies, are 'disrupting,' 'dominating,' or even 'violating' the inherent 'balance' of nature. In both instances, though, relatively unproblematized truth-claims are made about how nature 'really works.' Secondly, the three definitions of nature outlined above imply that it offers societies a set of possibilities and constraints that are more-or-less *unchangeable*. Aside from neo-Malthusian 'limits to growth' arguments, often used to justify population control, this idea of an intransigent nature frequently crops up in mainstream resource management, where restrictions on human activities are legitimated in terms of the need to conserve finite (nonrenewable) species or resources. Similarly, although ecocentrists dissent from the instrumental rationality of technocratic approaches to nature, they too often invoke the language of an unmalleable nature. In the 'deep ecology' of Arne Naess (1989), for example, a call is made to do away with all the paraphernalia of modern industrialism in order to 'be at one' (practically and spiritually) with a rapidly-vanishing 'first nature' before it's too late.

Finally, according to the three conventional definitions of nature commonly adhered to in geography and Western societies more generally, it is often invoked to ground value judgments about what is deemed 'good' and 'bad'/ 'normal' and 'abnormal'/'better' or 'worse' – either socially or ecologically. Examples of this abound in both the ecocentric and people-and-environment traditions. For instance, in the former case, the preservation of natural environments is usually taken to be inherently and self-evidently valuable. In the latter case, we can cite everything from Semple's egregious argument that 'difficult' environments produce 'inferior races' to the more subtle value claims built into modern physical geography research. Take the case of research into global warming, for instance, where it's sometimes simply *assumed* that such warming is intrinsically negative because it destroys the atmosphere's 'natural balance'.

The benefits of continued adherence to these deeply-ingrained ways of talking about nature are plain to see. In geography and beyond, whether one's perspective is technocratic or green, it's possible to (i) identify supposedly objective facts about nature and environment, leading to (ii) explanations of how far and in what ways societies are affecting, or being affected by them, in turn generating (iii) an evaluation of society–nature relations on scientific or moral grounds, leading to policy formulations or some shift in society–nature relations at one or more spatial scales. However, there are a number of potentially profound disadvantages with seeing nature as an external, intrinsic and/or universal domain whose 'essential' character can be objectively studied in order to ground value judgments. Three loom large.

Firstly, the 'facts' of nature never simply speak for themselves. In reality, what counts as the truth about nature *varies* depending on the perspective of the analyst. In other words, however rigorous and scientific one's investigations of the natural might be, there is no easy way to separate objective observations from social biases and political interests. As Raymond Williams (1980, p. 70) famously put it, "What is usually apparent [when reference is made to nature] is that it is selective, according to the speaker's general purpose." Secondly, it follows that statements about nature say as much about who is doing the talking, and what their individual group interests are, as they say about nature *tout court*. Thirdly, it's often the case that claims about nature – and actions based upon those claims – can serve as instruments of power and domination. Consider, for example, the wildlife conservation movement in the developing world, which has both an ecocentric and technocratic wing. For over a century, in countries like Kenya, indigenous peoples have been forcibly removed from, or denied access to, traditional territories because conservationists have argued that segregated 'wildlife parks' are required for species protection.

If we summarize these three problems, we might say that in each case the social dimensions of nature are ignored, denied, or effaced. But what does it mean to say that nature – which we typically define as nonsocial – is, in fact, social through and through? And what implications – for geographers and all those concerned about society–nature relations more generally – does it have for established ways of thinking about, and acting toward, resources, species, ecologies, and bodies?

Social Nature

As noted earlier, it's only in the last few years that geographers' understandings of how nature is socialized have deepened and expanded. As also noted, this outpouring of new work on social nature is associated with critical human geographers – and, as the chapters of this book testify, particularly those of a Marxist, post-Marxist, feminist, antiracist, poststructuralist, anticolonial, and actor-network persuasion. This association with critical thinking can, in fact, be traced back some three decades. For the counterintuitive idea of 'social nature' is not all new to geography – it originated with the first critical geographers like David Harvey (1974), writing in the context of public and governmental concern about global 'overpopulation' and resource scarcity during the mid-1970s. What is new, though, is the volume, diversity, and incisiveness of the recent work on social nature. In short, this work is now at the point where it can be described as distinct and influential approach to understanding nature and environment. Though it's not at all a unified approach – instead, it consists of multiple theoretical, thematic, and political strands – geographical research conducted under the social nature banner does share a set of important characteristics. These pivot on the claim that ideas of nature as either external, intrinsic, or universal are themselves social constructions, specific to Western social formations. To grasp nature's social character, we must therefore not only critique these ideas, but also find a way to see how, in both thought and practice, the natural and the social melt into one another. Simplifying deliberately, critical geographers have insisted that nature is social in three related ways:

1 Knowing nature

The first of these I've already touched upon: that is, the claim that knowledge of nature is invariably inflected with the biases of the knower/s. This is the same as saying that there's no singular, objective knowledge of nature, only particular, socially constituted knowledges, in the plural. What's so arresting about this argument is that it can be applied not only to how nature is understood by people, governments, and businesses out there in the wider world, but also to how geographers themselves see (and have seen) nature. It's an argument that's been made by critical geographers in a number of ways. It began life with the work of Marxists like Harvey and Neil Smith, writing in the 1970s and 1980s. Both were critical of the supposedly 'neutral' knowledge of environmental problems produced by the conventional 'human impact' school of geographical research, steeped as it was in the scientific tradition. For instance, in his germinal essay entitled 'Population, Resources and the Ideology of science,' Harvey scrutinized the neo-Malthusian arguments of 'scientific' resource analysts writing during the 1970s. Many of these analysts were predicting imminent global resource shortages – of oil, food and timber, for instance – and calling for drastic reductions in population growth, particularly in the developing world (see, for example, Meadows et al., 1972). Put differently, in the name of supposed 'natural limits' to population growth, poor developing nations were being asked to curtail their demographic expansion and conserve resources. In a biting critique, Harvey pointed out that there were, in fact, more than sufficient resources worldwide to feed and provision the entire global population to a high standard of living. The problem, though, is that these resources were controlled by Western nations. Therefore, for Harvey the 'overpopulation' argument was, in fact, a rhetorical cover designed to draw attention away from the real problem: the maldistribution of resources between the West and the rest. To use Smith's (1984, p. 1) terminology, it was an 'ideology of nature' that concealed the truth of social inequity behind the smokescreen of a purportedly scientific, value-free, resource-scarcity analysis.

Writing in the same vein, and at around the same time, a new, radical cohort of human geographers interested in so-called 'natural hazards' – like Kenneth Hewitt (1983) – began to argue that the very notion that earthquakes, tornadoes, and floods were *simply* natural events was deeply misleading. By showing that hazards impacted disproportionately on the most disadvantaged sections of society, these radicals argued that conventional hazards analysis was guilty of two things: first, diverting attention away from social vulnerability to hazards thus leading, secondly, to superficial hazard response policies. By social vulnerability, Hewitt and others were referring to the fact that it's typically only the poorest in society who lack the means to cope with the destruction caused by hazards. Therefore, the 'technofix' policies so beloved of conventional hazard managers – such as building flood defences or temporarily housing those displaced by a landslide – failed to address the deeper issues of why certain social groups, defined in class terms, are more vulnerable to hazards in the first place.

In these Marxian analyses, geographical knowledges of nature are seen as implicitly and explicitly reflecting the wider class interests of the most powerful groups in Western and non-Western societies. More recently, other critical geographers have argued that knowledges of nature also reflect other interests – especially those concerning gender, 'race,' and colonialism. For instance, feminist geographers Cathy Nesmith and Sarah Radcliffe (1997) have criticized the gender subtexts of a good deal of ecocentric thinking. Though such thinking seems politically progressive by virtue of being 'green,' they argue that it's often shot through with highly patriarchal notions of the environment as something to be 'protected' or something that is intrinsically 'nurturing.' By feminizing nature in this specific way, Nesmith and Radcliffe argue, certain ecocentric approaches to nature merely reflect and repeat the stereotypes of women that have allowed men to be the dominant gender for most of Western and non-Western history.

Similarly, others have argued that racial stereotypes and racial discrimination – both today and in the past – have been reproduced, in part, by way of attributing to different social groups certain 'inherent' characteristics. Indeed, as a university discipline, geography was implicated historically in what, a century ago, seemed perfectly normal ideas about the 'natural' superiority of Caucasians over non-Western peoples. Illicitly adapting the biologist Darwin's ideas about 'natural selection' among species to the supposed 'fight for survival' among different 'racial' groups, a form of 'social Darwinism' saturated geographical thinking during the early twentieth century. As Richard Peet (1985) has shown, it was thinking that routinely labeled aboriginal and native peoples in colonial territories as 'primitive,' 'uncivilized,' and 'backward' – all, of course, 'by nature.' More subtly, and in the contemporary era, Sian Sullivan (2000) argues persuasively that resource managers in many developing countries have perpetuated a set of 'environmental myths' about indigenous land-use habits. These myths – which, for instance, depict herders as 'irrationally' overstocking rangelands – are, Sullivan argues, designed to consolidate the 'expert authority' of the land managers, thus making their advice indispensable for Third World governments.

In their chapters, Jane Moeckli, Kay Anderson, Piers Blaikie, and Derek Gregory all explore these gendered, racialised and colonialised knowledges of nature. Where Marxists like Harvey and Smith talk of ideologies of nature – which hide the truth and which serve specific social interests – Moeckli, Anderson and Gregory show that knowledges of nature are more complex than this, in terms of their origins and outcomes. To begin, they prefer to talk of *discourses of nature*, drawing upon the so-called 'poststructuralist' theories of language proposed by the French intellectuals Derrida and Foucault. Here any claims about nature are seen to draw upon a wide repertoire of other social images and norms – whether of a gender, racial, colonial, national, or other type. Moreover, they argue that it's simply not possible to step outside these complex discourses in order to find out 'what's really going on' in relation to nature. For, as Moeckli, Anderson, and Gregory show, *all* claims about nature are discursively mediated. Knowledge and language are the tools we use to make sense of a natural world that is both different from us and yet which we are a part of. There is, therefore, no objective, nondiscursive way of comprehending nature 'in the raw.' We have to live with the fact that different individuals and groups use different discourses to make sense of the same nature/s. These discourses do not reveal or hide the truths of nature but, rather, *create their own truths*. Whose discourse is accepted as being truthful is a question of social struggle and power politics. Furthermore, many nature discourses become so deeply entrenched in both lay and expert ways of thinking that they themselves appear natural.

Whether one takes the ideology or the discourse line, the critical geographers mentioned above all agree on two things: first, that knowledges of nature (even scientific ones) frequently express social power relations and, second, that these knowledges have material effects, insofar as people may believe and act according to them. 'Deconstructing' these knowledges therefore entails 'denaturalizing' them: that is, showing them to be social products arising in particular contexts and serving specific social or ecological ends that ought to be questioned.

2 Engaging nature

Though knowledges of nature are social through and through, the social dimensions of nature are not reducible to knowledge alone. For the society–nature nexus, of course, has an insistently practical side to it: to wit, societies, past and present, always physically interact with nature. The form and consequences of this physical interaction is, as noted earlier, a key concern of both the technocratic and ecocentric approaches to nature in geography. However, as I also observed earlier, both approaches tend to see nature, in the physical sense, as nonsocial. It is this notion of a nonsocial nature that underpins the familiar geographical vocabulary of societies 'impacting on,' 'interfacing with,' or 'destroying' environments. Against this, many critical geographers insist that it's impossible to physically disentangle the social and the natural. In reality, all there is – to borrow Erik Swyngedouw's (1999, p. 443) apt neologism – is "socionature."

What does this mean? It is not at all a denial of the material reality of those things we routinely call natural – be they trees, rivers, animals, or anything else. Rather, it's an insistence that the physical opportunities and constraints nature presents societies with can only be defined *relative to* specific sets of economic, cultural, and technical relations and capacities. In other words, the *same* 'chunk' of nature – say the Amazon rainforest – will have *different* physical attributes and implications for societies, depending on how those societies use it. In this sense, the physical characteristics of nature are *contingent* upon social practices: they are not fixed. Critical geographers have, in recent years, made this important argument in four main topic areas.

The first of these is the above-mentioned field of hazards research, where it's now argued that hazards can only be defined relative to the vulnerability of different groups in society (see Blaikie et al.'s 1994 landmark book *At Risk*). This argument is explored in more depth in Mark Pelling's chapter in this volume. Second, and relatedly, several human geographers have sought to question conventional understandings of a particularly distressing phenomenon that, sadly, remains a reality for millions today: famine. For instance, Lakshama Yapa (1996), drawing upon the seminal work of radical economist Amartya

Sen, has argued that natural events like droughts merely trigger famines but do not cause them. Though this claim seems odd at first sight, Yapa's point is that famines often happen in situations of food surplus! Taking examples from the developing world, he shows that some people starve during droughts not because of absolute food shortages, but because they lack the economic wealth ('entitlements') to purchase much-needed food within their own country or community. Starvation is thus, for Yapa, a class-specific phenomenon.

Thirdly, this feeds into critical geographic work on 'Third World political ecology.' This work examines a plethora of society–nature relationships in developing countries, focusing particularly on the poor. One of the fundamental insights of this work is that the way poor communities use (and abuse) local resources depends as much upon extralocal economic, political, and social forces as it does upon the nature of the resources themselves. For instance, in *Silent Violence* – one of the early, key texts in political ecology – Michael Watts (1983) looked at Hausa agriculture in northern Nigeria. For centuries, the Hausa had successfully adapted their agronomy to the semiarid environment in which they lived. However, after the onset of British colonialism in the late nineteenth century, they suffered a series of major famines. The reason, Watts showed, was because the British had undermined traditional agriculture and replaced it with the commercial production of cotton and groundnuts for export. Thus, now dependent on two main cash crops, the Hausa lost their self-sufficiency and became subject to the vagaries of foreign markets. During times when exports were low, Watts revealed how the Hausa lacked the economic means to purchase adequate foodstuffs and so became vulnerable to drought. More recently, political ecologists have complemented this focus on the physical aspects of society–nature relations with a focus on knowledges of nature and their power-geometries. Raymond Bryant's chapter critically evaluates these two generations of political ecology perspectives.

Finally, and most recently, critical geographers have highlighted the phenomenon of 'environmental in/justice' in the developed world. In *Dumping in Dixie*, radical academic Robert Bullard (1990) showed some years ago that black and working-class Americans suffered a disproportionate exposure to toxic waste and pollution. Since then, many human geographers in the US, UK, and other Western countries have been concerned to show that this exposure is not 'accidental.' Rather, they have argued, it is due to the deliberate siting of noxious facilities – for instance, waste incinerators – in or near communities with the lowest capacity to contest them in the political or legal system (see the special issue of *Antipode* (1996) on 'Waste, Race and Class').

3 Remaking nature

It's one thing to say that societies physically engage with nature in ways that blur the boundaries between the two. But it's another to argue that societies *physically reconstitute* nature, both intentionally and unintentionally. Yet it's an argument many critical geographers have been prepared to make. Here, the natural – in a very material way – is seen to have become *internal* to social processes, particularly in advanced Western societies. Ideas of nature as external, intrinsic, or universal are, it's argued, therefore radically out of step with the reality of a nature that is social 'all the way down.' This argument has been made from three perspectives. First, from the mid-1980s, the already mentioned Marxist geographer Neil Smith argued that modern, industrial capitalism was, quite literally 'producing nature' in the narrow interests of profitability. Genetically modified organisms, manufactured by transnational agrofood companies, are only the latest example of what Smith was referring to. Today, a cohort of Marxist and neo-Marxist geographers, with interests in modern agriculture in particular, have taken Smith's ideas forward. In my chapter later in this book, I explain the idea of the production of nature at length.

Smith's account highlighted how science and technology were deeply implicated in capitalist development. But ultimately neither is reducible to the class interests of capitalist businesses alone. Hence, in the last few years, the roles of science and technology in remaking nature have become a focus of critical geographic attention in their own right. Drawing upon so-called 'sociology of scientific knowledge,' some have argued that scientists intentionally alter nature for very specific purposes that reflect more than simply 'scientific' interests. As science historian Ian Hacking (1983) said, science does not merely study the world but intervenes in it, physically and practically Scientists, both in the laboratory and the field, increasingly create what geographer David Demeritt (1998) calls "artefactual natures," ones that are purposefully engineered – even down to the genetic level. The question then arises: what types of artefactual natures exist today, for whose benefit and with what socioecological consequences?

This question brings me the final main perspective on how societies materially manufacture nature. It's a perspective first developed by German sociologist Ulrich Beck (1992) in his book *Risk Society*, and focuses on the powers of advanced industrial technologies. Beck's central point is that Western societies are now physically reconstituting nature in ways that, alarmingly, escape their control. Phenomena like acid deposition and the presence of pesticide residues in the food chain are, he argues, 'manufactured risks,' which are the unintentional and uncontrollable byproduct of mass industrialism. In geography, this argument has stimulated a good deal of debate (see, for example,

Eden 1998), and conjures up the apocalyptical idea that we're witnessing 'the end of nature' in the twenty-first century.

The Social *Construction* of Nature?

In the several ways outlined above, nature has come to be seen as never simply, or not even, natural. Understandably, the idea of 'social nature' has not been well received in all parts geography or, indeed, in other disciplines where it's been expounded – like environmental sociology. Notwithstanding the differences between the technocratic and ecocentric approaches to nature, advocates of both have expressed common concerns about the social-nature perspective. Chief among these is the accusation that this perspective licences the outlandish idea that nature is *nothing more* than a social construction. This idea is clearest in those arguments concerning the physical remaking of nature, where nature, it seems, is depicted as mere putty in the hands of modern science, technology, and business. But it also appears in arguments concerning knowledges of nature. Consider, for instance, the words of geographer William Cronon (1996, p. 69), in his deconstruction of the idea of 'wilderness': "[wilderness] is a profoundly human construction . . . , it hides its unnaturalness behind a mask that is all the more beguiling because it seems so natural."

Understandably, technocratic and ecocentric geographers worry that these kinds of arguments are intellectually misguided, and practically and politically debilitating. They are misguided because they apparently deny the physical reality and autonomy of nature from societies. In the case of the material construction of nature – *à la* Smith, Demeritt, Beck, and others – it appears as if the physical attributes of nature can be comprehensively manipulated by advanced Western societies. But this 'hyperconstructionist' view, its critics argue, ignores two facts: first, that some aspects of nature – like geology – are simply not amenable to physical alteration; and second, that even those that are – like GM seeds – are not *completely* subject to social control because their operation is not 100 percent predictable. Likewise, several technocratic and ecocentric geographers have been skeptical of the idea that nature is constructed ideologically/discursively. For if nature is *only* an idea – if it cannot be 'objectively' known – then, these geographers claim, we're led to the absurd conclusion that nature is whatever we want it to be.

If these criticisms are accurate, then it's clear why social nature arguments might seem practically and politically debilitating to some. They seem practically debilitating because they evidently prevent us from acting in and on nature in appropriate ways. For instance, if 'global warming' is simply a fabrication – a myth cooked-up by atmospheric scientists keen to secure large research grants for the kind of work they do – then we are led to conclude that polluting the atmosphere is okay, since we can never know the 'real' climatic effects of greenhouse gases. On the political front, the idea that nature is socially constructed seems to deny that nature can ground any value judgments about appropriate social or ecological behavior. How, for example, can eco-centrists claim that killing whales or destroying the Amazon is wrong, if we can no longer "appeal to nature as a stable external source of nonhuman values" (Cronon, 1996: p. 26)?

Though these criticisms are valid, they can only be made to stick if some or all of the geographical work on social nature is truly guilty of a hyperconstructionist view. However, as the contributors to this book show, this work generally eschews such an extreme stance. For however social nature is, it would be difficult to deny the reality of those myriad things societies define as 'natural.' The point, as David Demeritt shows in his chapter in this volume, is simply that there is never any way to access, evaluate, and affect nature that does not involve socially specific knowledges and practices (see also Proctor, 1998). We must live with this inability to know nature 'as it really is,' while still remaining commited to the idea that some knowledges of, and practices on, nature are better or worse than others.

This point can be taken even further. The questionable idea of nature being nothing more than a social construction not only exaggerates the power of societies but also arguably trades on the society–nature dualism that I criticized earlier in this chapter. For it implies that nature is a *tabula rasa* on which societies can write at will. Against this, critical geographers like Sarah Whatmore have drawn upon a new 'actor-network theory' to show that societies do not construct nature as they please. Rather, myriad 'social' and 'natural' entities are indissolubly conjoined as 'hybrids' in millions of actor-networks organized at multiple geographical scales. In this view, societies are 'in' nature (and vice versa) such that it becomes hard to understand who or what is doing the constructing. In the chapter written with Tom MacMillan, we explore and evaluate this exciting new perspective.

Theory, Practice, and Politics

Clearly, the new geographical ideas about social nature are as diverse as they are important. The chapters that comprise this book aim to give readers a comprehensive, though not exhaustive, critical introduction to these ideas. By way of a conclusion to this introductory essay, I want to signpost three key themes that run throughout the pages of *Social Nature*.

The first of these relates to theory. Theory is a complex and ambiguous word, but for many geographers – and particularly students – it often has a pejorative association with thinking that is abstract, conceptual, or just plain woolly. Against this, the chapters of *Social Nature* all show why theory is absolutely vital if we're to make proper sense of society–nature relations, past, present, and future. In this book, the term 'theory' refers to formal intellectual frameworks for explaining and evaluating myriad different society–nature imbrications. More specifically, the theories discussed in each chapter are critical, that is, ones concerned with questions of socionatural in/justice. They seek to question conventional understandings and practices regarding nature – technocratic, ecocentric, or otherwise – and they try, implicitly or explicitly, to envisage more progressive society–nature articulations.

Theory, however, can become irrelevant if it lacks direct connections to real world events. This is why, secondly, the chapters of *Social Nature* all seek to show how theory can make sense of the society–nature nexus in practice. This has two aspects. First, all the contributors show how many actors in society – from geographers themselves to the public to policy-makers – routinely misunderstand or misrepresent society–nature relations. Second, they show how the theories and concepts they present can illuminate what is so often denied: that is, nature's implication in social knowledge, practice, and power. In these two ways, readers will hopefully appreciate not only the 'power' of critical theory but gain empirical insights into nature's social dimensions.

Finally, all the chapters of this book are preoccupied with the politics of nature. For if nature is nothing if it's not social, it's also unavoidably political. Like theory, politics is a complex term. In *Social Nature*, the contributors unpack this term into three related meanings. The first of these is politics as *values*. Knowledge of, and action in/on, nature is unavoidably value-laden. It speaks volumes not only about who is doing the knowing and acting, but what kind of a world they are trying to forge. This is often subtle – as in the hidden values written into scientific knowledges of nature – but by no means always. *Social Nature* encourages readers to reflect carefully and critically upon the social value commitments involved in all society–nature relations. Second, we can understand politics as *moral or ethical statements* about nature. Morality and ethics are those principles societies use to determine what is 'right' and 'proper' thought or behavior. For instance, ecocentrists question the human-centered morals used to evaluate current society–nature relations worldwide and call for a less anthropocentric and more 'green' ethical code. In his chapter, James Proctor considers whether or not we can have an environmental ethics that 'defends nature' if all ethical judgments are inherently social and constructed. Finally, we can think of politics in the familiar sense of *formal governmental policies and decision-making*. Governments and bureaucracies – at a variety of scales – are responsible for both regulating and shaping society–nature relations. Typically, though not always, they deal with nature in technocratic ways. Several chapters in this book question the nonsocial view of nature written into state politics and policy, as well as the ecocentric criticisms of these politics and policies. They therefore insist that states, bureaucracies, and their ecocentric critics must all acknowledge nature's sociality from the very start, if adequate policy measures are to be developed over everything from deforestation to the patenting of life forms.

To sum up, in an era when nature is less natural than at any time in human history – an era when even the human body is becoming subject to social reengineering – it seems to me that geographers must become participants in, not spectators of, the momentous socionatural changes of our time. *Social Nature* is designed to give readers the tools to think critically about the dominant ideas and practices that circumscribe all manner of society–nature relations worldwide. The question it opens up for discussion is a crucial and profound one: what kinds of nature – or more properly natures, in the plural – do we want for what kind of future?

Notes

1   There are now many books in this 'people and environment' tradition of geography that are aimed at students. Two recent examples are Middleton's (1995) *The Global Casino* and Pickering and Owen's (1997) *An Introduction to Global Environmental Issues.*
2   The social and ecocentric appoaches to understanding society–nature relations do overlap in several substantive areas, in part because both approaches are internally diverse. However, for didactic purposes, I'm deliberately emphasizing the differences between them here.
3   See, for example, David Pepper's (1996) *Modern Environmentalism.* Though several texts like this now exist, ecocentrism is not, in fact, widely advocated by critical geographers. This is odd, since in the wider world it enjoys support among a significant minority of people, finding expression in the ideas and practices of many nongovernmental organizations and so-called 'new social movements' – like Green-peace, Earth First!, and genetiXsnowball.

Further Reading

For more on the concept of nature see Castree (2000), Gold (1984), or Smith (1998, ch. 1). Phillips and Mighall (2000, ch. 1) offer a useful overview of different approaches to society and nature. O'Riordan (1996) gives a good introduction to technocratic and ecocentric approaches.

References

Beck, U. (1992). *Risk Society*. London: Sage.
Blaikie, P., Cannon, T., Davis, I., and Wisner, B. (1994). *At Risk*. London: Routledge.
Bryce, J. (1886). The Relations of History and Geography. *Contemporary Review* 49: 426–43.
Bullard, R. (1990). *Dumping in Dixie*. Boulder: Westview Press.
Castree, N. (2000). Nature. In R. Johnston et al. (eds.) *The Dictionary of Human Geography*, fourth edn. Oxford: Blackwell, 537–40.
Cooke, R. (1992). Common Ground, Shared Inheritance. *Transactions of the Institute of British Geographers* 17: 131–51.
Cronon, W. (ed.) (1996). *Uncommon Ground*. New York: W. W. Norton.
Demeritt, D. (1998). Science, Social Constructivism and Nature. In B. Braun and N. Castree (eds.) *Remaking Reality*. London: Routledge, 173–92.
Eden, S. (1998). Knowledge, Uncertainty and the Environment. *Progress in Human Geography* 22: 425–32.
Gold, M. (1984). A History of Nature. In D. Massey and J. Allen (eds.) *Geography Matters!* Cambridge: Cambridge University Press, 12–33.
Hacking, I. (1983). *Representing and Intervening*. Cambridge: Cambridge University Press.
Harvey, D. (1974). Population, Resources and the Ideology of Science. *Economic Geography* 50: 256–77.
Hewitt, K. (ed.) (1983). *Interpretations of Calamity*. London: Allen and Unwin.
Huntington, E. (1925). *The Character of Races*. New York: Charles Scribner.
Lovelock, J. (1995). *The Ages of Gaia*. Oxford: Oxford University Press.
Lowe, M. and Bowlby, S. (1996). Population and Environment. In A. Mannion and S. Bowlby (eds.) *Environmental Issues in the 1990s*. Chichestrer: Wiley, 117–30.
McKibben, R. (1989). *The End of Nature*. New York: Vintage.
Meadows, D. et al. (1972). *The Limits to Growth*. New York: Universe Books.
Middleton, N. (1995). *The Global Casino*. London: Arnold.
Naess, A. (1989). *Ecology, Community and Lifestyle*. Cambridge: Cambridge University Press.
Nesmith, C. and Radcliffe, S. (1997). Remapping Mother Earth. In T. Barnes and D. Gregory (eds.), *Reading Human Geography*. London: Arnold, 195–210.
O'Riordan, T. (1996). Environmentalism on the Move. In I. Douglas et al. (eds.), *The Companion Encyclopedia of Geography*. London: Routledge, 449–78.
Peet, R. (1985). The Social Origins of Environmental Determinism. *Annals of the Association of American Geographers* 75: 309–33.
Pepper, D. (1996). *Modern Environmentalism*. London: Routledge.
Phillips, M. and Mighall, T. (2000). *Society and Nature through Exploitation* Harlow: Prentice Hall.
Pickering, K. and Owen, L. (1997). *An Introduction to Global Environmental Issues*. London: Routledge.
Proctor, J. (1998). The Social Construction of Nature. *Annals of the Association of American Geographers* 88: 352–76.
Redclift, M. (1996). *Wasted: Counting the Costs of Global Consumption*. London: Earthscan.

Semple, E. (1911). *The Influences of Geographic Environment*. New York: Henry Holt.

Smith, M. (1998). *Ecologism*. Milton Keynes: Open University Press.

Smith, N. (1984). *Uneven Development*. Oxford: Blackwell.

Soper, K. (1995). *What Is Nature?* Oxford: Blackwell.

Stoddart, D. (1987). To Claim the High Ground. *Transactions of the Institute of British Geographers* 12: 327–36.

Sullivan, S. (2000). Getting the Science Right, or Introducing Science in the First Place? In P. Stott and S. Sullivan (eds.) *Political Ecology*. London: Arnold, 15–44.

Swyngedouw, E. (1999). Modernity and Hybridity. *Annals of the Association of American Geographers* 89: 443–65.

Thomas, R. (ed.) (1956). *Man's Role in Changing the Face of the Earth*. Chicago: Chicago University Press.

Watts, M. (1983). *Silent Violence*. Berkeley: University of California Press.

Williams, R. (1980). *Problems of Materialism and Culture*. London: Verso.

Wolch, J. and Emel, J. (eds.) (1998). *Animal Geographies*. London: Verso.

Yapa, L. (1996). Improved Seeds and Constructed Scarcity. In R. Peet and M. Watts (eds.), *Liberation Ecologies*. London: Routledge, 69–85.

Chapter 2

Being Constructive about Nature

David Demeritt

"Nature," writes science critic Donna Haraway (1992: p. 296), "cannot pre-exist its construction." At first glance, that claim probably seems strange, even perverse. After all, 'nature' is frequently taken to mean the totality of everything that is *not* humanly constructed. In what sense can the land we see or the water we drink be called 'constructions'? And yet, an increasing number of human geographers now insist just this: that 'nature' is a social construction (Castree, 1995; Gerber, 1997; Harrison and Burgess, 1994; Kong and Yeoh, 1996; Olwig, 1996; Proctor, 1998). Wilson (1991: p. 12), for instance, claims:

> Nature is a part of culture. When our physical surroundings are sold to us as "natural" (like the travel ad for "Super, Natural, British Columbia") we should pay close attention. Our experience of the natural world – whether touring the Canadian Rockies, watching an animal show on TV, or working in our own gardens – is always mediated. It is always shaped by rhetorical constructs like photography, industry, advertising, and aesthetics, as well as by institutions like religion, tourism, and education . . . To speak uncritically of the natural is to ignore these social questions.

He is not alone. The claim that what we take for nature and environment is somehow socially constructed or produced has become very influential across the social sciences much more generally (Bird, 1987; Cronon, 1995b; Macnaghten and Urry, 1998; Scarce, 2000).

Such constructionist arguments are not restricted to just nature and the environment. Landscapes (Demeritt, 1994), environmental problems (Hannigan, 1995), AIDS (Patton, 1990), science (Golinski, 1998), facts (Latour and Woolgar, 1979), and even death (Seale, 1998) are also now said to be social constructions. But what do these claims entail? What, for instance, does Haraway mean by 'nature'? As I discuss below, the word is perhaps the most complicated in the English language. What is it, exactly, that she and others are claiming is being constructed? Our concepts of nature or the various things to which those concepts refer? What are the implications of those constructions – and of our understanding them *as* constructions?

My objective in this chapter is to answer these questions and clarify what being constructive about nature might imply, both politically and philosophically. I will begin by introducing the idea of nature as a social construction and explaining why it has sparked such an outpouring of academic interest and debate. Important political issues are at stake in questions about the social construction of nature and of environmental problems like global warming. Often, however, lack of terminological precision has meant that these debates have created more heat than light. One source of confusion has been the question of precisely what is meant by the term 'nature.' Making distinctions among different senses of the term can provide some badly needed clarity in debates about the social construction of nature. It also highlights a broad difference between those for whom the social construction of nature refers to the construction of our *concepts* of nature and those for whom the construction of nature refers to the process of constructing nature in *the physical and material sense*.

A second source of confusion concerns the philosophical implications of constructionist arguments. Social constructionism has become a popular, catch-all term to describe a variety of quite different approaches to understanding nature, knowledge, and the world. Different critics understand the idea of nature as a social construction, and its implications, in quite different ways. First, some people adopt constructionist rhetoric as a way of refuting particular claims about the environment as socially constructed and therefore false. I will discuss this first kind of social construction-as-refutation in more detail below. Those who invoke construction talk to refute particular beliefs about nature do not necessarily endorse wider claims that nature and the environment in general or our knowledge of them are socially constructed. By contrast, a second kind of construction talk – social construction-as-philosophical critique – is designed to do just that. Some people talk about the social construction of nature in order to advance much broader and more philosophical claims about the existence and nature of nature (or what philosophers call ontology) and about the status of our knowledge of it (what philosophers call epistemology). As we will see, these more philosophical questions about ontology and epistemology have some important political implications, but understanding the politics of these constructions of nature requires more attention to the different theories of nature's construction.

Contesting Social Constructions of Nature

Claims about the social construction of nature are important for two major reasons. First, social constructionist arguments challenge the apparent self-evidence of nature and the physical environment as pregiven things with certain fixed physical properties that exist independently of and apart from social practices. For example, one goal of my own research on the historical geography of New England forests has been to show how the abundant game populations that early European settlers looked upon as the Providential bounty of nature were in fact socially constructed (Demeritt, 1999; 2002). Native peoples used fire to encourage the growth of useful plants and animals. To call them 'natural resources' does not do justice to the way in which they were the intentional products of the ways native peoples cultivated the forest. Their use of fire to cultivate particular resources had unintentional effects as well. As a result of frequent burning, New England forests contained relatively more fire tolerant species such as white pine, so prized by European settlers for ships' masts and other timber, than might otherwise have been the case. Among the native peoples of northern New England, access to game resources was controlled by strict property rights, which allocated hunting territories to particular family groups. Hunting practices were regulated by a complex belief system of myth and origin stories that insured game species were not overexploited. None of this made any sense to English settlers. By refusing to recognize native property rights, they "both trivialized the ecology of Indian life and paved the way for destroying it" (Cronon, 1983: 57). As settlers advanced farther and farther into native territory, they disrupted the delicate ecological balance on which native life depended. Their fields encroached on native hunting grounds; their livestock foraged in the forest, competing with deer and the other animals on which native peoples relied, while white trappers poached relentlessly in native hunting territories killing off all the game they could find. As game populations fell so too did those of native peoples. In effect, colonial settlers actually brought about the kind of radically depopulated landscape – what the Puritan poet Michael Wigglesworth (quoted in Smith, 1950: 4) called a "waste and howling wilderness / Where none inhabited" – that they had imagined the forest as being all along.

My historical claims about the *material* construction of forest nature are slightly different from those concerned with the construction of *ideas of nature*. Cronon (1995), for instance, has shown that wilderness is not a thing, so much as an idea, and a socially constructed one at that. For seventeenth- and eighteenth-century settlers like Wigglesworth, wilderness represented Satan's home to be redeemed by improvement and agricultural cultivation. So relentlessly did frontier settlement progress that by the late nineteenth century American forests were in rapid retreat. Partly as a result American attitudes to

Figure 2.1:   In the late nineteenth century, the Maine Woods was constructed as a space of wilderness recreation in which visitors could shake off the deadening routines of urban life and re-create an essential 'primitive' self by getting back to nature

wilderness changed dramatically. Romantics like Henry David Thoreau imagined wilderness as God's own temple, a wondrous and unsullied wilderness refuge from a fallen civilization. To experience at first hand this sense of their own primitive pioneer past, tourists traveled great distances to visit the 'wild' forests of northern New England that Thoreau dubbed the Maine Woods (figure 2.1). Cronon (1995: 80) criticizes this wilderness idea as "a fantasy of people who have never themselves had to work the land to make a living – urban folk for whom food comes from a supermarket." The trouble with wilderness, he explains, is that it contributes to an all or nothing attitude about the environment. By longing for the pure and untouched wilderness spaces where they do not live, people tend to disavow any responsibility for the heavily urbanized environments in which they actually do live.

Second, arguments about the social construction of nature, despite some differences in emphasis among them, all pose a challenge to the authority of scientific knowledge. Since the dawn of modern science during the eighteenth-century Enlightenment, scientists have insisted that the scientific method offers a uniquely privileged vehicle to true knowledge about the world. While there are a number of somewhat different philosophical justifications of science, most come down to the general claim that unlike religious superstition, scientific knowledge is objective in the double sense that it is not based on subjective belief but on direct, impersonal, and, in that sense, objective observation of an independent reality. This Enlightenment understanding of scientific knowledge is founded on several important philosophical suppositions about knowledge (epistemology) and existence (ontology):

1   the objects of the physical world exist independently of our knowledge of them.
2   those objects can be observed directly such that knowledge of the world can be tested empirically by immediate reference to how it actually is.
3   Truth is defined by correspondence between our ideas about the physical environment and how it actually is (correspondence theory of truth).

Claims about the social construction of nature potentially challenge all three of these suppositions. If nature is socially constructed, its existence is not independent of our knowledge of it. Therefore nature cannot provide an independent foundation against which to test our knowledge claims. What's more the idea that nature is a social construction also suggests that even if there were an ontologically independent real world our empirical observations of it would still be biased by our socially constructed preconceptions of it. The upshot is that scientifically valid knowledge must inevitably be partial, in the sense both of incomplete and biased.

Many critics find this realization politically progressive. They have embraced social constructionism as a tool for challenging the apparent objectivity of certain politically undesirable scientific claims. For example, the political ecologists James Fairhead and Melissa Leach (1998) have attacked ideas of desertification as socially constructed and false myths. For a long time it has been assumed that increasing population pressure in West Africa leads inevitably to desertification and famine. According to this theory of desertification, population pressures force peasants and herders to expand onto marginal land, plow fragile soils, cut down trees for fuel wood, and overgraze pastures. These activities, in turn, lead to denudation of the vegetation, soil erosion and desiccation, and then ultimately to irreversible land degradation, which increases the population pressure on remaining resources and accelerates the process of desertification and the southward expansion of the Sahara desert onto former agricultural lands. This belief has led development agencies like the World Bank to press the governments of less developed countries into draconian schemes to restrict the access of rural populations to land so as to protect the environment from destruction (see Blaikie, this volume). Fairhead and Leach (1998) respond that this idea of desertification is a false construction of the environment. As they show through a careful analysis of air-photographs, historical surveys, and other evidence, claims about the scale of desertification in West Africa have been grossly exaggerated. In fact, larger human populations have been associated with more trees, not less, because villagers have cultivated and protected them. For Fairhead and Leach the idea of desertification is not simply a false construction of nature, but an ideological one, designed to conceal the true situation behind the smokescreen of purportedly objective science, thereby legitimating the actual dispossession of local villagers by state forestry agencies.

Similarly, a number of critics, like Cronon (1995), have adopted construc-tionist rhetoric to critique wilderness ideas. From a political ecology perspective (see Bryant, this volume), Neumann (1998) charges that wilderness is an ideological construction that was imposed, first by the colonial state and then by the independent government of Tanzania, on the Meru Peasant people of northern Tanzania. The creation of Arusha National Park as a protected nature reserve involved removing peasants from the land and depriving them of access to resources in the name of biodiversity protection. Willems-Braun (1997) makes many of the same general points about the effects of wilderness discourse in British Columbia, though from a somewhat different theoretical perspective. He points to the "representational practices through which 'nature' is made to appear as an empty space" (p. 7) in which the native peoples of Canada's West Coast have no place or voice (see also Braun and Wainwright, this volume).

However, other critics have worried that all this talk about the social construction of nature opens the door to relativism (Gandy, 1996; Soule and Lease, 1995; Worster, 1990). Relativism can involve one of two distinct philosophical beliefs. The first is the ontological claim that the actual conditions of reality are determined by and relative to the ideas and wishes of the observer. Thus the deep ecologist Gary Synder (1998) confesses:

> I am getting a bit grumpy about the dumb arguments being put forth by high paid intellectual types . . . [about] the idea of Nature as being a "social construction" – a shared cultural projection seen and shaped in the light of social values . . . A lot of this rhetoric, if translated into human politics, would be like saying, 'Black people are the construction of whites.' . . . Of course liberal critical theorists don't talk this way when it comes to fellow

human beings because they know what kind of heat they'd get. In the case of Nature, because they are still under the illusion that it isn't seriously there, they indulge themselves in this moral and political shallowness.

The second claim associated with relativism is an epistemological one: that what counts for truth and valid knowledge about the world is relative to the groups and individuals in question. Truth is therefore historically and culturally variable, not absolute. Social constructionists are often accused of both sorts of relativism. For instance, Soule and Lease (1995: xv) complain:

> certain radical forms of "postmodern deconstructionism" . . . assert that all we can ever perceive about the world are shadows, and that we can never escape our particular biases and fixed historical-cultural positions. Moreover some in the deconstructionist movement boldly assert that the natural world as described by scientists and conservationists, if it exists, is a human artifact produced by our economic activities.

Critics of social construction talk are hostile to it for both intellectual and political reasons, as physicist Alan Sokal (1996: 63–4) explains:

> Intellectually, the problem with such doctrines is that they are false (when not simply meaningless). There *is* a real world; its properties are not merely social constructions: facts and evidence do matter. What sane person would contend otherwise? And yet, much contemporary academic theorizing consists precisely of attempts to blur these obvious truths . . . Politically, I'm angered because most (though not all) of this silliness is emanating from the self-proclaimed Left . . . For most of the past two centuries the Left has been identified with science and against obscurantism . . . The recent turn of many 'progressive' or 'leftist' academic humanists and social scientists toward one or another form of epistemic relativism betrays this worthy heritage and undermines the already fragile prospects for progressive social critique. Theorizing about the 'social construction of reality' won't help us find a cure for AIDS or devise strategies for preventing global warming.

For Sokal and others on the traditional Left, the political problem with social construction talk is that it leaves no epistemologically secure foundation from which to speak truth to power. Their fear is that the powerful stand to gain the most from such relativism. Being constructive about nature, Worster (1985: 242, 241) fears, leads to an "environmental relativism" whereby it is impossible distinguish "between the balance achieved by nature and that contrived by man [*sic*]." Industrial polluters will be able to claim that environmental pollution is not real but socially constructed, and fears about it unfounded. As Synder (1998) notes, social constructionist "attacks on Nature and wilderness from the ivory towers come at the right time to bolster global developers, the resurgent timber companies (here in California, the Charles Hurwitz suits at Pacific

Lumber), and those who would trash the Endangered Species Act." Without being able to appeal to the higher authority of scientific truth, environmentalists will have no way to refute these false claims.

These concerns about the relativism potentially implied by being constructive have important parallels in other fields. Feminists, for instance, have also struggled with the political and philosophical implications of constructionism. On the one hand, many feminists have enthusiastically embraced constructionist arguments as a "strong tool for deconstructing the truth claims of hostile science by showing the radical historical specificity and so contestability of *every* layer of the onion of scientific and technological constructions" (Haraway, 1991: 186). Construction talk enables feminists to argue that apparently innate and therefore immutable differences between the sexes are in fact socially constructed *gender* differences that might be changed. On the other hand, however, they have also longed for a strong notion of objectivity on which to base their claims about the reality of women's oppression in male-dominated societies. Torn between these conflicting desires, feminists have experienced constructionism as a sort of "epistemological electro-shock therapy, which . . . lays us out . . . with self-induced multiple personality disorder" (Haraway, 1991: 186).

The Construction of What 'Nature'?

One way to resolve the arguments raging between constructionists and their critics is to be much more clear about the meaning of our terms. In the case of nature, the need for clarity is particularly important because the very word 'nature,' as the literary critic Raymond Williams (1983: 219) has famously observed, "is perhaps the most complex in the [English] language." Williams distinguishes three specific but closely intertwined meanings of the word:

i)   The ontologically essential or necessary quality of something.
ii) The inherent force which directs either the world or human beings or both. Insofar as these natural laws, in the sense of (ii), determine the quality and nature, in the sense of (i), of something, there is some overlap between nature (i) and (ii).
iii) The external, material world itself (e.g. the natural world).

While the question of what 'nature' is would seem to be strictly ontological, it also has important epistemological implications. All three of these senses of nature have been variously deployed to establish a foundation for distinguishing scientific knowledge from other kinds of belief. This, as I have suggested already, is one important reason why debates about the social construction of nature have become so heated. Claims about the social construction of nature are often understood – by proponents and critics alike – as assaults on the authority of science. First, scientific knowledge is sometimes defined as the explanation of what is natural, either in the sense of (i) ontologically necessary or of (ii) the inherent laws ordering the world. This naturalistic conception of scientific knowledge is common to many accounts both of the social and of the physical sciences. In this naturalistic view, what human and physical geographers share in common is a search for the essentially necessary and therefore scientifically predictable properties of their respective objects of study. Thus human geographers concerned with the nature (i) of economic growth would seek to identify the social and geographical conditions necessary to sustain it, while physical geographers might explain the nature (i) of hydrological systems (iii) and the natural laws (ii) governing the behavior of water in different sized catchments. Second, other senses of nature have been enrolled in constructing epistemological distinctions between the social sciences, concerned with meaningful human affairs, and the natural sciences, which study brute physical nature in the sense of (ii) or (iii) or both. This ontological difference between nature and society then forms the basis for distinguishing epistemologically between human geographers' subjective understanding of society and physical geographers' objective scientific knowledge of the natural world.

Distinctions among these different senses of nature can provide some badly needed clarity in debates about the social construction of nature. Marxist, feminist, and antiracist critics have long attacked the practice of explaining certain aspects of society in terms of natural (ii) or environmental (iii) determinism. These concerns about the construction of human nature are dealt with in greater detail by later chapters in this book (see Anderson; Gregory; Moeckli and Braun, all in this volume), but consider briefly the debates about race, class, and human intelligence sparked by the publication of Hernstein and Murray's (1994) *The Bell Curve*. On intelligence or IQ tests in the United States blacks tend on average to score lower than whites, poor people lower than wealthier people, and poor black people lowest of all. Sociobiologists like Hernstein and Murray (1994) explain these facts by arguing that human intelligence is an essential characteristic of human nature (i) and that it is scientifically measurable by IQ tests. Furthermore, they argue that intelligence is largely determined genetically (natural in the sense of (ii)) and varies regularly with racial and class groups. They conclude, therefore, that blacks are on average less intelligent than whites and the poor dumber than the rich; that measured differences in IQ explain differences in wealth among racial, class, and other social groups (i.e. the rich get richer because they are smarter); and, even more controversially, that since these IQ differences are natural, in the senses both of (i) and (ii), that there is no point in Affirmative Action, Head Start kindergarten programs, or other social services for socially disadvantaged groups because these groups are innately stupid and unlikely, on average, to improve. As Hernstein and Murray (1994: 17, 24) explain:

A society with a higher mean IQ is also likely to be a society with fewer social ills and brighter economic prospects . . . [T]he most efficient way to raise the IQ of a society is for smarter women to have higher birth rates. Instead, America is going in the opposite direction (i.e., dumber women are having babies in disproportionate numbers), and the implication is a future America with more social ills and gloomier economic prospects . . . This highlights the problem: the United States already has policies that inadvertently social-engineer who has babies (through programs like the Food Stamp program, Aid to Families with Dependent Children, etc.), and it is encouraging the wrong women.

Not surprisingly their conclusions were political dynamite and elicited an outpouring of political debate in the United States. Liberals condemned *The Bell Curve* as racist, while the Republican majorities in the US House and Senate pointed to it in support of their efforts to cut welfare programs. Among academics, Hernstein and Murray (1994) have been extensively criticized for the specific ways they misrepresent stastistics and ignore countervailing evidence (e.g. *New Republic*, 1994; Fraser, 1995).

But antiracist critics have also responded by arguing that human intelligence is not natural, in the sense of (i) and (ii), but socially constructed (e.g. Mitchell, 2000: 241–50). Such critiques would be more compelling if they were made more precisely. Arguments about the social construction of intelligence can work in a number of different ways. First, social construction arguments might be understood as denying the existence of intelligence altogether. Such a claim may sound totally outlandish, since what is it that distinguishes me from my dog if it is not human intelligence? But Hernstein and Murray (1994) assume that human intelligence is a singular quality – 'g' or general intelligence. Many psychologists insist that 'intelligence' is actually a composite of many different capabilities, like language, spatial reasoning, and so forth. This helps explain why students who excel in math classes may not also be the best in English. Whether or not these various 'intelligences' are genetically innate to individuals (natural in the sense of (i) and (ii)), a single IQ test does not measure them accurately, and so the conclusions of *The Bell Curve* are unsubstantiated. Second, antiracist critics might argue that since the outcome of any IQ test depends on social factors such as access to educational opportunities, intelligence is socially constructed rather than being determined naturally, in the sense of (ii). By this logic, Hernstein and Murray's (1994) public policy recommendations are completely backwards: what is required to achieve their goal and raise average IQ scores is more investment in public education necessary to socially construct higher IQ test scores among disadvantaged populations. Third, antiracist critics of *The Bell Curve* might argue that the test itself, by which IQ is defined, embodies important biases or assumptions that socially construct what we recognize as 'intelligence' (Staples, 2000: 73). Such arguments about the social construction of intelligence do not necessarily deny the existence of some essential human quality of intelligence. Instead they call attention to the way in which any empirical test for human intelligence depends on prior theoretical concepts that define for us what counts as human 'intelligence.' In the US, there have been longstanding debates about the extent to which SAT and other standardized aptitude tests administered to students for university admissions and other purposes incorporate cultural and ethnic biases that influence those scores to the disadvantage of minority groups. These social constructionist arguments directly challenge the independence, and thus the objectivity and credibility, of these empirical observations of human nature.

In trying to make sense of arguments about the social construction of nature, it is possible to make some further distinctions when we realize that all three of these interrelated meanings of 'nature' depend upon linguistic oppositions to that which is said to be cultural, artificial, or otherwise human in origin. This constitutive opposition of meanings of the natural to the cultural is particularly significant for (ii) and (iii), but it also applies to many senses of (i). Since the cultural references by which what is *not* nature and the natural are defined change over space and time, so too must ideas of what nature is.

This, then, is one very general way in which 'nature' might said to be a social construction: as a culturally and historically specific *concept*. Claims about the social construction of nature might be understood as claims about the social construction of our knowledge and concepts of nature. What are the epistemological implications of acknowledging that our concepts of nature are socially constructed and historically situated? Often, claims about the social construction of specific conceptions of nature are advanced as a way of refuting that knowledge and showing it to be false. But the latter does not necessarily follow from the former. Just because our knowledge of something is socially constructed and contingent does not mean that it must be false or unworthy of belief. The idea that our concepts are mental constructions is common to many philosophical viewpoints. Indeed, the vision of knowledge as a conditional construction that can be falsified by testing a hypothesis against observations of the real world is a cornerstone of empiricism, logical positivism, and realism. Proponents of these Enlightenment epistemologies are all opposed to wider philosophical claims about the construction of truth, objective reality, physical nature, or the empirical observations by which we gain access to the world and distinguish true claims about it from false ones. And yet they are also committed to the idea that our knowledge and concepts of nature are constructed. Thus social construction arguments are not necessarily as radical as they are sometimes imagined.

As a concept, 'nature,' in all three senses, must be always understood by reference to the social contexts in which the term has been given meaning. One longstanding ambiguity about these various concepts of nature is to what extent humans stand above or outside of nature. Historically the categorization of different social groups as either inside or outside nature has often been expressed in hierarchical or evolutionary terms. Whereas 'primitive' peoples are often represented as living in a state of wilderness nature (iii), in which they are subject to the universal laws of nature (ii), more modern people are imagined as having escaped these natural imperatives (ii) in a state of civil society that is based on dominating an external natural environment (iii) (Willems-Braun, 1997). This dualism between primitive people living within nature (iii) and 'civilized' people living outside it has alternatively been read so as to legitimate the dispossession of native peoples for failing to improve and cultivate wilderness nature (iii) or alternatively to critique modern people for dominating and destroying the natural environment (iii) (Demeritt 1999). Either way it is a dualism that lends itself easily to racial and colonial stereotyping (see Anderson and Gregory, both this volume).

There is also a second, much more material, way in which 'nature' might be thought of as a social construction. To provide for their needs, people have physically transformed the environment. Farmers, for instance, sow their crops, weeding out pests and other organisms deemed undesirable. Insofar as physiology and protein content are important, the cultural distinction between what we recognize as 'weeds' and as 'crops' is influenced by nature in the sense of (i) and (ii). Mostly, though, it is a cultural choice, imposed on the land by the people cultivating it. In this way nature and the environment are literally social constructions, things crafted and physically produced by the people inhabiting them. This material construction applies most obviously to nature in the sense of (iii), even if the term 'construction' is not always the metaphor of choice for describing the ways people materially change the physical environment. Increasingly through technologies like genetic engineering and global environmental changes like 'greenhouse warming', it is also possible to argue that nature in the sense of (i) and (ii) is also a material social construction. When Marxists use the term 'social nature' it is usually this sense of nature as a materially constructed and socially produced entity they have in mind. By contrast, when people in other schools of thought speak about the social construction of nature often what they mean is the conceptual categories by which we recognize what 'nature' in all three senes is.

Two Kinds of Constructionism: Political Refutation versus Philosophical Critique

Unfortunately these differences have not always been clear because the term construction has been applied to such an astonishing variety of different objects and ends. I have provided a fuller typology of this variety of elsewhere (Demeritt, 1998). But in trying to make sense of the debates about the social construction of nature, it is helpful to borrow a simple distinction from the work of Ian Hacking (1999). He distinguishes between two broad kinds of constructionism. The first is social construction-as-refutation. It is politically motivated. Its proponents use construction talk to help falsify particular claims about the world. Their specific arguments about the social construction of *particular* beliefs or entities do not amount to *universal* claims about the social construction of knowledge or entities, as indiscriminate critics of social constructionism so often imply. Indeed, people resorting to social construction-as-refutation arguments are frequently steadfast defenders of the three Enlightenment suppositions about knowledge and existence that I identified above. Nevertheless, they find construction talk useful because often the first step in the process of refuting a particularly well-established belief is to explain how that false belief was socially constructed and sustained in the first place.

Social construction-as-refutation arguments frequently work by 'denaturalization.' That is, critics seek to show that something, which is now understood as being natural, in the sense either of (i), essentially necessary, or of (ii), biologically determined, or of (iii), the external material world, is not natural at all, but instead is somehow socially constructed. Denaturalizing critiques usually carry an implicit political message as well. By denaturalizing this thing, the objective is to show that it is bad and that we would be better off if it were radically changed, which becomes conceivable once we begin to understand it as a social construction whose particular form and existence we need no longer take for granted (Hacking, 1999). Marxist geographer Smith (1984) has called such politically paralyzing false beliefs in the naturally (in the sense of (i) or (ii) or both) ordained state of things 'ideologies of nature.' But denaturalizing social construction-as-refutation critiques of them are hardly unique to Marxists. A great deal of feminist and antiracist scholarship has appealed to social construction talk in order to denaturalize our concepts of racial and sexual difference and thereby to raise consciousness about the possibility of changing what denaturalizing critiques help us recognize as socially constructed and therefore contingent and potentially reformed categories.

Although this first kind of social construction-as-refutation argument is politically motivated, it is difficult to identify with any coherent 'side' or political position. While both Sokal (1996) and Gross and Levitt (1994) matter-of-factly identified social constructionism with the 'Academic Left,' one of the most remarkable examples of social construction-as-refutation is the effort by conservative ideologues in the United States to refute scientific theories of global warming. They have sought to refute climate change science by exposing the socially negotiated assumptions, theories, and practices through which our knowledge of global warming is constructed. Dana Rohrabacher, new Republican chair of the House Subcommittee on Energy and Environment, which oversees the US agencies funding climate research, declared:

> Nowhere is scientific nonsense more evident than in the global warming programs that are sprinkled throughout the current year budget . . . but

there's a new gang in town ... Our '96 budget does not operate on the assumption that global warming is a proven phenomenon. In fact it is assumed ... at best to be unproven and at worst to be liberal claptrap; trendy, but soon to go out of style in our Newt Congress. (quoted in Brown, 1996: 33).

Rohrabacher is actually making two distinct claims here. The first is ontological. By denying that 'global warming' is a 'proven phenomenon,' he is claiming instead that it is a socially constructed and historically contingent *idea*. His second argument is epistemological and political. By showing that concepts of 'global warming' are socially and historically constructed, Rohrabacher is seeking to refute them. These two arguments are often advanced together. Indeed, Rohrabacher has collapsed the distinction between them entirely. But they are logically independent. Rohrabacher's second claim – that ideas of 'global warming' do not warrant our belief – does not necessarily follow from his first one that it is a socially constructed idea. As I have already explained, Enlightenment epistemologies are committed to truth and reality and yet also subscribe to the belief that our concepts are mental constructions.

The ambiguity of the term construction leaves the epistemological implications of denaturalizing arguments somewhat unclear. Like most English words with the suffix 'tion,' construction is a noun that describes both a process (of constructing) and the outcome of that process (the construction itself). There is an important issue here about the extent to which the social process of conceptual construction has any bearing on the epistemological status and credibility of the resulting knowledge. In popular parlance, socially constructed is synonymous with artificial and untrue. This is certainly what Rohrbacher and other climate skeptics are hoping to suggest by highlighting the role of scientific theories and practice in constructing our knowledge of global warming. Such a reaction is born of age-old distinctions between nature and society. It leaves us with an inflexible, take-it-or-leave-it understanding of scientific knowledge: *either* real, objective, and therefore true *or* artificial, subjective, and thus socially constructed.

My own view is somewhat different. Concern about the relativism of social construction talk is something of a red herring. Demystifying scientific knowledge and demonstrating the social relations its construction involves does not imply disbelief in that knowledge or in the phenomena it represents. The image of a dangerously warmer global climate is unquestionably a social construction – after all, it would not exist, nor, arguably, would the present-day concern with global warming, without the intervention of scientists and their theoretically-based computer models of the climate system (Demeritt, 2001). But they are certainly not free to construct or invent them any way they choose. To dispel any hint of ontological relativism, some constructionists have tried to outline theories of 'constrained construction' (Hayles, 1991) and to insist on the active role of nature 'in negotiating reality' (Bird, 1987). These approaches then raise important questions about what exactly it is that is being constructed. Nature? Our ideas about it? The relationships between the two?

These philosophical reflections provide a hint of the concerns underwriting the second broad variety of social constructionism. In contrast to the first kind of construction-as-political-refutation, a second broad variety of construction talk involves a philosophical critique of the Enlightenment's presumptions about knowledge and existence. Insofar as different critics object to different suppositions, this second variety of social construction talk is somewhat heterogeneous. Many varieties of social constructionism are concerned with situating human knowledge socially and historically. Haraway (1991: 187) has proposed the idea of 'situated knowledge' as a solution to the apparent contradiction involved with advocating "*simultaneously* an account of the radical historical contingency for all knowledge claims and knowing subjects . . . *and* a no-nonsense commitment to faithful accounts of the real world." Such situated knowledge is partial, both in the sense of incomplete and of subjectively biased, and yet still critical and politically accountable because it is reflexive about its own location and construction.

Others use construction talk to advance more ontological claims about specific entities as socially produced, rather than as simply given with fixed ontological properties. Whatmore (1997: 34), for instance, emphasizes the ontological implications of social constructionism. By dissolving the binary distinction between nature and society (as well as those dualisms closely associated with it: objective/subjective, natural/social science, mind/body, reality/representation), theories of social construction help us to "recogni[ze] the intimate, sensible, and hectic bonds through which people, organisms, machines, and other elements make and hold their shape in relation to each other in the business of everyday living" (see Castree and MacMillan, this volume).

Still others would use construction rhetoric to undermine the implicit distinctions I have set up throughout this essay between epistemology and ontology and between conceptual and material constructions of nature. Haraway (1991), for instance, embraces 'cyborg' imagery to unsettle the ontological purity of nature and society. They are instead, Haraway (1997: 141) suggests, contingent and artefactual constructions that emerge from the practical "inter-actions of humans and nonhumans in the distributed, heterogeneous work processes of technoscience." By emphasizing the process of making nature intelligible, Braun and Wainwright (this volume) also seek to make a similar point about the contingency of nature's construction and impossibility of ever finally distinguishing questions of ontology from epistemology.

It is important to recognize the degree to which even the more explicitly philosophical forms of constructionism are necessarily political as well as philosophical in their effects. Hacking (1999), for instance, vastly underestimates the degree to which social construction as philosophical critique can be political as well as philosophical in its aims. The reason that the debates about constructionism have become so contentious is that "questions of epistemology are also questions of social order" (Latour, 1993: 15–16). For instance, it is the hotly contested intergovernmental politics of climate change that make philosophical questions of how the social construction and warranting of scientific knowledge should be understood so politically contentious. Though simplistic, my distinction between social construction as refutation and as philosophical critique is still a useful one because it helps to identify some major differences between two broad varieties of construction talk. These different kinds of social constructionism imply very different epistemological, ontological, and political commitments. They should not all be tarred (or lauded) with the same brush.

Conclusion

Debates over the social construction of nature have created more heat than light. Instead of illuminating the political and philosophical stakes at issue, constructionism has become largely a symbolic term. For its proponents it is a sign of modish radicalism, while others advertise their commitment to rationality and reasonableness by trashing it. This situation has tended to encourage careless and unreflexive usage of the term. There are important issues as stake in the debates over the construction of nature, both political and philosophical. Other essays in this book have more to say about the politics of nature. I have tried to concentrate here on the philosophical ones. Arguments about the construction of nature are ambiguous because of the slipperiness of both terms. I have tried to clarify that ambiguousness by defining those terms more closely. I have identified a number of distinct senses of the word 'nature' and two broad ways in which the construction of 'nature' might be imagined: the construction of our concepts of nature and the material construction of the physical environment. I have also demonstrated the variety of construction talk and explored the similarities and differences between two broad varieties: social construction as refutation and as philosophical critique.

In so doing I have also identified two philosophical sticking points. The first concerns the epistemological implications of understanding our concepts as socially constructed, historically and geographically situated, and in that sense contingent. Although constructionists are not always as explicit as they might be on this issue, it is clear that there are a variety of views on it. The second sticking point concerns the metaphysical implications of understanding 'nature' as an ontologically contingent and socially constructed phenomenon. For many critics of constructionism, 'nature' is precisely that which is *not* socially contingent. These are difficult philosophical questions, and the variety of constructionisms suggests that it is possible to answer them

in a number of different ways. But until constructionists start to engage with
them more explicitly, the politics of constructionism will be no clearer than
the philosophy.

Further Reading

For an overview of construction debates, see Demeritt (1998) and Hacking (1999). In
addition to the other chapters in this book, Demeritt (1999), Wilson (1991), and
Macnaghten and Urry (1998) provide good introductions to the ways in which nature
has been socially constructed.

References

Bird, E. (1987). The Social Construction of Nature: Theoretical Approaches to the
    History of Environmental Problems. *Environmental Review* 11: 255–64.
Brown, G. E. (1996). *Environmental Science Under Siege: Fringe Science and the 104th
    Congress. A Report by Rep. George E. Brown to the Democratic Caucus of the Committee
    on Science, US House of Representatives*. Washington: Democratic Caucus, US House
    of Representatives (http://www.house.gov/science_democrats/archive/envrpt96.htm).
Burningham, K. and Cooper, G. (1999). Being Constructive: Social Constructionism
    and the Environment. *Sociology* 33: 297–316.
Castree, N. (1995). The Nature of Produced Nature. *Antipode* 27: 12–48.
Cronon, W. (1983). *Changes in the Land*. New York: Hill and Wang.
Cronon, W. (1995a). The Trouble with Wilderness; Or, Getting Back to the Wrong
    Nature. In W. Cronon (ed.), *Uncommon Ground: Toward Reinventing Nature*. New
    York: W. W. Norton, 69–90.
Cronon, W. (ed.) (1995b). *Uncommon Ground: Toward Reinventing Nature*. New York:
    W. W. Norton.
Demeritt, D. (1994). The Nature of Metaphors in Cultural Geography and Environ-
    mental History. *Progress in Human Geography*, 18: 163–85.
Demeritt, D. (1996). Social Theory and the Reconstruction of Science and Geography.
    Transactions of the Institute of British Geographers 21: 484–503.
Demeritt, D. (1998). Science, Social Constructivism, and Nature. In B. Braun and N.
    Castree (eds.), *Remaking Reality: Nature at the Millennium*. New York: Routledge,
    173–93.
Demeritt, D. (1999). Nature, Environment, and the Cultures of Nature in North
    America. In F. W. Boal and S. A. Royle (eds.), *North America: Environment and
    Society*. London: Edward Arnold, 37–54.
Demeritt, D. (2001). The Construction of Global Warming and the Politics of Science.
    Annals of the Association of American Geographers 91, forthcoming.
Demeritt, D. (2002). *Property and the Production of Nature in Thoreau's Maine Woods*.
    New York: Cambridge University Press.

Dunlap, R. E. and Catton, W. R., Jr. (1994). Struggling with Human Exceptionalism: The Rise, Decline, and Revitalization of Environmental Sociology. *The American Sociologist* 25: 5–30.

Eder, K. (1996). *The Social Construction of Nature*. London: Sage.

Escobar, A. (1996). Constructing Nature: Elements for a Post-Structural Political Ecology. In R. Peet and M. Watts (eds.), *Liberation Ecology*. New York: Routledge, 46–68.

Fairhead, J. and Leach, M. (1998). *Reframing Deforestation: Global Analyses and Local Realities with Studies in West Africa*. London: Routledge.

Fraser, S. (ed.) (1995). *The Bell Curve Wars: Race, Intelligence, and the Future of America*. New York: Basic Books.

Gandy, M. (1996). Crumbling Land: The Postmodernity Debate and the Analysis of Environmental Problems. *Progress in Human Geography*, 20: 23–40.

Gerber, J. (1997). Beyond Dualism – The Social Construction of Nature and the Natural *and* Social Construction of Human Beings. *Progress in Human Geography* 21: 1–17.

Golinski, J. (1998). *Making Natural Knowledge: Constructivism and the History of Science*. New York: Cambridge University Press.

Greider, T. and Garkovich, L. (1994). Landscapes: The Social Construction of Nature and the Environment. *Rural Sociology* 59: 1–24.

Gross, P. R. and Levitt, N. (1994). *Higher Superstition: The Academic Left and Its Quarrels with Science*. Baltimore: Johns Hopkins University Press.

Hacking, I. (1999). *The Social Construction of What?* Cambridge, Mass.: Harvard University Press.

Hannigan, J. A. (1995). *Environmental Sociology: A Social Constructivist Perspective*. New York: Routledge.

Haraway, D. J. (1991). *Simians, Cyborgs, and Women: The Reinvention of Nature*. New York: Routledge.

Haraway, D. J. (1992). The Promises of Monsters: A Regenerative Polics for Inappropriate/d Others. In L. Grossberg, C. Nelson, and P. A. Treichler (eds.), *Cultural Studies*. New York: Routlege, 295–337.

Haraway, D. J. (1997). *Modest_Witness@Second_Millennium*. New York: Routledge.

Harrison, C. M. and Burgess, J. (1994). Social Constructions of Nature: A Case Study of Conflicts over the Development of Rainham Marshes SSSI. *Transactions of the Institute of British Geographers* 19: 291–310.

Hayles, N. K. (1991). Constrained Constructivism: Locating Scientific Inquiry in the Theatre of Representation. *New Orleans Review* 18: 76–85.

Hernstein, R. and Murray, C. (1994). *The Bell Curve: Intelligence and Class Structure in American Life*. New York: Basic Books.

Kong, L. and Yeoh, B. (1996). Social Constructions of Nature in Urban Singapore. *Southeast Asian Studies* 34: 402–23.

Latour, B. (1993). *We Have Never Been Modern*, trans. C. Porter. Cambridge, Mass.: Harvard University Press.

Latour, B. and Woolgar, S. (1979). *Laboratory Life: The Social Construction of Scientific Facts*. London: Sage Publications.

Macnaghten, P. and Urry, J. (1998). *Contested Natures*. London: Sage.

Mitchell, D. (2000). *Cultural Geography: A Critical Introduction*. Oxford: Blackwell.

Neumann, R. P. 1998: *Imposing Wilderness: Struggles over Livelihood and Nature Preservation in Africa.* Berkeley: University of California Press.

New Republic. (1994). Special Issue on Race and IQ. 211(4), Oct. 31.

Olwig, K. (1996). Environmental History and the Construction of Nature and Landscape: The Case of the 'Landscaping' of the Jutland Heath. *Environment and History* 2, 15–38.

Patton, C. (1990). *Inventing AIDS.* New York: Routledge.

Proctor, J. D. (1998). The Social Construction of Nature: Relativist Accusations, Pragmatist and Critical Realist Responses. *Annals of the Association of American Geographers* 88: 352–76.

Scarce, R. (2000). *Fishy Business: Salmon, Biology, and the Social Construction of Nature.* Philadelphia: Temple University Press.

Seale, C. (1998). *Constructing Death: The Sociology of Dying and Bereavement.* New York: Cambridge University Press.

Smith, H. N. (1950). *Virgin Land: The American West as Symbol and Myth.* Cambridge, Mass.: Harvard University Press.

Smith, N. (1984). *Uneven Development.* Oxford: Blackwell.

Sokal, A. (1996). A Physicist Experiments with Cultural Studies. *Lingua Franca* 6 (May/June); 62–4.

Soule, M. E. and Lease, G. (eds.) (1995). *Reinventing Nature?: Responses to Postmodern Deconstruction.* Washington, DC: Island Press.

Staples, W. G. (2000). *Everyday Surveillance: Vigilance and Visibility in Postmodern Life.* Lanham, Md: Rowman & Littlefield.

Synder, G. (1998). Is Nature Real? *Whole Earth Magazine* (winter), http://www.wholeearthmag.com/ArticleBin/188.htm.

Whatmore, S. (1999). Hybrid Geographies: Rethinking the 'Human' in Human Geography. In D. Massey, J. Allen, P. Sarre (eds.), *Human Geography Today.* Cambridge: Polity, 22–39.

Willems-Braun, B. (1997). Buried Epistemologies: The Politics of Nature in (post)colonial British Columbia. *Annals of the Association of American Geographers* 87: 3–31.

Williams, R. (1983). *Keywords: A Vocabulary of Culture and Society,* 2nd edn. London: Flamingo.

Wilson, A. (1991). *The Culture of Nature: North American Landscape from Disney to the Exxon Valdez.* Toronto: Between the Lines.

Worster, D. (1985). *Rivers of Empire: Water, Aridity, and the Growth of the American West.* New York: Pantheon.

Worster, D. (1990). The Ecology of Order and Chaos. *Environmental History Review,* 14: 1–18.

Chapter 3

Nature, Poststructuralism, and Politics

Bruce Braun and Joel Wainwright

What is it to think the present in its presence?
Jacques Derrida (1982: 23)

Introduction: Nature and Legibility

This chapter seeks to contribute to, and extend, our understanding of the *culture* and *politics* of nature. To investigate this we will shift the focus of our analysis from questions of nature's material existence and transformation to questions of epistemology.[1] How is it that something called 'nature' comes into being as an object of knowledge? How are certain understandings of nature stabilized? And with what consequences? These questions lead us into much more than debates over meaning; they take us into a complex terrain of power and politics. As we will see, the very possibility of speaking of nature with some level of certainty – and by extension, of acting upon the physical world – entails foreclosing on other possibilities. This is because what *counts* as nature is never a closed question. Further, the concepts through which we know nature are deeply implicated in the kinds of nature that we produce: *social nature* is produced at these epistemological/ontological junctures where concepts, actions, and matter get mixed together (Haraway, 1997; Escobar, 1999; Braun, 2000). As we argue in this chapter, how nature comes to be stabilized as an object of knowledge has concrete effects, both social and ecological. This leads us to see the need to rigorously question our concepts of nature even as we must still speak 'of' nature, as well as to see how environmental politics are always entangled with a cultural politics of knowing.

Before proceeding it will be helpful to foreground the central issues raised in this chapter, and to clarify how these issues complicate dominant research paradigms in the study of human–environment relations. Our most important point is that the very thing that is taken to be the object of environmental studies and politics – namely, 'nature' – is an effect of power. This represents somewhat of a departure from existing work in the field which assumes nature to be an unproblematic category, in the sense that it is a thing that is self-present to knowledge. Our goal here is to change the very terms in which interactions with, and struggles over, nature are understood. To argue that environmental disputes merely reflect competing 'interests' assumes that what is perceived as natural is self-evident, and exists *external* to the domain of power and politics that geographers and political ecologists set out to study. In a similar fashion, to assert that environmental issues are primarily about 'ethics' (how to act *toward* nature) is to assume that it is only our attitudes and values that are at stake, not the 'thing' to which the ethical relation is to be fostered (but see Proctor, this volume). In contrast to this we will argue that such debates are always enabled by a set of discursive practices through which what counts as nature is made intelligible.

All this has important consequences for how we think about environmental politics. It forces us to recognize the fundamental openness, or undecidability, of what counts as nature in environmental conflicts, and in turn reveals the urgent need for critical analysis of how the stabilization or normalization of any particular understanding of nature is achieved. It also prods us to attend to the ways in which constructions of nature are non-innocent, since as we will see in the examples we discuss, they carry with them certain (disavowed) political commitments. Finally, it suggests that the discussion of environmental ethics is often the wrong place to begin: to the extent that discussions over ethics assume nature to be a pregiven category, they fail to recognize the ways in which relations of power are already present. Or, to say this differently, environmental ethics, by framing the matter in terms of human relations *to* nature, often fail to take into account the cultural politics *of* nature.

We will develop these arguments in the pages that follow. As we do so we will introduce one further element to this chapter. To justify our arguments we will rely heavily on a set of concepts often referred to as 'poststructuralist.' Although we will later find reasons to problematize this term, one of our objectives is to examine what new questions for research and politics this body of thought introduces to the study of social nature. What is gained by drawing on poststructuralist concepts? We can begin to answer this question by turning to an example of the politics of nature drawn from a set of struggles around the temperate rainforests on Canada's west coast.

The Fate of the Forest in British Columbia

Biogeographers have long considered the heavily treed, mountainous region from Alaska to Northern California a unique climatic and vegetation zone. Although the terminology for these forests – and what has been considered their most important characteristics – has changed over time, they are today commonly referred to as 'coastal temperate rainforests', a term that differentiates the region from other ecological zones, including 'tropical rainforests' with which these forests share very little except exceptionally high levels of precipitation. Although there were antecedents, forestry became a major industry in the region only in the early to mid-twentieth century, at first in association with local mining and agriculture for which it supplied needed timber, but eventually serving markets for softwood lumber and pulp and paper across the country, as well as in the United States, Europe, and more recently Japan and east Asia. In the late 1940s, the provincial government of British Columbia (in Canada's decentralized federalist system provinces hold constitutional powers over natural resources) established a system of sustainable yield units (SYUs) that covered virtually the entire extent of the province. These were leased to forestry companies who, through various forms of state regulation, were compelled to manage their operations for 'maximum sustainable yield.'

Between the mid-1940s, when this system of forestry was initiated, until the early 1980s, when its terms began to be seriously challenged, this arrangement formed a relatively stable regime of accumulation based upon the distribution of forest wealth between the state, forest companies, and workers, and upon a vision of modernist social planning in which controlling nature was understood as a means by which to produce a rational society (see Scott, 1998). On the British Columbia (BC) coast, sustained yield forestry was organized according to a plan whereby bounded 'forest spaces' were first constructed and then 'harvested' at a rate that equaled the annual incremental increase in tree fiber in the region as a whole. At least in theory, for each tree cut, an equal amount of fiber would be added to the forest elsewhere (figure 3.1). The spatial metaphor of a 'working circle' exemplified this rationality; by the time one 'cycle' of the circle was completed, the areas cut initially would be ready to be harvested again, and it was thought that this could go on in perpetuity. Many thought that this would lead to stable capitalist development: forest workers and forest communities would no longer be subject to boom–bust cycles; forestry companies would have long-term access to forest resources; and the state would receive revenues from taxation that would support the management and maintenance of this regime, as well as contribute to the development of the social fabric of the province.

Three related developments disrupted this socioecological order and helped produce a crisis in BC's forests in the 1980s and 1990s. First, for a variety of reasons ranging from inaccurate inventories to falling rates of profit, levels of tree cut were set far too high, such that as the first cycle neared completion, second-growth forests were not yet commercially viable. Second, with increased mechanization, employment in the forest industry dropped, with drastic effects on the communities whose fate was directly linked to sustained-yield forestry. These two developments increased pressure to log more remote or less accessible

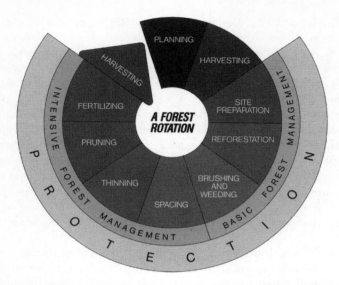

Figure 3.1: Working circles: constructing the rational forest in sustained-yield forestry

forests in order to sustain corporate profits, government revenues, and community stability. Third, and related to these developments, with each additional cut, the remaining uncut forest took on added significance for a number of different actors, especially environmentalists who increasingly saw the 'pristine' forests under threat of 'disappearance.' Thus, by the 1990s, what had previously been local conflicts over specific industry actions gathered intensity, becoming a broad-based campaign to 'save' the remaining uncut forests, including numerous global actors such as Greenpeace, the Sierra Club, and the Natural Resources Defense Council.

Until this point, we have presented these struggles in relatively conventional terms. That is, we have treated the conflict in terms of a struggle between development and conservation, in which an increasing scarcity runs up against competing forest values. Around this central conflict can be arrayed a series of different actors with specific 'interests': forest companies, state forest managers, local communities, workers, local First Nations peoples, environmentalists, and so forth, each of which might be said to have a 'stake' in how the dispute is resolved. In turn, such an analysis might posit a set of social and economic dynamics that shape the struggle: a logic of capital accumulation, state rationality, forms of cultural identity, and so on, which may be said to *inform* the actions of different actors. Arguably, this is precisely how these struggles have been represented, both in accounts provided by social scientists (Barnes and Hayter, 1997; Marchak, 1997) and in the media (Matas, 1993).

Here we wish to register two reservations. First, what we have termed 'conventional' interpretations of forest struggles place actors in pregiven categories and view them as the conscious bearers of particular, objective interests. What we will argue is that these subject positions do not prefigure these conflicts, but emerge *within* them (Moore, 1999). Second, what is left unquestioned in such accounts is the ontological status of the 'rainforest' itself. The struggle is framed as being 'over' the rainforest, that is, over its fate as a source of (economic or aesthetic) value. Yet, this leaves unexamined the very ways that the 'rainforest' is constructed and stabilized as an object of economic and political calculation in the first place, and therefore hides from view an important arena for the operation of power.

In answer to the question – what is this conflict about? – conventional analysts may very well answer: it is about the fate of the rainforest and who benefits from its use. But to this, we must immediately ask, *what* rainforest? What are we referring to when we speak of the 'rainforest'? How is it that we are able to speak of something called a 'rainforest'? What is included in this thing, and what is excluded from it? Ultimately, what are the political consequences of framing the forest in these terms?

Interrogating 'Nature'

The argument we have started to sketch is that the 'forest' cannot preexist its construction (cf. Haraway, 1992). This draws heavily on arguments put forward by a number of writers often grouped together as poststructuralist. As we will explain shortly, for these writers the 'truth' about the world is not something that is self-evident, but instead is an *effect* of practices of signification, including the very distinction between nature and society. Before proceeding, however, it will be helpful to discuss some common misunderstandings. First, to speak of 'truth' as a discursive effect is not to deny the materiality of the world, but to insist that there is no way to talk about this reality before the entry of this 'reality' into discourse, i.e. without words and concepts. Note here that we place 'reality' in scare-quotes not because we are ambivalent about the existence of 'a real world' – rest assured, we believe in reality! – but because there is no innocent, prediscursive metalanguage for us to use to describe that 'reality'. Thus we reject the 'strong constructivist' view that language precedes and produces the world and that denies any part in the construction of knowledge to the material world itself (see Demeritt, 1998 and the chapter above; arguably very few strong constructivists exist outside of the imagination of critics who fail to differentiate between types of constructivism). If we return to our example of the 'rainforest,' a constructivist argument would be that there is no place external to, or outside, language (or the practice of producing meanings) from which the 'forest' can be objectively known. The 'forest' is the outcome of practices of signification, not their immediate cause.

If we accept this, a number of implications follow. We can see, for instance, that the very idea of 'human interactions with nature' is always already predicated on one particular (cultural) way of understanding nature. Moreover, the continuous remaking of nature through social practices is always in part a cultural process, for it is only through cultural practices of knowing and representing that action is possible. This is only more the case in the heavily scientized world we inhabit today (Haraway, 1997; Wright, 1998). We can also see that when social practices are contested in defense of 'nature,' the nature defended is also already a cultural artifact, since what counts as nature emerges in and through discursive practices (Cronon, 1995). Thus, environmental politics of every kind always involve framing nature in ways that have particular consequences.

'Nature' as an effect of discursive practices

The insight that the forest emerges through historically specific discursive practices, and the broader point that 'reality' is never transparent to us but accessible only in particular ways, owes a considerable debt to poststructuralist thought, and especially the work of the historian and critic Michel Foucault. Foucault's studies on the historical emergence within everyday thought of such categories as 'madness,' 'sexuality,' the 'body,' and so on, showed that there are always a given set of understandings, metaphors, expressions, statements, and gestures – that is, discursive practices – that govern what can be said about entities in the world at any given time and place. These discursive practices in turn were shown by Foucault to be tied to the work of institutions, such as prisons, hospitals, and schools, through which certain ways of relating to the world were made possible. In other words, Foucault asked his readers to consider the ways in which knowledge was produced as an effect of power (rather than an innocent discovery), and in turn how power operated through knowledge.

We can refer to Foucault's approach as 'epistemological constructivism,' meaning that knowledge is socially and historically produced rather than found (see also Haraway, 1991; Demeritt, 1998). Many writers have extended Foucault's analysis to other domains and disciplines. Donna Haraway (1992), for instance, insists that we understand biology as a discourse, not as life itself. Biology, as a set of discursive practices, constitutes a way of knowing through its particular rules and regularities, as well as its gaps and silences. Indeed, as we will see later, such silences are not simply a result of 'incomplete' knowledge, but are necessary for any knowledge to achieve its status as 'truth.' While

Haraway developed her ideas through a series of challenging studies of late modern technoscience, Foucault focused on earlier periods. In *The Order of Things* (1970), for instance, he explored how the relationship between 'words' and 'things' came to be systematically rethought in the early modern period, and dwelt at some length on the emergence of 'natural history' as a discourse that governed what could (and what could not) be said about living beings. For Foucault, ways of knowing were always historical and contingent. Natural history, for example, departed from earlier systems of knowledge: with its emphasis on taxonomy and distribution it placed objects in a grid of knowledge by which different entities could be related or differentiated (see also Pratt, 1992; Gregory, 1994). This approach held sway up to the end of the eighteenth century – and was an integral element of European imperialism which thrived on such universal taxonomic systems – after which it was displaced in part by other knowledge systems, most prominently biology and its study of 'life.'

Foucault, of course, did not conjure these notions out of thin air. Nor was he the only one working within this philosophical ethos. Indeed, what we today call poststructuralism – a term that suggests a far more unified body of theory than actually exists – has a complicated history that deserves at least a brief detour. The term, with its prefix 'post,' suggests that it is a set of ideas that replaced something called structuralism, but we need to be cautious in making this claim, partly because there were different structuralisms, and partly because the 'post' in poststructuralism suggests the existence of a radical break when there are actually many continuities.

Structuralism, in its various forms, entailed an approach to studying social practices that rethought the relationship between the world, meaning, and action. Structuralists borrowed heavily from the work of a Swiss linguist, Ferdinand de Saussure, who proposed a highly original way of thinking about the relationship between language and meaning. Saussure's major insight was that language was a structured system and that this system could be studied through the operation of linguistic signs. For Saussure, a sign had two aspects, a signifier and a signified. The signifier was that which was perceived (a symbol in the case of writing, a sound in speech); the signified was the meaning or concept that was understood. To use one of Saussure's examples, 'arbre' is a signifier, and the concept of 'tree' is the signified. The sign as a whole is therefore a combination of concept and sound pattern (Saussure 1983: 66). Saussure's work contributed to structuralist thought by suggesting that language, and linguistic meaning, were undergirded by a structured system of signs. The key insight to be gathered from this was that 'beneath' all cultural practices were sign-systems that afforded to meaning a certain stability.

What we now refer to as structuralism emerged as this set of ideas came into contact with anthropology, political economy, literature, psychology and other related disciplines in the humanities and social sciences. The effect was to introduce new questions for research. Although the form that structuralism took in each discipline differed, they all shared an approach to understanding social processes that looked 'behind' the everyday actions of human subjects in order to uncover the hidden or underlying structures that guided human behavior. The anthropologist Lévi-Strauss, for example, proposed that the cultural-symbolic realm was structured like a language, and thus governed by universal rules, such as the incest taboo. One result of the structuralist turn was to complicate theories of human agency (or intentionality) to emphasize structures that circumscribe the actions of individuals.

Poststructuralism emerged both from attempts to push these structuralist insights to their limits, and as a response to them. Foucault retained some aspects of structuralist thought, especially during the period of his 'archaeological' inquiries in which he sought to trace the outlines of *epistemes* – the underlying structures of thought specific to certain historical periods – which he tended to present as a unified totality. His later work, in contrast, provided more room for the *instability* of forms of knowledge, explicitly undermining the notion of a single, universal, or timeless, structure. This obtained far greater expression in the work of Jacques Derrida. Derrida and Foucault share certain similarities, such as the fact that they are both French theorists who studied with the Marxist philosopher Louis Althusser. But their work is actually quite different in ways that are often overlooked by social scientists. Foucault's ideas have also been more readily taken up and used by geographers and political ecologists than have Derrida's. This is unfortunate, because, as we will argue, Derrida's approach to philosophy offers us useful ways of rethinking how geography and political ecology have been done.

Derrida is probably best-known for two words – 'deconstruction' and '*différance*' – which stand for key philosophical interventions. Although these concepts are difficult, they are tremendously important, and deserve careful attention. Deconstruction is sometimes (incorrectly) treated as a method, or dismissed as merely a procedure for *destroying* meanings. It can be understood instead as an approach to reading that constantly and rigorously challenges the possibility of achieving *closure* of meaning, since there is no center or core from which meaning radiates:

> To deconstruct is a structuralist and anti-structuralist gesture at the same time . . . an artifact is taken apart in order to make the structure, the nerves, or as you say the skeleton appear, but also, simultaneously, the ruinous precariousness of a formal structure that explained nothing, since it is neither a center, a principle, a force, nor even the law of events, in the most general sense of this word. (Derrida 1995: 83)

This notion of deconstruction owes a considerable debt to the work of another philosopher, Martin Heidegger, who rigorously thought through ideas of being and existence as developed in the Western philosophical tradition.

These efforts have profoundly influenced many of the thinkers we refer to in this chapter (Foucault, Derrida, Butler, and Haraway). One way to understand how Heidegger inspired these thinkers is to turn to his notion of the 'crossing-through.' In an essay on "the question of being" written in 1955, Heidegger argued that in order to think through the question of humanism – i.e. what is human essence? – one would have to first confront the question of the essence of 'being.' This leads Heidegger to look back, with some nostalgia, to a time before language was corrupted by the 'problems' of nihilism, essence, and humanism, and to generate new grammatical strategies that enable him to think 'being' (*Sein*) differently. Heidegger does this by writing or 'crossing through' *Sein* as ~~*Sein*~~; in doing this, he is *not* saying that 'being' does not exist, but that being is placed under erasure (placed in question). Thus, he is not negating being, in the sense of simply destroying the concept. We can still read the word 'being' under the mark of crossing-through, but only while knowing that it cannot be accessed as a stable concept. We are left with a 'being' that is revealed in its effacement, that is, only known as it is taken away. This may seem paradoxical – since 'being' is both necessary for our thinking yet impossible – but paradox is productive because it allows us to think at/about the limits of our metaphysical traditions.

With this gesture Heidegger opened a powerful strategy for rigorous thinking among whose practitioners Derrida figures prominently. In some sense, Derrida's work with 'deconstruction' entails the 'putting under erasure' of the entire Western philosophical tradition. Since we have already mentioned semiology, let us see (rather superficially in the space available) how this works as Derrida 'reads Saussure against himself.' A crucial moment in Saussure's theory occurs where Saussure defines the relationship between signified and signifier as unmotivated and arbitrary; that is, there is no absolute, necessary relationship between the signified and the signifier (see above). But Derrida shows that, if we rigorously accept Saussure's starting-point – i.e., the arbitrariness of the sign relation – then there can be no "relationship of natural subordination, [or] any natural hierarchy among signifiers or order of signifiers" (1976: 44). Thus, meaning is always potentially mutable, an effect of the play of différance.

Like deconstruction, *différance* is sometimes seen as a neologism 'invented' by Derrida (from the French word *différence*, but with an *a*). This 'a' is a subtle intervention in the word French *différence*, which has two meanings: to differ and to defer. With *différance* Derrida gestures to a play of deferrals and differentiations within meaning. Crucially, Derrida argues that *différance* has been, in some sense, always already 'in' Western metaphysics. By using this nonconcept *différance*, Derrida is gesturing to undecidability at the apparent 'center' of writing, sense, and meaning. Like deconstruction, Derrida 'uses' *différance* to interrogate what makes Western metaphysics work. This project has been called antifoundationalism, because it shakes the philosophical basis of our tradition. But such a formulation is limited because it only emphasizes the aspect of *negation* in Derrida's work – as if Derrida were out to destroy all sense. But one can also think of his project as 'positive deconstruction,' in the sense that by embracing the undecidability of meaning we can open up new possibilities for thought and politics.

This brings us back to the question of nature, but in a new way. Geographers and political ecologists have traditionally taken 'man and land,' or more recently 'nature and society' as the point of departure for environmental studies. Taking up Derrida's insight that "what is put into question is precisely the quest for a rightful beginning, an absolute point of departure" (1982: 6), we argue that it is precisely this point of departure – nature and society – that needs to be interrogated. Instead of simply accepting traditional formulations of environmental studies, we instead ask what 'cognitive failures' are necessary to make this starting-point seem self-evident. What is forgotten by this way of framing the problem? As we demonstrate in what follows, it is not only the conjunction nature *and* society that must be placed in question, but also the ontological presuppositions contained in both terms. These two seemingly separate things – 'nature' and 'society' – are perhaps neither separate nor stable categories of being.

The 'Forest' and its Constitutive Absences

1 Producing the 'forest'

We can put these ideas to work by returning to the forest conflicts on Canada's west coast. As we explained earlier, recent conflicts over the 'fate' of the forest have pitted environmentalists against industry, First Nations against the state, environmentalists against First Nations, even the state against industry, in a complex, shifting matrix of political actors. Although commonly represented as a struggle over the 'temperate rainforest,' these struggles are also in part an effect of, and waged over, the very concepts used to discuss these landscapes. It is on the production of the 'rainforest' as an object of political calculation that we wish to focus our attention.

We can begin by turning to what arguably has been the most important document in the history of forestry on Canada's west coast, *The Royal Commission Report on the Forest Resources of British Columbia*, written for the BC government by Justice Gordon Sloan in 1945. This report recommended, and provided the blueprint for, a 'modern' system of 'sustained-yield forestry,' and the many recommendations Sloan made were incorporated with little change into the province's Forestry Act over the next three years.

Sloan's report was at the time, and remains today, an item of considerable debate. At the time it was written, the debate turned the question of whether the ownership of the resource should remain in public hands, or be handed to private business (see Drushka, et al., 1993). Sloan's report and subsequent forestry legislation fell somewhere in between, with the state retaining ownership of the resource and private corporations provided with long-term leases. In subsequent years this system of tenure has come under attack, mostly at the hands of critics who have suggested that the system reduced diversification in the province's forest industry, and that it represented a deep distrust of 'ordinary citizens' of the province by bureaucrats, resource professionals, and others, including industry (ibid.). As important as these debates are, we want to focus instead on the manner in which Sloan's report, and subsequent debates over forestry, have turned on framing the forest in particular ways, while at the same time placing on the margins other cultural and political understandings of these landscapes.

Let us explain by examining the master concept of sustained-yield forestry announced in Sloan's report: the 'working circle.' Rather than focus on how such a program might be instituted, we ask instead what presuppositions operate unannounced in its tidy rationality? What underlying assumptions about the 'forest' allowed Sloan to frame the forest, and forestry, in this way? Here we will leave aside the important question of whether such sustained-yield forestry is ecologically viable in order to focus instead on three related issues: what this diagram – and the discourse of sustained-yield forestry that it embodied – assumed about the 'forest' as an ontological entity; the discursive practices that enabled the construction of such a diagram; and, ultimately, the degree to which Sloan's ordering of the 'forest' was predicated on the *prior* construction of the 'forest' as both a *natural* and *national* resource.

To say this differently, our question is not whether sustained-yield forestry was the most rational way to proceed; rather, we ask what understandings about the forest enabled this ordering of the forest to *appear* rational. To what extent was this regime of forestry predicated on the forest being framed in some ways and not others? Tracing the many forces that have shaped the emergence of the temperate rainforest in political discourse is a daunting task, but we can get a sense of what it might entail, and what might be at stake in such a project by beginning to unpack Sloan's working circles. Sloan's understanding of the forest, for instance, owed something to the development of the science of conservation at the end of the nineteenth century, most closely associated in North America with the figure of Gifford Pinchot. Such a science could never have emerged, however, without an array of representational practices through which the forest could appear as a spatial and statistical object, and thus something that could be known, measured, and conserved. Here we have in mind innovations in cartography, developments in mensuration (the science of quantifying the quantity of wood fiber in a forest), techniques of accounting, and so on. In other words, the emergence of a discourse of conservation in

state planning was indebted far less to individual actors like Pinchot, who is
often presented as a heroic figure in these stories, than it was a result of a series
of practices through which it was possible to render visible the extent of the
forest, rates of growth and deforestation, threats to its renewal, and so on.
Crucially, the 'forest' in conservation discourse is not something that existed
independently from the maps, tables, techniques, and practices that made it
available to forms of economic and political calculation. One must first see the
forest before one can rationalize it.

2 "If there were a mountain"

The working circles were one set of discursive practices that 'constructed' the
forest as a space of economic and political calculation. Here we wish to suggest
that there is another, equally important way in which Sloan 'constructed' the
forest. This time, however, we will attend to what is left unsaid or unthought
in his understanding of the forest, as well as how this comes back to haunt the
system of forestry that his report helped set in place.

In what appears to be an innocent passage located early in his report Sloan
invites his readers to accompany him on a journey up an "imaginary mountain"
in order to grasp the spatial character of the province's forests:

> If there were a mountain near Vancouver with a gently ascending slope, the
> climber would find as he progressed upward that beyond the 2,000 foot line
> a gradual change in the forest species was encountered. He would notice the
> Douglas fir was thinning out and the stand was now made up of cedar,
> hemlock, and balsam, in that order of importance. Still climbing, he would
> find himself in a forest of hemlock, cedar, spruce and balsam. Higher up his
> forest would now be hemlock, balsam, spruce and cedar. Soon the cedar is
> left below and the hemlock, spruce, and balsam remain in that order. Should
> he persist in his climb, he would get into scrub and non-commercial
> mountain species.
>
> Now, let us conceive of our gradually ascending slope, not as a mountain
> near Vancouver, but as the coastal plane of the province, stretched out from
> south to north. Let us assume our climber is traveling north up the latitudes
> instead of up the mountain. He would come upon the same general
> classification of forest-cover in the same order of species as we encountered
> on our imaginary Vancouver mountain. (Sloan, 1945: 19)

Although it reads as a departure from the more scientific tone of the rest of his
report, the passage deserves further comment (historians have generally ignored
it). Its first paragraph begins with Sloan asking his readers to take part in a
thought experiment ("if there were a mountain"). Now, we might chide Sloan

for inventing a forest that does not exist; but the fact that he invokes an imaginary forest here is a serious, productive moment, one that makes possible a truth about 'the forest.' This 'truth' is made explicit in the second paragraph, where Sloan asks us to shift from the 'imaginary' mountain to the 'reality' of the coastal rainforest. Whereas the first paragraph is supposed to be read as fictional, the second purports to describe the 'real.' But are the two different in the ways that Sloan suggests? Or, is the second forest – the one that Sloan juxtaposes to his "imaginary Vancouver mountain" – as metaphorical as the first?

To answer this question, it is important to note that Sloan's 'forest' was not something that one could 'discover' at the time. Sloan imagines a landscape that consists merely of a mix of different species of trees: hemlock, cedar, balsam, spruce, and so on. This is not only a remarkable simplification of what we now recognize through the language of ecology to be a complex ecosystem; it also posits the forest as an entirely 'natural' entity – a domain that existed separate from the people and communities that were in part constitutive of it. Read today, after years of blockades, protests, and court challenges by First Nations, the absence of any discussion of the forest as anything *other* than a 'natural' entity may strike many readers as remarkable, even naïve. At the time of its writing, however, the 'naturalness' of the forest was simply *assumed*, at least in the minds of BC's non-Native population.

Here we can interject a series of questions. How was it possible that in 1945 Justice Sloan, and the predominantly white settler society that lived in the province, could understand the 'forest' in these terms, as a place devoid of history and culture? What were the consequences of framing the forest in these terms? And in what ways has this 'underlying fiction' of the natural forest been subsequently challenged? The first point we need to make is that depicting the forest in this way was not an intentionally malicious act by Sloan designed to diminish other claims to land and resources. Sloan may well have sympathized with the province's capitalist class, and some have argued that he had close ties to the politicians leading the BC government at the time, but this does not concern us here. Rather, what is important to note is that Sloan drew upon widely-held assumptions about what constituted the 'forest.' Thus, while the system of forestry that emerged in the years after Sloan's report was a matter of great contention, the image of the 'forest' on which it was predicated received no comment. Instead, since the forest was framed as a *natural* rather than a *social* entity, First Nations were not invited to participate in the Sloan Commission proceedings.

What allowed Sloan's forest to appear under the guise of the 'real' was the acceptance of a particular understanding of the forest as common-sense, that is, its sedimentation as 'reality' through processes of iteration. By the late nineteenth century – some fifty years before Sloan's report – it had already become common practice to divide BC landscapes into two separate domains: a domain of 'primitive culture' (native village sites, totem poles, and artifacts), and a domain of 'nature' (geology, climate, and biogeography). This can be seen in the work of individuals like George Dawson, a geologist and natural historian, who on the one hand cataloged in great detail native 'culture' (its folklore, rituals, material artifacts, architecture, and so on), and on the other gave remarkable descriptions of the 'physical landscape' (Braun, 1997). The effect was to separate 'resources' from their cultural relations and from the communities who relied on them (see, for instance, Dawson's map of the geology of Skidegate Inlet, a region heavily populated by the Haida, figure 3.2). This discursive separation authorized the mapping of 'resources' without any reference to the activities and practices of Native peoples. While Dawson was a geologist, he also enumerated the 'forest wealth' of the province, constructing it as a natural entity, governed by 'natural history' rather than infused with culture and politics. With this constitutive absence it became all the more possible to understand these 'forest spaces' as empty, and thus to incorporate them as the sovereign territory of the Canadian state. As this separation was accomplished by discursive means, it facilitated the exercise of colonial state power, through the segregation of Natives on small reserves. This example demonstrates how colonial narratives of indi-geneity and conquest enabled particular ways of thinking about the state–First Nations relations; the discursive separation of Natives and land was one of the conditions that led to their physical separation.

By the time of Sloan's 1945 report the disavowal of the forest's cultural histories was so complete that it simply operated unannounced across the province's public, political, and legal arenas. We can say, then, that what could count as the 'the forest' had come to be constrained within certain discursive norms that governed its appearance. Over time this 'forest' would become so deeply woven into the social, economic, and political organization of the province as a whole that redefining the forest as a cultural landscape would be a subversive and threatening move.

Yet, the legibility of the forest – as 'the forest' – was, and can only ever be, a *provisional* achievement. Moreover, as we saw in this example, this intelligibil-ity was achieved through a 'cognitive failure' (Spivak, 1988), which is to say that it was achieved by leaving something out. What is left out is not simply excluded, it exists through its absence as a constitutive element of what 'is.' The feminist philosopher Judith Butler (1993) refers to this as the 'constitutive outside' which must be excluded in order for any entity or identity – the body, sex, nature – to achieve its apparent coherence. In Butler's work the object in question is 'sexuality,' and she explains how heterosexuality is normalized through the 'casting-off' of that which does not fit within its conceptual frames (e.g. homosexuality). It is that which is excluded – and the disavowal of this act of exclusion – that enables heteronormativity to appear as 'natural.' The same can be said for any other object or identity. In BC state forestry discourse, but also occasionally in environmentalist rhetoric as well, what is excluded are

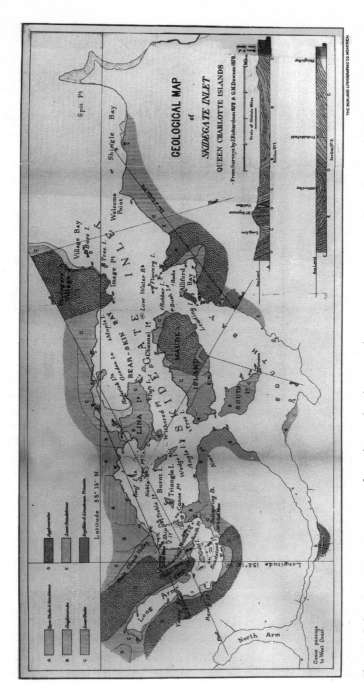

Figure 3.2: Separating 'resources' from their cultural surrounds: George Dawson's geological map of Skidegate Inlet, British Columbia, Canada (1878)

the complex ways that First Nations' territorial and material practices are interwoven with the surrounding physical landscape. This combination of separation with exclusion must be read against the broader history of the British colonial project in British Columbia. What we call 'colonial' forestry – which exists even after the end of official colonialism – appears as a technical problem of management, rather than as a political question of justice, precisely because it disavows this founding exclusion (Spivak would say that it operates with a kind of 'sanctioned ignorance'). Indeed, it is only when this constitutive absence begins to be called into question that forestry comes to take on the prefix 'colonial'; before this, it is simply 'forestry.'

Here we can pause to reflect further on the value of certain poststructuralist concepts. First, while poststructuralist thought is often discussed in terms of its emphasis on the *impossibility* of 'fixing' meaning within an objective grid of logic and reason, it also alerts us to the way that forms of closure, however provisional and unstable, are *achieved* in everyday practices. In turn, it points to the always-present possibility of other articulations. By destabilizing the notion that there is an 'outside' to discourse – where an ahistorical or universal metalanguage could be used as a reference to 'interpret' the truth of this particular discourse – poststructuralist thinking attunes us to the contingency of what comes to count as the 'real,' as well as its political effects.

(Hau)ntologies

In the preceding section we suggested that closure is always a provisional achievement that works through iteration or repetition. This is not merely a matter of speech or writing; such norms become institutionalized in state and legal practice to such a degree that social life would be placed in crisis if they were all to be questioned at once. Yet, it is also the case that every articulation of the colonial 'forest' is *haunted* by its constitutive disavowals which threaten to return to disrupt the truths that work through their absence.

This is worth exploring further, both theoretically and through a specific example. As we noted earlier, our ability to speak of the world relies on referencing existing systems of signification. Derrida asks:

> Could a performative utterance succeed if its formulation did not repeat a 'coded' or iterable utterance, or in other words, if the formula I pronounce to open a meeting, launch a ship or a marriage were not identifiable as conforming with an iterable model, if it were not then identifiable in some way as a 'citation'? (Derrida, 1988: 18)

As we saw in the case of Sloan, his invocation of the 'forest' was citational: it drew upon an archive of 'forest-images' through which his readers – predominantly white settlers – could and did understand the landscapes of the West Coast. To speak of the 'intertextuality' or 'citationality' of any utterance, then, is not to make the claim that all that exist are texts, but rather that any utterance derives its power from a discursive tapestry that is woven in, through, and around the language and concepts that enable the statement to make sense. In other words, for signifying practices to work – as in the case of Sloan's 'forest' – *other* texts and concepts must work through it. Meaning in textual practices requires repetition or citation, a continual (re)calling of meanings from other texts.

To return to an earlier point, the iterative nature of discourse is also why closure can never be finally achieved. While any invocation of the 'rainforest' today necessarily draws on an archive of 'forest' images that provide a horizon of intelligibility, a temporal 'gap' exists between the act of speech (writing, cartography, etc.) and the *prior* texts which the present act reiterates. This 'gap' is important because it introduces the possibility that iteration may fail. In Derrida's (1976: 66) words, it "divide[s] the present in and of itself." Butler (1993: 10) states this in slightly different terms: it is "by virtue of this reiteration that gaps and fissures are opened up." These 'gaps and fissures' allow for the possibility that what has been excluded – the constitutive outside that is a necessary component of meaning – might 'return' to destabilize existing norms. It is for this reason that Derrida substitutes for 'ontology' the neologism 'hauntology.' The silent 'h' renders the difference undecidable, such that all 'ontologies' are also 'hauntologies': all things that appear as 'being' – or as 'being natural' – are haunted, and potentially disrupted, by that which has been excluded.

Over the past 20 years, the colonial forest institutionalized in Sloan's report and subsequent Forest Acts, has become increasingly haunted by its disavowed exclusions. We can see this in a later Commission headed by the resource economist Peter Pearse (1976), who was asked by the Provincial Government in 1972 to convene meetings across the province into the state of the forest industry. While the mandate assumed the same assumptions about the 'forest' and state sovereignty that were found in Sloan's earlier report, Pearse found himself consistently facing First Nations witnesses who called into question the founding presuppositions of the province's forestry system. Another more recent example brings this point home. In 1984 the multinational forestry company MacMillan Bloedel (acquired by Weyerhauser in 1999 in a major forest industry merger) announced plans to log portions of Meares Island, located in Clayoquot Sound on the west coast of Vancouver Island. The company's plans were challenged on numerous fronts. Residents of nearby Tofino argued that it endangered the town's water supply, since the island served as the town's watershed. Environmentalists complained that the logging threatened to destroy a pristine environment that contained some of Canada's largest trees. But perhaps the most effective protests were made by a Tla-o-qui-

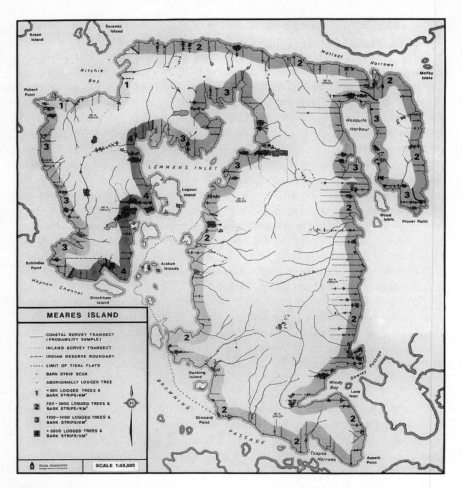

Figure 3.3: Forest (hau)ntologies: Tla-o-qui-aht forest use on Meares Island. Used by permission of Arcas Consultants and *BC Studies*

aht band who claimed the entire island as their 'traditional territories.' Joined by environmentalists, the Tla-o-qui-aht band blockaded the island in order to prevent MacMillan Bloedel workers from landing equipment. The company asked the court for an injunction against the blockades. The protesters, in turn, asked the court to impose a moratorium on logging until issues of sovereignty could be settled.

Key to the court battles was a map of 'culturally modified trees' produced by archaeologists for the Tla-o-qui-aht (see figure 3.3). The significance of this map was that it challenged the erasures, or 'cognitive failures,' that had underwritten forestry since the 1940s. Where forestry officials had always seen a 'natural' landscape without political-cultural claims, the Tla-o-qui-aht inter-jected a landscape worked-over by many centuries of Tla-o-qui-aht land use. With this map the exclusions that were constitutive of colonial forestry on the coast returned to disrupt the smooth workings of colonial power. This was not merely about competing 'texts,' but rather competing systems of signification. These practices do not operate on their own, independent of social processes; signification involves work. In this case, the map was produced with the help of a team of archaeologists and anthropologists who worked closely with the Tla-o-qui-aht to collect material and oral histories of land use. The work by the archaeologists was particularly important. Employing a series of transects and statistical methods of extrapolation, the archaeologists concluded that the island has been extensively and intensively used by the Tla-o-qui-aht from well before contact with Europeans through to the present. Far from 'pristine nature' – or a mere collection of trees – this is a landscape infused with meaning and intent.

In 1985 the British Columbia Court of Appeal issued an injunction against further logging on Meares Island, an important decision that had reverberations throughout the province (as have a number of other decisions on First Nations' rights to land and resources; see Tenant, 1990; Persky, 1998). Other First Nations soon followed the Tla-o-qui-aht, producing similar maps for their traditional territories. The point we wish to draw from this is that this result was achieved not through revealing the final 'truth' about nature. For the Tla-o-qui-aht to press their claim – for them to disrupt the smooth workings of colonial forestry – they also needed to present an *intelligible* image of reality that 'made sense.' In other words, there is a complex 'intertextuality' that informs the intelligibility of this map too, from cartographic conventions (which allow this object to obtain the status of an 'objective' representation) and Lockean discourses of 'property' (which link land *use* and *ownership*) to norms of archaeological research and notions of 'indigeneity.' We have not arrived at the forest's final meaning, but at a representation of the forest that through its intertextuality has both displaced another, and achieved a measure of stability. We remain, as we always must, within thickets of discourse and practices of signification (see Latour, 1999).

Significantly, it was not only the 'forest' that was remade through these struggles. In the crucible of environmental politics (a phrase that we borrow from Moore, 1999) all manner of identities and relations were remade. Meares Island became something new. But so also did the Tla-o-qui-aht, whose coherence as a collective identity was strengthened, and whose cultural memory was refashioned to emphasize links with its surrounding landscape in ways, and through language, that had previously not been available. Struggles over nature, land, and meaning are simultaneously struggles over identity and rights. Such struggles do not exhaust First Nations politics in Canada – these struggles extend to language, culture, economic justice, and other areas. But questions of land, resources, and environment remain central to the future of First Nations peoples.

Differential Nature and the Politics of Poststructuralism

[T]o question a form of activity or a conceptual terrain is not to banish or censor it; it is, for the duration, to suspend its ordinary play in order to ask after its constitution. I take it that this . . . [provides] the important backdrop for Derrida's own procedure of 'placing a concept under erasure.' I would only add, in the spirit of more recent forms of affirmative deconstruction, that a concept can be put under erasure and played at the same time. (Butler, 2000: 264)

Our purpose in this chapter has been both political and theoretical. In terms of the former, we have sought to identify the way that the operation of colonial power operates through discursive practices, including the 'forest discourses' that shape political struggles over the 'fate' of the forest. In terms of the latter, we have attempted to explore the critical purchase of poststructuralist approaches to 'nature.' In important ways the two projects converge: poststructuralist thought offers us not only a different way of thinking about nature, but a different way of understanding and doing environmental politics. To begin, the domain of politics is no longer understood as limited to political institutions – parliament, law, etc. – but enlarged to include the concepts and knowledges that inform debates within these arenas. Foucault, for instance, was not concerned with achieving the optimal conditions for the operation of *reason* in politics, but instead with understanding how some knowledges come to qualify as *truth*.

Perhaps more than anything else, poststructuralist thought alerts scholars and activists to the instability of the categories and identities that undergird our politics and practices. Poststructuralism emphasizes a world in flux, where meanings and identities, forces and relations are fixed only in a provisional sense (Doel, 1999). This emphasis on undecidability has, as its corollary, an equal emphasis on how closure is achieved, on how certain forms of thought and identity are relegated to the 'unintelligible'. This does not mean that poststructuralism is political in any predictable way; rather, poststructuralist thought inaugurates a politics of the 'open end' (Spivak, 1990). Or, as Haraway has argued (1994), such a politics is about 'queering' that which seems to be common sense in order to open up to scrutiny the possibilities foreclosed. This does not mean giving up on the project of making sense of the world, but rather focusing attention on how some meanings come to be momentarily stabilized. As the example of the Tla-o-qui-aht map of culturally modified trees shows, this does not bring us a final 'truth' of the forest, but instead opens up ways of seeing the forest differently.

Some might regard our analysis of the productivity of constitutive absences in colonial discourse as 'too strong,' ontologically speaking, for a pair of epistemological constructivists. They may propose, alternatively, to 'use' discourse analysis as a supplement to a 'more grounded' materialist approach. We would argue that those who embrace constructivist approaches to 'nature' but stop short of accepting the radical undecidability of meaning often end up making arguments that are too rigorous, or too 'clean,' in their separation of ontology and epistemology. The ontology/epistemology relation, we have argued, cannot be casually upheld after Heidegger, Derrida, and Butler. We prefer to question, rather than simply accept, this relationship between ontology and epistemology (which is always *at work* in Western metaphysics), as a step towards rethinking social/nature. For geographers concerned with the politics of nature, there is much to gain from this tension-fraught work.

Note

1   An epistemology is a theory of knowledge – a set of implicit or explicit principles and practices by which one comes to know the world. All people have epistemologies, but few reflect critically on the taken-for-granted ways they come to know the world. Epistemologies are related to ontologies. These are beliefs about what is real in the world or what exists. Again, all people possess ontologies and, as with epistemologies, these are usually unexamined and taken-for-granted.

Further Reading

For a wide-ranging, accessible discussion of the 'culture' of nature see Wilson (1991). A number of the essays collected in Cronon (1995) and Bennett and Chaloupka (1993) examine the relationship between nature, culture and politics. Critical understandings of the environment that draw on Michel Foucault can be found in Darier (1999). For a discussion of poststructuralism and its relevance to geography, see Dixon and Jones (1998).

References

Barnes, T. and Hayter, R. (eds.) (1997). *Troubles in the Rainforest: British Columbia's Forest Economy in Transition*. Victoria: Western Geographical Press.

Bennett, J. and Chaloupka, W. (eds.) (1993) *In the Nature of Things: Language, Politics and the Environment*. Minneapolis: University of Minnesota Press.

Braun, B. (1997). Buried Epistemologies: The politics of Nature in (Post)colonial British Columbia. *Annals of the Association of American Geographers* 97: 3–31.

Braun, B. (2000). Producing Vertical Territory: Geology and Governmentality in Late-Victorian Canada. *Ecumene* 7: 7–46.

Butler, J. (1993). *Bodies that Matter: On the Discursive Limits of 'Sex.'* New York: Routledge.

Butler, J. (2000). Dynamic conclusions. In J. Butler, E. Laclau, and S. Žižek, *Contingency, Hegemony, and Universality: Contemporary Dialogues on the Left*. New York: Verso Press, 263–80.

Cronon, W. (1995). The Trouble with Wilderness: Or, Getting Back to the Wrong Nature. In W. Cronon (ed.) *Uncommon Ground: Toward Reinventing Nature*. New York: Norton, 69–90.

Cronon, W. (ed.) (1995) *Uncommon Ground: Toward Reinventing Nature*. New York: W. W. Norton.

Darier, E. (ed.) (1999) *Discourses of the Environment*. Oxford: Blackwell.

Demeritt, D. (1998). Science, Social Constructivism and Nature. In B. Braun and N. Castree (eds.), *Remaking Reality: Nature at the Millennium*. London: Routledge, 173–93.

Derrida, J. (1976). *Of Grammatology*, trans. G. Spivak. Baltimore: Johns Hopkins Press.

Derrida, J. (1982) [1968]. Différance. In *Margins of Philosophy*, trans. Alan Bass. Chicago: University of Chicago Press.

Derrida, J. (1988). Signature, Event, Context. In G. Graff (ed.), *Limited, Inc.*, trans. S. Weber and J. Mehlman. Evanston: Northwestern University Press.

Derrida, J. (1995). *Points . . . interviews, 1974–1994*, ed. E. Weber, trans. P. Kamuf. Palo Alto: Stanford University Press.

Dixon, D. P. and Jones, J. P. (1998) My Dinner with Derrida, or Spatial Analysis and Poststructuralism do Lunch. *Environment and Planning A* 30, 247–260.

Doel, M. (1999). *Poststructuralist Geographies: The Diabolical Art of Spatial Science*. Edinburgh: Edinburgh University Press.

Drushka, K., Nixon, B., and Travers, R. (1993). *Touch Wood: BC Forests at the Crossroads*. Maquira Park, BC: Harbour Publications.

Escobar, A. (1999). After Nature: Steps to an Anti-essentialist Political Ecology. *Current Anthropology* 40: 1–30.

Foucault, M. (1970). *The Order of Things*. New York: Random House.

Gregory, D. (1994). *Geographical Imaginations*. Oxford: Blackwell.

Haraway, D. (1991). *Simians, Cyborgs and Women: The Reinvention of Nature*. New York: Routledge.

Haraway, D. (1992). The Promises of Monsters: A Regenerative Politics for Inappropriate/d Others. In L. Grossberg, C. Nelson, and P. Treichler (eds.), *Cultural Studies*. New York: Routledge, 275–332.

Haraway, D. (1994). A Game of Cat's Cradle: Science Studies, Feminist Theory, Cultural Studies. *Configurations* 1: 59–71.

Haraway, D. (1997). *Modest_Witness@Second_Millennium*. London: Routledge.

Heidegger, M. (1998) [1955]. The Question of Being. In *Pathmarks*. New York: Cambridge University Press.

Latour, B. (1999). *Pandora's Hope: Essays on the Reality of Science Studies*. Cambridge, Mass.: Harvard University Press.

Marchak, P. (1997). A Changing Global Context for British Columbia's Forest Industry. In T. Barnes and R. Hayter (eds.), *Troubles in the Rainforest*. Victoria: Western Geographical Press.

Matas, R. (1993). Clayoquot: The Sound and the Fury. *Toronto Globe and Mail*, May 22.

Moore, D. (1999). The Crucible of Cultural Politics: Reworking 'Development' in Zimbabwe's Eastern Highlands. *American Ethnologist* 26: 654–89.

Pearse, P. (1976). *Timber Rights and Forest Policy in British Columbia: Report of the Royal Commission on Forest Resources*. Victoria: Royal Commission on Forest Resources.

Persky, S. (1998). *Delgamuukw*. Vancouver: Greystone Books.

Pratt, M. L. (1992). *Imperial Eyes: Travel Writing and Transculturation*. London: Routledge.

Saussure, F. de (1983). *Course in General Linguistics*, eds. C. Bally and A. Sechehaye, trans. R. Harris. London: Duckworth

Scott, J. (1998). *Seeing Like a State*. New Haven: Yale University Press.

Sloan, G. (1945). *Report of the Commissioner Relating to the Forest Resources of British Columbia*. Victoria.

Spivak, G. (1988). Deconstructing Historiography. In *In Other Worlds: Essays in Cultural Politics*. London: Routledge.

Spivak, G. (1990). Practical Politics of the Open End. In *The Post-Colonial Critic: Interviews, Strategies, Dialogues*. New York: Routledge.

Tenant, P. (1990). *Aboriginal Peoples and Politics: The Indian Land Question in British Columbia, 1849–1989*. Vancouver: UBC Press.

Wilson, A. (1991) *The Culture of Nature: North American Landscape from Disney to the Exxon Valdez*. Toronto: Between the Lines Press.

Wright, S. (1998) Molecular Politics in a Global Economy. In A. Thackray (ed.), *Private Science: Biotechnology and the Rise of the Molecular Sciences*. Philadelphia: University of Pennsylvania Press, 80–104.

Chapter 4

The Nature of 'Race'

Kay Anderson

'Race': A Fact of Nature?

For most human geographers today, and many liberal-minded people in society at large, visual images likening a mountain gorilla to an Australian Aborigine (see figure 4.1) are sure to disturb, if not wholly offend. Juxtaposing any human with an animal conjures up all kinds of monstrous meanings, and to do so with a racial motivation would be viewed very dimly indeed. For some years now, from within many branches of the human sciences, we have come to think of 'race' as something that is wholly separate from the natural and animal world. Race is an idea, this corpus of critical work informs us. It is a cultural concept, a label used to define and differentiate people: anything but a biological or genetic fact of nature fixed at birth.

This was certainly not the case in the thinking of people like Carleton S. Coon, Harvard University physical anthropologist and adventurer, who, not so many years ago, published his influential book *The Origin of Races* (1962). In that book, Coon expounded ideas that would probably now be considered unthinkable. And yet in other ways, as I will go on to outline, traces of Coon's thinking can be found smuggled into our received understandings about biology, culture, and humanity that live on in various forms in Western societies today. To the extent that he looked to "the animal condition" as the departure point for "the races of man," and the animal connoted such negative meanings as things bestial and outside of history, his understandings of race were inflected by a most partial perspective indeed. I shall thus proceed to outline the debt within that perspective of peculiar discourses of animality (savagery) and civilization – ones that I will be claiming provide a useful set of narrative tools for bridging the opposed spheres of the human and nonhuman, and for deepening our understanding of white normativity in Europe and its settler colonies abroad. But, first, some discus-

Australoid subspecies: a Tiwi from Melville Island   Mountain Gorilla

Figure 4.1: Two of a series of photographs in a section of C. Coon's (1962) *The Origin of Races* describing "prehuman primate society" and the "beginnings of human society" (p. 84)

sion of Coon's (1962) work will help to place these objectives in intellectual context.

From Apes to Humans/From Hunter-gatherers to City-dwellers

In an attempt to understand the natural history of the species of modern man called *Homo sapiens*, Coon traced the "ancestry of man's living races." Each such "subspecies," he declared, had "reached its own level on the evolutionary scale" (p. vii). Accepting strands of Charles Darwin's work in the 1870s, which argued for evolutionary continuity between humans and animals, Coon saw fit to locate certain "geographical races of *Homo sapiens*" not only anatomically "closer" to the likes of the mountain gorilla, but also at the more "simple" end of the vast geological time scale during which primates had inhabited the earth's surface. The taxonomic and temporal axes came together for Coon in his claim that the evolutionary threshold, when primitive Neanderthal man

(*Homo erectus*) crossed into modern *Homo sapiens*, was marked by measurable changes in brain size and cranial shape (see figures 4.2 and 4.3).

The transition from primate form to modern man was also recorded in what he described as "ecological adaptations." The "simplest grade" was collecting wild foods and hunting among what he called "Stone Age cultures"; followed by agriculture, when man [*sic*] alone gained control over subsistence and commenced village life; and finally, "the birth of cities, kingdoms and empires" (p. 307). In this developmental sequence from "biological" to "cultural events," evolution mutated into, and became independent of, what Coon called "culture history." The "pertinent cultural grades" for Coon were therefore those preceding agriculture, since *by then*, "all the known subspecies of man had reached their present anatomical forms" (p. 307).

On these measures, and using samples of body remains, Coon determined the following. *Homo erectus* of the Pleistocene's Oriental fauna region – whose skull size was slightly bigger, but whose shape Coon likened to a female gorilla and which evolved into modern, living "Australoids" – had the lowest cranial capacity of the five lines of human descent across the globe. And the cranial capacity of living, female Aborigines (including one measured by Coon himself – see figure 4.4) was "even less," Coon noted, than that of Western *homo erectus* who evolved into the modern Caucasoids, the agriculturalists of Paleolithic Europe. It followed, Coon wrote not even 40 years ago, that "the Australian aborigines are still in the act of sloughing off some of the traits which distinguish the grade of *Homo erectus* from *Homo sapiens*" (p. 411).

It would matter much less had such claims been the meandering reflections of a lone scholar. But Carleton Coon's work was only one of the numerous pieces of nineteenth- and twentieth-century science that saw race as a key to understanding the natural history of humankind. *Arguments about Aborigines* (Hiatt, 1996) coursed their way with disturbing regularity through Victorian and post-Victorian scientific and anthropological treatises on humanity's early forms. Coon's conjectures would also matter less were elements of his evolutionary thinking not still with us today, presenting a stumbling block to improved race relations, and with those inferiorized beings that carry the title of "animals." Although as stated earlier, most liberal-minded people today would recoil in horror at any attempt to conflate Animal and Aborigine, discourses of animality nonetheless are latent in many popular understandings of human and racial difference. Displacing the basis for this will be my major ethical concern in this chapter.

Connecting Social Race and Social Nature

Leaving aside the complex issues of human biological evolution – ones which continue to attract much science, speculation, and controversy among palaeoan-

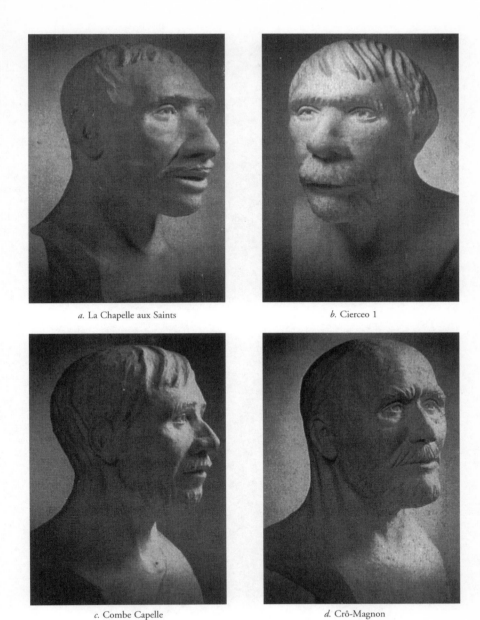

a. La Chapelle aux Saints

b. Cierceo 1

c. Combe Capelle

d. Crô-Magnon

FLESH RECONSTRUCTIONS OF FOSSIL MEN
By Maurice Putnam Coon

Figure 4.2 One of a series of representations in Coon's book invoking the evolutionary transition to modern *Homo sapiens*

Figure 4.3: Zinjanthropos is the name Coon used to refer to a "fossil manlike primate" of the Lower Pleistocene, here compared with the palate of a contemporary Aboriginal

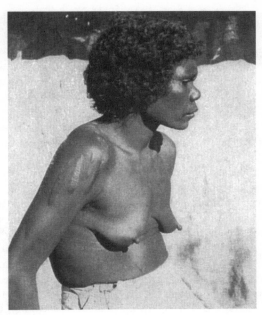

The Alpha and Omega of *Homo sapiens:* An Australian aboriginal woman with a cranial capacity of under 1,000 cc. (Topsy, a Tiwi); and a Chinese sage with a brain nearly twice the size (Dr. Li Chi, the renowned archaeologist and director of Academia Sinica)

Figure 4.4: Plate in a section of Coon's book on "an introduction to fossil man" and "the evidence of cranial form" (p. 341)

thropologists (e.g. Wolpoff and Caspari, 1997) – there is a wealth of judgement that lies buried in Coon's account which is of central significance to this chapter. Turning, then, to the concerns of this essay, it is important to first acknowledge two things that will be elaborated in more detail below. First, I take as given the value of extricating the study of race from that of biology and nature. Second, I endorse the recent efforts of critical nature theorists to socialize those life-forms that have come to be called 'nature.' This includes scholars of human–animal relations who remind us that the boundary people are so quick to draw between humans and animals is not so simply drawn (e.g. Elder, Wolch, and Emel, 1998).

Taking both these developments as points of departure, my primary objective is to attempt to reconnect the study of what we might call 'social race' with that of 'social nature.' As we have seen, race was a key concept through which Western science and society came to conceive of the relationship among humanity, society and nature. A crucial platform through which that set of relations was conceived was the notion of "culture" or "civilization" to which I shall pay close attention. We shall see that the crucial "missing link" in the analysis I present is not the Australian Aborigine, as many interpreters of Darwin including Coon proposed, but rather the notorious hybrid figure of part man/part beast who we have already met in the work of Carleton Coon. But first, I wish to contextualize these arguments within some relevant bodies of work in human geography: first, those concerning social nature and social race; and second, those devoted to conceptualizing culture.

The attempts among social scientists to disturb the divides in Western thought between society and nature, on the one hand, and race and nature on the other, have to date largely taken place in isolation from each other. Two separate literatures have evolved in geography and other human sciences, as follows.

Social nature

Social scientists from a range of different critical directions have in recent years observed the end of external nature. The notion of nature as an essence existing independently of human thought and action, and whose operations can be understood in the light of humanity's powers of reasoning, has been challenged and overturned. Theoretical perspectives among geographers, anthropologists, environmental historians, political economists, scientists, and others have differed, but the abiding claim has been consistent (for a review, see Braun and Castree, 1998). There is no 'natural' conception of nature, no stable inventory of the products that count as nature, and no universal register of questions timelessly posed by it. In the words of Donna Haraway (1992: 296), nature does not "pre-exist its construction." Nature's life-forms inhabit that wildly elastic range of designations that are united only by their opposition to critical aspects of humanness – notably culture, knowledge, intentionality, and agency.

In the case of critical nature theorists, their primary object has been the social production of the life-forms we think of as "nature," including not only the likes of forests and hurricanes, but also the so-called "hybrid" entities of acid rain, genetically modified food, medical implants, and so on. Critics inspired by Marx have made particularly forceful claims for nature's sociality (e.g. Fitzsimmons, 1989; Castree, 1997). Further to Smith's (1984) pioneering work, the production of nature has been seen as integral to the historical geography of capitalism – its labor process, commodification imperative, and pattern of uneven development (on this see Castree's chapter 10 below).

Other more culturally-oriented commentators, noting the examples of the 'hedge,' the zoo, the 'wilderness,' and so on have also observed the end of external nature (e.g. Wilson, 1992; Anderson, 1995). They have dispensed with a model of nature as somehow independent of time and culture-bound ways of seeing, acting, and judgment. Nature, they argue, belongs at least in some senses to human imagining and practice. There are also so-called 'actor-network theorists' who have evolved a different set of analytical tools for understanding nature's social constitution. Tracking the networks through which organic and inorganic entities are scripted, fabricated, and transformed, these researchers focus on the mixes of social, technical, institutional, military, scientific, political, economic, and organic relations of production and consumption. In the interstices between these relations, hybrid or "quasi-objects" – whether cows, roses, microbes, human and nonhuman bodies, machines, oil, and other artifacts – are stitched together and exert their being (see Castree and MacMillan, this volume).

These reconceptualizations of nature, as something shaped by society rather than existing outside of it, grow out of and transform a long tradition of geographic learning and labor variously referred to as human–environment and man–land geography (Mathewson, 1999). A place for all life-forms in an interconnected, non-binary world has been envisaged by a more relational line of thinking than is permitted by dualistic models of, for example, human impact *on* the environment.

Social race

These developments at the nature–society interface have, as stated above, taken place largely in isolation from those geographers working on the subjects of race and racialization. The primary focus of geographers working in the field of ethnic and racial studies has been the cultural politics of *identity*. Their critical focus has been the cultural habits of mind and practice of people and institutions, markets and politics – in short, the social formations that make and remake the 'racialization process' (e.g. Anderson, 1991; Smith, 1989; Jackson and Penrose, 1993). Foremost in their analyses have been the imaginings and practices that constitute (or rather are thought to constitute) the very antithesis of nature.

A cursory inspection of the social race literature reveals that this oppositional referent to human agency is an insistently nonsocial nature. Nature is seen as something that is exclusive of humans, as a closed field of instinct, of biodeterministic impulse from which the majority of race scholars have recoiled. Here recent scholars have followed a long tradition of viewing the problems of race and racism as strictly sociological, at least since the 1920s when American sociologist Robert Park first argued that steep social distance gradients operated between blacks and whites in urban America.

More recently, efforts to denaturalize race have enclosed the sociological frame of reference more tightly. Critical race theory has figured race as a set of material and discursive practices that perpetuate power relations between populations presumed to be essentially different. Markers of difference, notably skin color, take their meaning not from anything natural or innately relevant – but from belief systems that are best understood as 'cultural.' In that sense, as mentioned earlier, race is said to be an idea. It is a concept in which people invest in order to draw boundaries between themselves and 'others,' between ingroups and outgroups. This practice has occurred at least since the fifteenth century in Western cultures when European empires began to extend their reach into the 'New World,' encountering unfamiliar people and livelihoods. It follows that race is not just any social construction or set of beliefs, but one that is intimately linked to the exercise of power. Indeed critical race scholars insist on a distance from nature in order to underscore the political potency of racialized difference and conflict. Nature as 'the biological' is assumed by them to stand for all those things that human agency, power, and politics are not. This maneuver enables them to glimpse the end of 'race' as a category of distinction and inequality.

The power of this explanatory strategy continues to be demonstrated in the range of sophisticated critical investigations. The advances of the constructivist position over static models of race and racism have by now been convincingly detailed. Yet it is also the case that constructionism in its current form works with a strained, and by now untenable, opposition between the human (sociocultural) and nonhuman spheres. It follows that the full potential of its own antiessentialist stance has been blunted. Indeed although the reinsertion of debates about nature into geographies of race and racism needs careful reflection, the prospect can no longer be ignored. Among other things, we shall see the move casts fresh light on the genealogy of systems of thought we have come to call racial and racist.

Rethinking Culture

From evolutionary to symbolic conceptions

What does it mean for critical race theorists to say that 'race' is cultural, that it is a concept that belongs to culture rather than nature? To answer this question, we need to read back into the recent history of theories of culture in the human sciences. There we shall find a version of the story of nature as the passivity on which culture does its work.

Typically, critical race scholars have turned for inspiration to the work of anthropologist Clifford Geertz (1973), who argued culture is a human field of meaning and signification, universal in capacity, yet variable in character across the world's populations. Culture is understood by Geertz as the mediating tissue between the world's perception by different human groups, and the world's physicality. That is, humanity mediates its world through symbolic or knowledge systems. By way of a relevant example to this chapter, and as mentioned earlier, critical race scholars working with a Geertzian idea of culture have argued that the visible differences in skin colour between the world's populations have been made to represent far more significance in Western (and other) societies than their mere physical reality would suggest. Instead of being viewed by people in the more neutral way of differences among us all in, say, height or eye color, skin color differences are thought to mark out something far more profound. They are given the cultural meaning of something biologically innate and unchanging. More than that, in the eyes of some people, such as yesterday's and today's Nazi-inspired activists, racialized markers are believed to imply differences in worth and intelligence.

In geography, the symbolic conception of culture (which lies at the heart of this more critical perspective on race) has had a major impact. In 1980, Geertzian ideas formed the basis for a path-breaking critique by James Duncan of the model of culture that had informed the influential work of Carl Sauer, and other scholars in the group known as the Berkeley School of Cultural Geography. Some abbreviated attention to Sauer's work on culture is needed here to contextualize (and in turn, push further) Geertzian-inspired models of culture.

Sauer (1944, 1952) had conceived of culture as the evolutionary force behind the unique imprints that diverse groups of people had left on the face of the earth. The richness of Sauer's empirical work lies in his keen attention to the diverse expressions of this force in different regional contexts. In his enquiries into the origins of agriculture, for example, Sauer (1952) argued that in Malaysia and India, certain animals were selected for domestication as gifts to spirits or for the purposes of ritual reenactments of divine combat. His overriding point was the instrumental role of culture as a "universal capacity" of "even the most primitive people, including the obtuse Tasmanians" (1952: 11) to effect landscape changes. For Sauer (1956: 2) "[m]an alone ate of the fruit of the tree of Knowledge and thereby began to acquire and transmit learning, or culture." It followed that the domestication by humans of animals and plants was a "cultural advance," in Sauer's eyes, one that saw humanity's rise to ecological dominance as "lord of creation" (1952: 104).

This said, Sauer was not uncritical of humanity's impacts on its diverse cultural landscapes. By 1955, he was part of a major symposium in the United States convened to assess the deleterious attrition of agriculture, pastoralism, and settlement on vegetative cover and soils. These were the impacts, stated Thomas (1956: viii), that had transpired since "man supplemented organic evolution with a new method of change – the development of culture." By this he meant "man's growing knowledge of and control over forces external to himself."

It was the determinism in this model of culture – the idea that people were in the grip of a controlling force handed down in the transition from 'organic' to 'cultural' evolution – with which Duncan (1980) took issue. Duncan's concerns were not the conceits in the Sauerian tradition about humanity's self-regard in the world, or the privileging of a specific characterization of human development (points to which I shall return). Rather, Duncan took issue with Sauer's 'superorganic' conception of culture. By this he meant the false attribution of causal power to culture, as if culture were an agent that functioned somehow independently of individuals and over which they had little control. Duncan thus proposed an alternative view of culture we have already encountered in this chapter. Following Geertz, he argued that culture was not a black-box 'thing' governing human beings, but rather a network of shared ideas whose meanings people participate in shaping, transforming and resisting. In this way Duncan provided a much more activated sense of people's agency in shaping their worlds.

Beyond the idea of a nature/culture divide

Working with this conception of culture, cultural geographers have unveiled the shared meanings surrounding key, socially constructed categories – like race, gender, and age – and wider discourses, such as those concerning development, heritage, progress, and so on. These geographers have also, as mentioned above, queried what *counts* as 'nature' in Western thought. Instead of taking nature for granted as an external set of 'things' out there, they have displaced the discourses surrounding it into the sphere called 'culture.'

But, turning now to an alternative direction, we need to ask one, seemingly simple, question as follows: to *whose* culture does the *idea* of a divide between nature and culture belong? What domain does "culture" occupy, and for whom? Much more attention has been paid by culture–nature criticism in geography in recent years to the category of 'nature' than the reverse pole of 'culture.' Since the time of the superorganic critique of Sauer's evolutionary model – which paved much of the way for the 'new cultural geography' – critical attention to the sphere of culture has tended to close down. And yet, in conflating culture with the universal category of humanity – as do *both* symbolic and superorganic conceptions of culture – some problems for nature–culture critique have arisen, to which I now turn.

The first problem, ironic for culture–nature criticism, is one of speciesism. Culture's cherished moorings in a sealed, species-specific sphere of humanity are left intact by the humanistic move to embrace nature within what is taken as 'culture'. While it is true there are things that human beings can do which are apparently impossible for any other creature, the move to conflate culture with 'the human' ignores the many convincing claims for language, sentience, consciousness, sociability, and intentionality of creatures additional to the human (e.g. Birke and Hubbard, 1995; Gates, 1996). It is now common for groups of zoologists and biologists to acknowledge the variably rich cultural and linguistic life of animals; their use of tools; their species-specific cognitive, even emotional, states (e.g. Masson and McCarthy, 1996). Others too are working hard to break the rigid anthropocentrism that closes its gates tightly around the human reference point; also, the stale model that defines animal behavior *only* in terms of nature, instinct, and biology has come under attack (see the introduction to Philo and Wilbert, 2000).

For that matter, there have been compelling efforts to rethink, and render artificial, the series of distinctions people and scientists have made between culture and biology, history and evolution (see the thought-provoking piece by Tim Ingold, 1995). The line dividing what humans are said to acquire after birth (e.g. reading, writing, and cycling), and that which is assumed to be biologically innate (e.g. the capacity for language and walking upright), collapses when all such activities are seen as learned, embodied skills that "develop in the relational contexts of a child's involvement in its surroundings" (p. 192). Ingold's argument does not (in my view) discredit the model of culture as a symbolic system of ideas and practices. But it does undercut the assumption that there is a bedrock of biological nature that preexists that cultural system. It is the assumption of this bedrock, as if there exists a universal baseline in biological nature from which modern humanity *emancipated itself*, that presents a major stumbling block to a move beyond not only speciesism, but also racism.

The second, equally serious problem, then, is ethnocentrism. In the following section, I explore critically Western society's concept of 'civilization' where I elaborate the arguments in more detail. But it is helpful to first anticipate the major points. Overlooked in existing nature–culture critique in geography and other human sciences, has been the sense in which the Western conception of what it is to be *properly 'human'* developed in the light of the achievements of particular, provincial forms of humanity (Soper, 1995: 66). Recall the value-ridden model of humanity's developmental path out of Stone Age savagery that we met in Carleton Coon's work (which as we shall see has a much older ancestry in classical landscape mythology; Cosgrove, 1993).

These narratives of human transformation have themselves been variously set against a backdrop of discourses surrounding the 'lowly' animal condition. In recurring contexts, through classical, medieval, biblical, colonial, and modern settings, the condition of the more beastly humans or 'savages' has consistently been likened to an animal state whose oppositional referent has been an essentialized humanity. The ideal bearer of this privileged station has been civilized and rational Man [*sic*] – an agent of technological change, a maker of history. This model of humanity grew especially resistant in European colonial encounters with unfamiliar people, and in connection with developments in science in the nineteenth century, when scientists turned their attention to the natural history of humanity (see Bowler, 1992, ch. 8). Increasingly, the so-called 'races of man' became drawn into the effort of people and scientists to better understand the history of humanity as a species.

It will be clear by now that one of my primary concerns in this chapter is to find a pathway for reuniting the study of the human and nonhuman worlds. Interestingly, a deeper understanding of the geneaology of the 'race' concept *demands and enables this bridgework*. On the one hand, to address the historical question of *why* racialized markers of difference were invoked so readily, and with such confidence by European colonizers, we need to unsettle the discourses of culture, humanity, savagery, and animality that gave those markers much of their meaning. The instrumental Imperial will to power does not alone explain why the modern race idea was so seductive to colonizers. The maneuver to historicize race in this way, in turn, depends upon a critique of the speciesism that lies at the heart of the human/animal distinction.

By 'speciesism' is meant not only the set of attitudes that license human exploitation of animals. Primarily I am referring to the mind-set, scientific as well as popular, Western though not exclusively so, which conceives of humanity as an essential condition existing on a plane above animals (Glendinning, 1996). Still today, there is a widespread sense among many, if not all, people that 'the human' designates a whole different order of being from 'the animals.' To get a sense of how entrenched this sense is in Western-derived societies, think of how often we hear it proclaimed, including by judges and journalists, that someone 'lives like an animal,' or worse, has become one through their behavior. By interrogating, therefore, the conceits that lie buried within received understandings of what it is to be 'human,', we inch our way toward an ethical reason for this chapter's excavations into the history of ideas. This is to advance the case for a more inclusive, 'communicative paradigm' (Plumwood, 1992; see also Elder, Wolch, and Emel, 1998) that draws into its moral frame the variegated bodies of all humans *and* nonhuman animals.

Culture as the Transcendence of Nature

How did we come to think of ourselves as most of the things that animals are not? Why have we so persistently been concerned with what makes us human? This impulse has seen elaborate effort devoted to specifying how we are different from animals (and machines), rather than ones to understand what *kind* of animal humans are (Haraway, 1992). And yet, as soon as the questions are posed, another one is raised. And that is, for whom do such questions make sense? One quickly confronts the inescapable reality that there are multiple views across the globe on such matters, notably among certain indigenous groups for whom a more species-specific and less hierarchical awareness of human and nonhuman is the norm (Milton, 1997: 488–9). The point here is not to privilege such worldviews, but rather to note that an animal baseline is not necesssarily or everywhere (or for all time) the departure point for understandings of what it is to be properly human.

From where, then, did such boundary conventions arise in Western cultural formations, including ones that covertly identified the 'human' side of the humanity–nature distinction with 'civilized' humanity? To answer this question, we need to examine some building blocks of European worldviews, including the notions of 'culture' and 'civilization.' This is less by way of tracing the 'origins' of their meanings, as if their vast history can be threaded together like a string of beads leading seamlessly from the ancients to the present. Rather the interest is more strategic: to reread past meanings with a narrative toolkit that holds the potential to think *across* axes of difference (human and nonhuman, civilized and savage).

At least since the early modern period, and within that assemblage of territories occupied by 'Europe,' to be properly 'human' was assessed in the light of the capacity for *cultura*, conceived in terms of cultivating something – usually animals and crops (Thompson, 1990: 124–7). Such activities of cultivation had long before then, and at least 11,000 years from today, seen human communities in South Asia and parts of Europe selectively breeding particular plants and animals for characteristics that were suited to them (including for food, warmth, and companionship). This process, of 'bringing in' animals and plants to the human *domus* was foundational to the philosophical writings of Greek scholars on human identity and agency (Anderson, 1997). Aristotle, for example, conceived of a universalized human race – or civilization – in opposition to a homogenized animal category whose lowly condition justified human use (Sorabji, 1993). The rational art of selectively breeding other life-forms including dogs, goats, pigs, sheep and so on is known as 'domestication,' and the cultivated landscapes made in its image have been read as a marker of human transcendence of nature by many generations of evolutionary thinkers.

According to Greek myths of landscape, for example, human civilization had – in cultivating the earth, tending flocks, and more generally transforming the wilderness into the landscapes of 'garden' and ultimately city – ascended *out* of a state of nature (Cosgrove, 1993). Man – as mind – had freed himself from the primal struggle in which animals were inescapably lodged. Whereas animals would remain fixed in nature's sphere of instinct, man figured in the storyline as unique in being set on a course of 'civilization.' (Here we might also recall the evolutionary thinking of much later scholars we have already met in this chapter, such as Carl Sauer and Carleton Coon.)

In time, under the influence of ancient and biblical thinking, this notion of 'civilization' as a concept linked to the self-constitution of the human species (Rundell and Mennell, 1998), became entangled with a parallel notion of civilisation derived from the Latin word *civilis*. Meaning of, or belonging to citizens, the Latin idea of *civilis* referred to a model political community of free individuals. Its spatial correlate was the city which, as we have seen, had pride of place in the temporal narrative of humanity's civilizing path. Recall the trajectory plotted in Greek landscape myths from the wilderness of pristine nature, through the pastoral and cultivated agrarian garden, to the spaces of the city. Note also that in this developmental trajectory, each stage represented progressively greater intervention by human design and labor (Cosgrove, 1993: 292–3). Each stage would release humanity on its singular path of self-realization leading to the supremely evolved space of citizenry in cities.

The two discourses on civilization – the one a universalistic reference to the condition of being human, the other linked to the identity of the West – thus came to be conjoined through the idea of improvement. Both discourses were located within a most potent narrative of human self-transformation which had the animal condition in nature as its starting point, nature's cultivation as its driving force, and the city as its endpoint. Perhaps it is no surprise, then, that the classical idea of *cultura* as the human cultivation of the earth transmuted into a still more triumphal, human-centered, and ethnocentric idea, in fifteenth- and sixteenth-century Europe. By then culture came to be understood as the raising of human faculties through works of scholarship and invention, or more simply, the cultivation of the human mind (Thompson, 1990).

Voyages beyond the Mediterranean world from the fifteenth century brought Europeans into contact with worlds quite different to their own. Sometimes such worlds were called cultures, other times civilizations, and by the late eighteenth century, 'race' was the prevailing descriptor (Rundell and Mennell, 1998). Yet the premise of a unified category of humanity whose defining characteristic was its capacity for self-transformation along a specific develop-mental path, slipped all too easily into a framework for perceiving 'other' human groupings, not to mention the inferiorized animal condition from which the entire human race had apparently 'departed.'

In the context of European encounters with difference and the emerging discipline of anthropology in the 1800s, the concept of culture was stripped of some of its ethnocentric connotations. It was adapted to the task of describing the customs of 'other' societies. German scholars such as Herder preferred to speak in the 1780s of 'cultures' in the plural, signalling the particular character-istics of different groups and nations. However, as mentioned, this relativist notion of the world's diverse culture(s) did not unseat – and unfortunately continued to co-exist with – the idea that there was a universalized human condition with an animal baseline as its departure point.

Nature/native: the stasis of the savage

The notion of the universal human who had transcended nature, including his own biological nature – the generic man, the unspecified subject – has carried all manner of exclusions. Not least, it has provided the justification behind a complex mix of relationships, from exploitation to endearment, with those life-forms classed as 'animals.' Of more immediate relevance to this chapter are the idealized models of human livelihood that shaped Western differentiations and valuations of human groupings.

In the case, for example, of the Aboriginal people encountered by British colonists in the late eighteenth-century colony of New South Wales (Australia), they were seen as being bereft of not only cities, governments, and laws. More fundamentally still, they lacked crops, herds, and gardens and all the proud props of 'cultivation' and its spatialities of 'settlement.' In that sense they were even less civilized than the indigenous people of America and New Zealand (see e.g. Morgan, 1877). Many colonists thus construed the Australian Aborig-ine as a subhuman part of nature beyond civilization, lodged in the implacable bedrock of deep time (Anderson, 1998). As the site of the original aspects of humanity when people apparently 'lived in nature,' the Aboriginal savage testified to the primeval origins of modern man. As either noble, in eighteenth-century depictions, or as ignoble, in nineteenth-century portrayals, the savage was taken as living evidence of the stage of universal man's development *before* the cultivation of crops and animals. As the site of *pre*history, he stood on the threshold of the realization of the human race's capacities. This view persists in subtle forms even today in the claim in many quarters of Australian society, that Aborigines are 'out of place' in the built spaces of cities; that they more properly belong in the open spaces of the vast undeveloped 'outback.' In contrast, Chinese immigrants to Australia and other white settler colonies have sometimes been considered 'overcivilized,' as effete and unmanly.

I have been attempting in a most preliminary way here, to excavate the contours of a peculiar model of civilization shaping real and archetypal landscapes, initially at home in northwestern Europe, and in turn abroad in the white settler colonies of the New World. My interest is not in reviewing the vast constituents and variants of this model *per se*. Rather it is to suggest that the ideologies of race and progress associated with Europe's (diverse) imperial ventures, drew on much older discourses of nature's improvement that deserve more critical attention from students of ethnocentrism and colonialism.

Conclusion

While it is universally recognized that humans and animals do manifestly differ, not all cultures have worked with a simple or strict classification of human versus nonhuman (Ingold, 1994). The species divide is not solely a behavioral or biologically-determined distinction, but a cultural and historically changing attribution (Noske, 1989). And yet in western Judeo-Christian traditions – and despite Darwin's influential claims for continuity between the human and animal worlds – humanity has persistently been seen *not* as a species of animality, but rather as a condition operating on a fundamentally different (and higher) level of existence to that of 'mere animals.'

In this chapter, I have taken this conceit as my starting point for reading back into processes of human self-definition in Western thought. And as we saw in these excavations into the history of ideas, the norm of 'the human' became identified not with humanity in all its manifest variability. Rather it became identified with the achievements of 'civilized' Western humanity measured (especially under modernity, but also for the ancients) in terms of acquiring technological control over nature. If, in so transcending nature, humans became in Sauer's words 'lords of creation,' I have tried to suggest there was no evolutionary inevitability to this status; that there are other ways of 'being human' (as for example existed among the noncultivators on the continent of Australia for some 50,000 years prior to European settlement).

My way into this vast subject has come through trying to find clues as to *why* the modern idea of race had such a force and appeal in the era of European colonization of the New World. While the Imperial drive for power accounts for much of the allure of the myth of racial difference during this era, problematizing European superiority in terms of its discourses of civilization and savagery is also productive. By enlarging the storyline to take in a critique of Western humanity's characterization of human development as an ascent out of nature, we are forced to confront some cherished ideas about culture, biology, humanity, and animality. We also, however, advance the case for more diverse and inclusive models of 'progress' on earth.

Further reading

Critiques of the idea of 'savage races' in knowledge-making about the New World are abundant. See for example the different perspectives of Pagden (1982), Goldie (1989), and Spurr (1993). Much less abundant are critiques of animality discourses in colonial understandings of the natural history of humanity – understandings that used 'the races of man' as their primary differentiating category. For leads, see the excerpts from Enlightenment texts in Eze (1997).

References

Anderson, K. (1991). *Vancouver's Chinatown: Racial Discourse in Canada, 1875–1980.* Buffalo and Kingston: McGill-Queen's University Press.

Anderson, K. (1995). Culture and Nature at the Adelaide Zoo: At the Frontiers of 'Human' Geography. *Transactions of the Institute of British Geographers* 20(3): 275–94.

Anderson, K. (1997). A Walk on the Wild Side: A Critical Geography of Domestication. *Progress in Human Geography* (21)4: 463–85.

Anderson, K. (1998). Science and the Savage: The Linnean Society of New South Wales, 1874–1900. *Ecumene* 5: 125–143.

Birke, L. and Hubbard, R. (eds.) (1995). *Reinventing Biology: Respect for Life and Creation of Knowledge.* Bloomington: Indiana University Press.

Bowler, P. (1992). *The Fontana History of the Environmental Sciences.* London: Fontana Press.

Braun, B. and Castree, N. (eds.) (1998). *Remaking Reality: Nature at the Millennium.* London: Routledge.

Castree, N. (1997). Nature, Economy and the Cultural Politics of Theory: 'The War against the Seals' in the Bering Sea, 1870–1911. *Geoforum* 28: 1–20.

Coon, C. S. (1962). *The Origin of Races.* New York: Knopf.

Cosgrove, D. (1993). Landscapes and Myths, Gods and Humans. In B. Bender (ed.), *Landscape, Politics and Perspectives.* Providence: Berg, 281–305.

Davidson, A. (1991). The Horror of Monsters. In J. Sheehan and M. Sosna (eds.), *The Boundaries of Humanity: Humans, Animals, Machines.* Berkeley: University of California Press, 36–67.

Duncan, J. (1980). The Superorganic in American Cultural Geography. *Annals, Association of American Geographers* 70: 181–98.

Elder, G., Wolch, J. and Emel, J. (1998). Race, Place and the Bounds of Humanity. *Society & Animals* 6: 183–202.

Eze, E. (ed.) (1997). *Race and the Enlightenment.* Oxford: Blackwell.

Fitzsimmons, M. (1989). The Matter of Nature. *Antipode* 21: 106–20.

Gates, P. (1996). *Animal Sense.* Cambridge: Cambridge University Press.

Geertz, C. (1973). *The Interpretation of Cultures.* New York: Basic Books.

Glendinning, S. (1996). Heidegger and the Question of Animality. *International Journal of Philosophical Studies* 4: 67–86.

Goldie, T. (1989). *Fear and Temptation: The Image of the Indigene in Canadian, Australian and New Zealand Literatures.* Montreal: McGill-Queen's University Press.

Haraway, D. (1992). *Primate Visions.* London: Verso.

Hiatt, L. (1996). *Arguments about Aborigines: Australia and the Evolution of Social Anthropology.* Cambridge: Cambridge University Press.

Ingold, T. (1994). Humanity and Animality. In T. Ingold (ed.), *Companion Encyclopedia of Anthropology: Humanity, Culture and Social Life.* London: Routledge, 14–32.

Ingold, T. (1995). 'People Like Us:' The Concept of the Anatomically Modern Human. *Cultural Dynamics* 7(2): 187–214.

Jackson, P. and Penrose, J. (eds.) (1993). *Constructions of Race, Place and Nation.* London: UCL Press.

Masson, J. and McCarthy, S. (1996). *When Elephants Weep: The Emotional Lives of Animals.* New York: Random House.

Mathewson, K. (1999). Cultural Landscape and Ecology II: Regions, Retrospects, Revivals. *Progress in Human Geography* 23: 267–81.

Milton, K. (1997). Ecologies: Anthropology, Culture and the Environment. *International Social Science Journal* 154: 477–95.

Morgan, L. (1877). *Ancient Society, or Researches in the Lines of Human Progress from Savagery to Barbarism to Civilisation.* Chicago: Charles H. Kerr & Co.

Noske, B. (1989). *Humans and other Animals: Beyond the Boundaries of Anthropology.* London: Pluto Press.

Pagden, A. (1982). *The Fall of Natural Man: the American Indian and the Origins of Comparative Ethnology.* Cambridge University Press: Cambridge.

Philo, C. and Wilbert, C. (eds.) (2000). *Animal Spaces, Beastly Places.* London: Routledge.

Plumwood, V. (1992). *Feminism and the Mastery of Nature.* London: Routledge.

Rundell, J. and Mennell, S. (1998). *Classical Readings in Culture and Civilization.* London: Routledge.

Sauer, C. (1944). A Geographic Sketch of Early Man in America. *Geographical Review* 34: 529–73.

Sauer, C. (1952/1969). *Seeds, Spades, Hearths and Herds.* American Geographical Society; reprinted in 1969. Cambridge, Mass.: MIT Press.

Smith, N. (1984). *Uneven Development.* Oxford: Blackwell.

Smith, S. (1989). *The Politics of 'Race' and Residence.* Cambridge: Polity Press.

Soper, K. (1995). *What is Nature?* Oxford: Blackwell.

Sorabji, R. (1993). *Animal Minds and Human Morals: The Origins of the Western Debate.* Ithaca, NY: Cornell University Press.

Spurr, D (1993). *The Rhetoric of Empire: Colonial Discourse in Journalism, Travel Writing and Imperial Administration.* Durham and London: Duke University Press.

Thomas, W. (1956). *Man's Role in Changing the Face of the Earth.* Chicago: University of Chicago Press.

Thompson, J. (1990). *Ideology and Modern Culture.* Cambridge: Cambridge University Press.

Whatmore, S. (1999). Hybrid Geographies. In D. Massey et al. (eds.), *Human Geography Today*. Cambridge: Polity, 22–40.

Wilson, A. (1992). *The Culture of Nature*. London: Routledge.

Wolpoff, M. and Caspari, R. (1997). *Race and Human Evolution: A Fatal Attraction*. New York: Simon & Schuster.

Chapter 5

(Post)Colonialism and the Production of Nature

Derek Gregory

All three terms in my title are contested concepts, but in this short essay I have had to make choices. I begin by describing the characteristic emphases of postcolonialism, an intellectual approach and a political project that had its origins in literary and cultural studies but which has since spiralled out across the field of the humanities and the social sciences as a whole. One of its central concerns has been the production of what Edward Said calls 'imaginative geographies' as one of the enabling conditions and material effects of colonial rule. Its analysis of their construction and consequences has for the most part been concerned with productions of space and has had comparatively little to say about productions of nature. In this chapter I try to show how postcolonial theory might intersect with ideas about 'social nature.' More specifically, I identify two major constellations of meaning and practice that have been woven around culture–nature as part of the formation of a distinctively colonial modernity: the domination of nature and the normalization of nature. As we will see, each is at once elaborately imaginative and acutely material, embedded in and giving substance to images and texts, practices and performances.

Postcolonialism and its Imaginative Geographies

'Postcolonialism' can mean many things. If, like the postmodern, it is used to identify an historical period, you might be surprised to find that many writers have argued that its beginning ought not to coincide with the end of formal colonialism. Such an approach not only runs the risk of concealing the ways in which colonial norms and forms extend into the present, but it also fails to account for the historical reach of the postcolonial once it is also understood, like the postmodern, as a critical strategy (in other words, it fails to explain *post*colonialism's preoccupation with interrogating *colonialism*). The

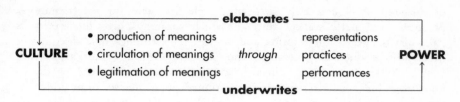

Figure 5.1: Culture and power

most productive response to these concerns may be to trace the curve of the postcolonial from the inaugural moment of the colonial *encounter*. Moreover, there have been many different colonialisms, so that this arc is inscribed in different histories and different geographies. All have been made in the shadow of colonialism, but they have been made in the shadows of other formations too, which makes it important to avoid the sort of explanation that reduces everything that subsequently happened to the marionette movements of colonialism. Even so, its impositions and exactions have often been lost from view – suppressed or simply forgotten – so that one of the central tasks of postcolonialism is to recover the impress of colonialism: to retrieve its shapes, like the chalk outline at a crime scene, and to remind ourselves of the living bodies they so imperfectly summon to presence (Gandhi, 1998).

That act of recovery is difficult: it is partly for this reason that postcolonialism has accentuated (some critics would say aggrandized) the power of *theory*, because theory in its critical mode can challenge our 'commonsense,' taken-for-granted understandings. In this case, theory can help to reveal the ways in which colonialism is still abroad in the world. Postcolonialism theory, like any other sort of theory, is partial and situated, however, and no matter what some of its architects and advocates might claim, it does not offer a complete survey of the (post)colonial condition. In this essay I will be concerned with its characteritic *cultural* emphases, but this does not mean that I am indifferent to its points of connection and contention with other theoretical systems, most of all with political economy and political ecology.

A central concern of postcolonialism is to elucidate the relations between culture and power. It aims to do so in such a way that culture is seen not as superficial, or as a screen for supposedly more fundamental (which for its critics typically means politico-economic) relations, and above all not as a 'reflection' of the world. Culture is seen instead as a series of representations, practices, and performances *that enter fully into the constitution of the world* (figure 5.1).

Postcolonial theory often seeks to map the circuits through which culture underwrites power and power elaborates culture by working with the concept of *discourse*. A discourse is a specific, collective series of representations, practices, and performances through which meanings give the world its particular shapes – their forms and norms. This implies that discourse is inherently productive, generative, and 'object-constituting': or, as Prakash (1995: 202) puts it more directly, "discourse does not restrict or distort knowledge but generates, encodes and arranges it in diverse forms and locations." It doesn't do so by magic. Discourses have their own rules and protocols about what can properly be regarded as knowledge, but these conventions are grounded. By this I mean that they are encased in apparatuses – in books and journals, in instruments and equipment, in interactions and procedures – which are produced and reproduced through interlocking networks of individuals and institutions, and their physicality, materiality, and durability help to naturalize particular ways of being in and acting in the world. This is extremely important because it means that discourse is always about more than the production of *representations*, and this explains why *practices* and *performances* appear in figure 5.1.

These are general characterizations. One of the preoccupations of a specifically *colonial* discourse is the production of imaginative geographies that construct and calibrate a distance between colonizing and colonized societies: constructions that "help the mind to intensify its own sense of itself by dramatizing the distance and difference between what is close to it and what is far away" (Said, 1978: 55). What is crucial about this process is that it is *asymmetrical*. Said frames his critique of Orientalism with an epigram from Marx that says it all: "They cannot represent themselves; they must be represented." In other words, colonial discourse confers the power to represent upon the agents of colonizing societies, who are supposed to have the self-evident right, critical capacity, and even bounden duty to exhibit otherwise inarticulate or inchoate subaltern populations before the gaze of metropolitan audiences. Imaginative geographies are thus *orderings* in the double sense of both bringing an essentially external order to colonial societies – subaltern populations are defined by their nominal 'lack' of attributes which are present in and valorized by metropolitan societies – and of commanding their members to make themselves present as intrinsically colonial subjects. But there is nothing axiomatic or automatic about this, whatever colonial discourse might claim. Subaltern populations are neither silenced nor silent, and colonizer and colonized are drawn into a reciprocal and contradictory process of 'transculturation.' In consequence, the production of colonial knowledges *of* other cultures – through the spiral of representations, practices, and performances – also depends *on* the active involvement of those other cultures.

Seen like this I expect it is not very difficult to see how postcolonial theory intersects with ideas about 'social nature.' Here, for example, is the French anthropologist Claude Lévi-Strauss gazing down on the landscape of central India from an aircraft:

When the European looks down on this land, divided into minute lots and cultivated to the last acre, he experiences an initial feeling of familiarity. But the way the colours shade into each other, the irregular outlines of the fields and the rice-swamps which are constantly rearranged in different patterns, the blurred edges which look as if they had been roughly stitched together, all this is part of the same tapestry, but – compared to the clearly defined forms and colours of a European landscape – *it is like a tapestry with the wrong side showing*. (Lévi-Strauss, 1992: 132–3; emphasis added)

This extraordinary passage captures the reflexes of colonial discourse with raw precision: the European gaze on another landscape from a distance; the uncanny reflection of the European ideal that yields to the imperfections of the alien landscape; and, finally this other 'culture-nature' revealed as an image in a mirror. To Lévi-Strauss this other 'culture' and its 'nature' lack the order and clarity of his own European landscape.

Yet in practice postcolonial analysis of imaginative geographies has privileged the *production of space* and been drawn to the multiplication of enclosures and partitions that demarcate the colonizing from the colonized. These are immensely important considerations. But these geometries were not featureless planes: they were topographies rather than topologies – 'geographies' in the fullest of senses – and, as I want to show, it is important to explore how colonial productions of space were hinged to colonial *productions of nature* (as can be seen in the passage from Lévi-Strauss).[1] In considering these connections, it will be necessary to move beyond poststructuralism by investing not only nominally 'cultural' practices with the capacity to make a difference but also by allowing that nominally 'natural' organisms and physical systems also have the capacity to make a difference. This possibility assumes a special force in colonial discourse in which other natures are frequently endowed the gigantesque or monstrous powers that threaten to overwhelm colonial cultures and to exceed the space available for their presentations.

Culture, Nature, and Colonial Modernity

From the sixteenth century the triumph of European modernity came to be represented as in some substantial sense the triumph of 'culture' over 'nature.' The scare-quotes remind us that this was an imaginative achievement: that both 'culture' and 'nature' here, whatever else they may be, are conceptual constructions, the product of imaginative cuts in the fabric of the world (see Demeritt, this volume). There were voices that dissented from the discourse of domination, to be sure, but in general 'culture' and 'nature' were prised apart within the modern European imaginary and the advance of European culture was usually measured by the distance it was supposed to have traveled from its own nature.

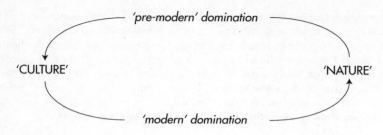

Figure 5.2:   'Culture,' 'nature,' and modernity

It was widely assumed that European nature has been forced to yield its secrets to the intimate probings of a new experimental European science – especially physical science and natural history – and to release its energies through the inventions of a new mechanical European technology. Other sciences and other technologies were by no means as inferior as these assumptions made out, but the achievements of the 'Scientific Revolution' and the 'Industrial Revolution' helped to create and calibrate an imaginative distance between a self-consciously modern Europe and the rest of the world (Adas, 1989). Modern cultures were supposed to have dissected nature so deeply and to have imposed themselves upon nature so forcefully that they were no longer at its mercy, whereas premodern cultures were regarded as creatures of their containing natures whose institutions, practices, and possibilities were conditioned and limited by the caprice of their local ecologies (figure 5.2).

This imaginary produced, and was in part produced through, a culture of nature in which 'nature' was constructed as an external and eternal domain lying *outside* the historical trajectories of 'culture.' Smith (1984) calls this an "ideology of nature" because it obscures the ways in which the restless dynamics of capitalism *enter fully into* the *historical* production of nature. In concealing these connections, Smith argues this culture of nature is so indelibly marked by class that it can be described as a bourgeois imaginary. Modern colonialism has often been described as a bourgeois project by its radical critics, so such a conjunction is scarcely surprising. But this culture of nature is marked in other ways that also bear directly on European colonialism. For 'nature' was not only dominated: it was also *domesticated*. This had two other dimensions of acute significance that further served to situate discourses about social nature produced under the sign of colonialism.

In the first place, these modern productions of nature were *feminized*: They were codified in an imaginary that was intricately gendered and sexualized. If appeals to 'Mother Nature' were a commonplace of European thought, however, they were by no means constants. Merchant (1980) suggests that in the course of the seventeenth century established "constraints against penetration" – taboos that derived from the Renaissance image of nature as a beneficent, nurturing 'earth-mother' who busily provided for the needs of humankind in an ordered universe – were transformed, in large measure through the active elaborations of empirical, experimental science and technology, into what she calls "sanctions for denudation." These switched signals were not mute metaphors; rather, they helped to fashion a fluid and evolving 'rape-script' in which *Natura* was no longer able to complain "that her garments of modesty were being torn by the wrongful thrusts of man" (Merchant, 1980: 189). While Merchant's argument unfolds in a Europe riven by the scientific revolution of the sixteenth and seventeenth centuries, there were close connections between the maps of nature made by that 'New Science' and the colonial mappings of the 'New World' (Albanese, 1996), and later and in a different register between the cultural authority of natural science and (post)colonial projects in South Asia, Africa, and elsewhere (Adas, 1989; Prakash, 1999).

In the second place, modern productions of nature were codified in an imaginary that defined European nature as *temperate* nature: a nature that was moderate, constant, and continent, without extremes of excesses. It was acknowledged that there were interruptions to its harmonies and cycles, like the Lisbon earthquake of 1755 that devastated much of the city or the volcanic spasms of Vesuvius that excited so many Victorian tourists, but a nature whose instabilities were chronic and generalized was located elsewhere (cf. Johns, 1999). The capricious eruptions, violent extremes, and monstrous deformations of nature at large were supposed to be removed from modern Europe either by the passage of time (the catastrophic floods and ice ages of the remote past) or by physical distance: Enlightenment and post-Enlightenment adventurers and explorers may no longer have feared remote regions and many-headed monsters, but their scientific journals and travel writings conveyed to an enthralled public a vivid sense of the *excesses* of other natures – wild, luxuriant, and tangled; harsh, empty, and barren – and hence produced those other natures *as* other. Through the emerging partitions and divisions of global space European nature was constructed as 'normal' nature, while other, nontemperate natures were diagnosed as abnormal, pathological, and even 'unnatural' natures.

This double discourse of domination and normalization presented modern colonialism with a dilemma. On the one side, it was possible to attribute the advance of European culture not only to the distance it had traveled from nature but also, paradoxically, to its embeddedness in its own, temperate nature. In his lectures on the philosophy of world history first delivered in 1822–3, the German philosopher G. W. F. Hegel had this to say:

> Man uses nature for his own ends; but where nature is too powerful it does not allow itself to be used as a means ... The torrid and frigid zones, as such, are not the theatre on which world history is enacted ... All in all, it is therefore the temperate zone which must furnish the theatre of history. And more specifically the northern part of the temperate zone.

These were not exceptional views in northern and western Europe. On the other side, however, it was possible to feminize non-European nature not as a nurturing mother but as a wild, seductive, and unruly siren, which implied not only that these other natures lacked the order that could only be brought to them from the outside by a masclinized Reason that forced them to submit to its will, but also that their excesses posed a real threat to the virile powers and integrities of European culture as it penetrated those other natures.

I want to bring this dilemma into sharper focus by considering the discourses of domination and normalization in turn. This analytical separation is for the purposes of exposition alone: both the powers and the predicaments that attended them derived in very large measure from the ways in which they were entangled with one another, and it will be impossible to keep them wholly separate.

Colonizing Cultures and the Domination of Nature

Colonialism was involved in a distinctive cultural politics of nature, but this does not mean that the precolonial past was a 'golden age' of ecological equilibrium. "By making the arrival of the Europeans the center of our analysis," Cronon (1986: 164) warns, "we run the risk of attributing all [ecological] change to their agency" and rendering native inhabitants "as passive and 'natural' as the landscape." Famine, deforestation, and environmental degradation were not the exclusive products of colonial modernity. Neither did modern colonialism inevitably issue in ecological apocalypse: colonial ecologies were not always and everywhere exploitative and destructive and, at least before the 1870s, there was a space for what Grove (1995) calls a "green imperialism."

We can gain some sense of what was distinctive about a colonial politics of nature by turning to the novelist Joseph Conrad. The protagonists of his short story 'An Outpost of Progress,' first published in 1897, are two agents of a European trading company in Africa:

> They lived like blind men in a large room, aware only of what came in contact with them (and of that only imperfectly), but unable to see the general aspect of things. The river, the forest, all the great land throbbing with life, were like a great emptiness. Even the brilliant sunshine disclosed nothing intelligible. Things appeared and disappeared before their eyes in an unconnected and aimless kind of way. The river seemed to come from nowhere and to flow nowhere. It flowed through a void.

"Blind," "unable to see the general aspect of things," this nature appeared to both men as "a great emptiness," "a void." It was a nature without limits or boundaries, an unmappable and hence unmasterable space, where a river could come from nowhere and flow to nowhere.

Later the hapless pair chance upon a faded European newspaper containing an article on 'our colonial expansion':

> It spoke much of the rights and duties of civilisation, of the sacredness of the civilising work, and extolled the merits of those who went about bringing light, and faith, and commerce to the dark places of the earth. Carlier and Kayerts read, wondered and began to think better of themselves. Carlier said one evening, waving his hand about, "In a hundred years, there will perhaps be a town here. Quays, and warehouses, and barracks, and – and – billiard rooms. Civilization . . ." (Conrad, 1991: 42–3)

Here at last was the prospect of dominating nature through the production of a different, *differentiable* space, of bringing this unruly nature within the disciplined, regulated, and ordered perimeter of culture.

The same themes reappear in Conrad's novella *Heart of Darkness*. In this scene Marlow has just arrived at a trading station in the Congo:

> When near the buildings I met a white man, in such an unexpected elegance of get-up that in the first moment I took him for a sort of vision. I saw a high starched collar, white cuffs, a light alpaca jacket, snowy trousers, a clear necktie, and varnished boots. No hat, hair parted, brushed, oiled, under a green-lined parasol held in a big white hand. He was amazing, and had a penholder behind his ear.
>
> I shook hands with this miracle, and I learned he was the Company's chief accountant . . .

This extraordinary European figure presented a stark contrast to what Marlow saw as "the great demoralization of the land" and the encroachments of its savage nature on the space of the trading station itself:

> Everything else in the station was in a muddle – heads, things, buildings. Strings of dusty niggers with splay feet arrived and departed; a stream of manufactured goods, rubbishy cottons, beads and brass-wire sent into the depths of darkness, and in return came a precious trickle of ivory.
>
> I had to wait in the station for ten days – an eternity. I lived in a hut in the yard, but to be out of the chaos I would sometimes get into the accountant's office . . . [where], bent over his books, [the chief accoutant] was making correct entries of perfectly correct transactions. (Conrad, 1985: 45–7)

Marlow's overwhelming sense is one of disorder – and yet, in the middle of all this, he glimpses (and seeks refuge in) a space of rationality, of calculability, the space of capital accounting.

Here was the central predicament of colonial modernity: how could nature 'out there' – savage and undomesticated – be brought 'in here'? How could such a 'nature' be made to submit to 'culture'? The immediate answer does *not* lie in the clearing of forests and the fencing of fields, the laying of roads and railways, and the building of barracks and barrages. These were concrete achievements – some of them spectacular signs intended to be taken for wonders – but to understand how *they* were possible, conceptually and imaginatively, it is necessary to understand the process of *enframing* through which the discourse of domination was articulated.

Enframing nature

'Enframing' means both to set the world up as a picture and to treat the world as a picture. This looks deceptively simple, but its implications are so far-reaching that the German philosopher Martin Heidegger once declared that "the fundamental event of the modern age is the conquest of the world as picture." This is a large claim, so let me try to unpack what is involved. As a first aproximation, we can say that the modern domination of nature depends upon the successful production of a space of constructed visibility within which three objectives have to be fulfilled: 'nature' has to be held at a distance, set up as an object, and structured as a more or less systematic totality. If we look more closely at what this involves, we can see that there is something theatrical about it. It's a sort of performance that involves a 'staging' – an artful 'organization of the view' – by means of which an audience is persuaded that the representations made available to it provide a privileged (or 'truthful') access to the real. The connections between power, space, and visuality here are complex, but Mitchell (2000) summarizes their diverse histories as so many stagings of 'the world-as-exhibition' or 'the world-as-picture,' each of which turns on a distinction between 'representation' and 'reality.'

You probably think there is nothing exceptional about this, but its obvious-ness is precisely the point that Mitchell seeks to sharpen: how is such an 'obvious' distinction brought about? Within this imaginative theater, he suggests, both actors and audience conduct themselves as though the world is divided in two. On one side, *reality* is taken to be 'an object that exists prior to any representation, as something given, material, fixed in its unique time and space'; on the other side, *representation* promises its practitioners endless, serial, replicable entries into the presence of the real which is thereby made available (or 're-presented') for them within a unified and fully legible space. Colonial modernity, Mitchell argues, "involves creating an effect we recognize as reality, by organizing the world endlessly to represent it." Hence, the real – in our case, 'nature' – is endlessly made available to us through multiple practices and performances, each of which is made to 'stand for' the objective, original, and enduring structure of the natural world (Mitchell, 2000: 16–24).

It is now possible to see why Heidegger, Mitchell, and others firmly believe that 'the world-as-exhibition' is structurally (not accidentally) implicated in the *general* operations of colonizing power: in 'the conquest of the world as picture.' For the dualism put in place through the process of enframing endows the modern viewing subject, constructed as a disembodied and distanced observer, with the exclusive privilege and the extraordinary power to dis-cover the 'real' order of what will appear to other, nonmodern actors and audiences as an otherwise errant universe. Seen like this the modern enframing of nature is inherently colonizing no matter where it takes place: coercive, invasive, appropriative in all its sites, it makes nature available for inspection, codification, calculation, and regulation. And, as I've said, it is a central concern of Marxist materialism to identify the instrumentalities by means of which this ever more effective domination of nature under a restlessly globalizing capitalism sustained the ever more effective domination of one class by another.

Making colonial natures visible

But in its *specific* operations colonial discourse trades on the dualism between 'representation' and 'reality' in such a way as to produce (and reproduce) a second dualism – *between 'colonizer' and 'colonized'* – that turns on more than class filiations and which thus prompts different questions. If colonial 'nature' is held at a distance, set up as an object, and structured as a totality, how does this enframing accommodate the double positions of colonizer and colonized? In what ways does the colonial domination of nature sustain the power of the colonizer over the colonized? And to what extent is the colonial will-to-power compromised, interrupted, even reversed?

To fashion a preliminary answer to these questions I want to examine two strategies by means of which colonial discourse attempted to enframe non-European natures as particular landscapes. The concept of landscape was focal to modern colonialism and imperialism (Mitchell, 1994), but I can discuss only symptomatic examples here, and it is extremely important not to homogenize colonial ways of seeing. Different travelers with different purposes had different perspectives and different priorities. More than this, enframing was not simply a matter of packing one's cultural baggage at home, unpacking it elsewhere and returning with its contents unchanged and intact. As Martins (2000: 21) remarks, representations, practices, and performances were always contingent affairs, in process as well as in transit, and freighted with the traces of their passage. Although my examples are drawn from nominally 'artistic' and 'scientific' registers, these should not be construed as opposites; each informs and even depends on the other. Still more important, their terminus is much the same. By these means nature is made to appear within a space of order and organization and, in the end, made available for calculation and commodification.

In her critique of the 'imperial eyes' deployed by European cultures of exploration and travel in the nineteenth century, Pratt (1992) has drawn attention to what she calls 'the monarch-of-all-I-survey-scene.' Here, in an exemplary passage originally published in 1860, is the British explorer Richard Burton describing his first view of Lake Tanganyika:

> Nothing, in sooth, could be more picturesque than this first view of the Tanganyika Lake, as it lay in the lap of the mountains, basking in the gorgeous tropical sushine. Below and beyond a short foreground of rugged and precipitous hill-fold, down which the foot-path zigzags painfully, a narrow strip of emerald green, never sere and marvellously fertile, shelves towards a ribbon of glistening yellow sand, here bordered by sedgy rushes, there cleanly and clearly cut by the breaking wavelets. Further in front stretch the waters, an expanse of the lightest and softest blue, in breadth varying from thirty to thirty-five miles, and sprinkled by the crisp east-wind with tiny crescents of snowy foam. The background in front is a high and broken wall of steel-coloured mountain, here flecked and capped with pearly mist, there standing sharply pencilled against the azure air . . . [The landscape], like all the fairest prospects in these regions, wants but a little of the neatness and finish of art – mosques and kiosks, palaces and villas, gardens and orchards – contrasting with the profuse lavishness and magnificence of nature . . .

Nature is here visibly made over into a picture, and in this passage pictorial imagery achieves several things.

First, Burton's ability to deploy the picturesque was a triumphant affirmation of what Ryan (1996: 60) calls "the portability of [European] visual taste." Just think: an aesthetic popularized by an English country parson was seemingly able to contain the vastness of the African landscape and to render it in familiar terms.

Secondly, once the landscape is framed as a painting, constructed as a sketch, and filled in with a palette of watercolors (the 'steel-coloured mountain sharply pencilled against the azure air'), the scene of visual mastery becomes almost palpable. "If the scene is a painting," Pratt (1992: 205) remarks, "then Burton is both the viewer there to judge and to appreciate it, and the verbal painter who produces it for others."

Thirdly, Burton not only organizes the view, he also orders the *landscape* as a composition of elevations, planes, and colors: an order which turns out to be necessary if the landscape is to be seen at all. During his travels through central Africa, the French novelist André Gide (1929) was once driven to despair at "the impossibility of differentiation." Looking out over a wide stretch of country, "everything is uniform," he wrote, so that "there can be no possible predilection for any particular site . . . From one end of the horizon to the other, there is not a single point to which I wish to go." Without 'points' there was nothing to see: no particular 'sights' and so no particular 'sites.' But those 'points' had to be produced. The land had to be summoned to presence, made to submit itself as a series of 'points' to the observing gaze in order for it to appear *as* a landscape.

Fourthly, this order is not static. The scene is a 'prospect' partly because the view unfolds before Burton's uninterrupted gaze but partly too because it allows him to present an unobstructed vision of its future: a vista of palaces and villas, gardens and orchards, whose cultivation will at once contrast with and complement the abundance of an undomesticated nature. The picturesque not only invited this sort of correction; it positively required it. If the landscape did not conform to the protocols of the picturesque, the artist was given license to 'improve' the prospect. But the explicitly *colonial* picturesque vested the power to do so in the totalizing dispositions of the colonizer alone. If local people left only "scratches on the face of the country," feint "traces on the landscape," these were superficial signs to be taken for vacant possession, tacit invitations to colonial possession and appropriation (Pratt, 1992: 60).

Science made many of the same discursive moves, and often enrolled art in order to do so. In the course of the eighteenth century the maps, sketches, and illustrations that were folded into the projects of natural history, topographical survey, and cartography made visible a colonial 'order of things' by means of a thoroughgoing spatialization of knowledge that brought various non-European natures within the sovereign grid of European scientific culture. Those 'natures' were dis-placed in order to be re-placed within a taxonomy: "One by one," Pratt (1992: 31) remarks, "the planet's life forms were drawn out of the tangled threads of their life surroundings and rewoven into European-based patterns of global unity and order." Plates in books and journals, specimens in botanical gardens and zoos, displays in museums and exhibitions: "nature and its geographies were enframed in these ways for a variety of audiences" (Withers, 1995: 148). In their turn these orderings made possible a second dis-placement and re-placement that confirmed the power of colonial productions of nature. A spectator at the zoological gardens in Regent's Park, for example, was able to occupy a dual position: at once physically in London, where 'the natural world lay at John Bull's feet,' and also figuratively elsewhere, each exhibit standing for the place from which it originated. "The Zoo works metaphorically here as a moment of transportation," Jones (1997: 8) explains, "while simultaneously acting metonymically to condense the globe into the space of the gardens." It is this double passage – from 'there' to 'here' and back again at will – that marks the operations of colonizing power.

But these condensations and displacements revolve around individuals – plants or animals – whereas science, like art, also worked to produce other, aggregative kinds of 'natural objects.' Consider geology. In the eighteenth century European explorers had noticed the morphological particularities of the coast of the Pacific North West, but these were represented as individual profiles or idiosyncratic sites. It was the achievement of nineteenth-century geology to read them instead as signs standing for a larger structural order:

> In the span of less than 100 years a dramatic shift had occurred, from collecting specimens and viewing the physical outlines of landscapes, to 'seeing geologically.' What was visible in nature had changed irrevocably: one no longer attended to scattered mineral samples or other curiosities, but to the 'inner architecture' of the earth. (Braun, 2000: 22).

This process of scientific enframing was generalizing in another sense too. Braun (1997: 16) argues that it was only after the land was staged as a "theater of nature" in this way that it could be made available to political and economic calculation. As soon as it became possible to convey the fixities and particularities of solid geology in a general calculus of private property and speculative valuation, this 'nature' was able to enter a world where 'all that is solid melts into air': the circuits of global capital where it could be endlessly transformed. "From London, New York or Montreal, it was now possible to view the 'true structure' of Canada's nature without having to be there in person; the circulation of one inscription, the geological map, permitted the circulation of another, money" (Braun, 2000: 25). This process of commodification was underwritten by the colonial state which structured systems of property, lease, and concession, and systems of regulation, surveillance, and enforcement, so that individuals would be compelled to follow the script of rational accounting.

But to stage colonial governmentality through such a theatrical production of the state's 'vertical territory' required some of the principal actors to withdraw to the wings. When George Dawson, a surveyor for the Geological Survey of Canada, made his way through the Pacific Northwest in the 1870s and 1880s, he routinely relied on the assistance of the Haida people. Although his journals describe their cultural practices in great detail, these ethnographic inscriptions are separated from his parallel inventory of the physical landscape. In effect, Dawson's texts detach indigenous 'culture' from 'nature,' and thereby stage "the unveiling of nature's 'plan,' a plan which both *preceded* and lay *external to* a native presence" and which for this reason could be fulfilled through "the judicious mixing of European (Canadian) capital and labor" alone (Braun, 1997: 14).

There were other ways in which scientific discourse allowed the colonial domination of nature to extend the power of the colonizer over the colonized. When the British annexed the Punjab they chose to work *with* local populations and local rulers, respecting their knowledges and working to enhance existing systems of irrigation. Although the results were deemed successful, however, neither the East India Company nor the Presidencies quite knew how to measure their effect or estimate the results of future irrigation schemes (Headrick, 1988: 181). For this, water had to be 'disenchanted' so that "all mystery disappears from its depths, all gods depart, all contemplation of its flow ceases" (Worster, in Gilmartin, 1995: 211). This involved not only filtering cultural residues from 'water' *but also replacing them with others*. Thus, in the second half of the nineteenth century a new discourse of hydrology and hydraulic engineering emerged which translated 'nature' into mathematical formulae. In these there would be no place for 'local' knowledge and the hydraulics of irrigation channels and the mechanics of dam construction could be made the same the world over.

Crucially, the production of nature through the production of ever more abstract spaces raised other possibilities for the consolidation of colonial power. If movements of water and sediment could be made visible and literally brought to account through cascades of equations, was it possible to bring 'culture' within the same calculus? Was it possible to enframe *both* culture *and* nature – a colonized 'culture-nature' – within a system of *simultaneous* equations? One answer sought to reduce culture to nature by treating local actors as so many (other) objects to be controlled with the same dispassionate efficiency that calibrated flow models and turned valves. Accordingly, rules of conduct were published setting out penalties and punishments for infractions of the irrigation code. As Gilmartin (1994: 1139) observes, this was "an attempt to impose individual 'discipline' within an irrigating 'machine.'" But the colonial order was vested in collectivities rather than individuals, and the state's powers of surveillance and sanction were hopelessly inadequate to the task. An alternative solution was to naturalize 'culture' within the calculus of equilibrium economics by modeling local people as self-interested actors whose transactions were governed by the abstract and instrumental rationality of the market. This too erased the collective, communal world of local cultivators, but it proved to be problematic for the colonial state on quite other grounds:

> If the model of market rationality promised theoretically to integrate irriga-
> tors on a micro-level into a system of colonial environmental control, it also
> threatened to undercut the theoretical separation of the British, both from
> the environment *and* from Indian society, that was so central to their
> position as a ruling community. Indeed, the alliance between large-scale
> government control of the environment and profit-maximizing individuals
> held the potential to define political foundations for a community *linking*
> the state and society, a community forged through a common relationship to
> the environment. But this was not a vision of community for which colonial
> rule provided a structural foundation. For the British, the scientific definition
> of the environment served to legitimize the state's separation not only from
> the natural world that it sought to control, but also from the customary,
> community-based structure of Indian society. (Gilmartin, 1995: 226)

It should now be clear how the process of enframing enabled the conversion of other 'natures' into more or less domesticated 'landscapes.' By the turn of the twentieth century the concrete forms made possible through these transformations often amounted to spectacular stagings of the power of colonialism to dominate other natures – mines and plantations; canals and railways; barrages and dams – and, through these practices and performances, other cultures. But colonial enframings were not always as secure or stable as they seemed. Not only could colonial stagings of a supposedly domesticated nature be interrupted by unforeseen side-effects and by extreme physical events like flash-floods, but they could be subverted through everyday acts of resistance and collective protests (Guha, 1989). These grandiose projects could also be co-opted by political movements that reactivated indigenous knowledges, in concert with modern Western traditions, to redirect colonial technoculture to avowedly *anti*colonial, nationalist ends (Prakash, 1999). More recently still, postcolonial states have been obliged to confront demands from marginalized populations over their complicities in technocultural dominations of nature that have licensed multiple forms of resource-based repression (Moore, 1997; Watts, 1997). Postcolonial theory has had much less to say about any of these counter-possibilities than political ecology or subaltern studies but, as I now want to show, colonial discourse – still the main object of postcolonial critique – could itself confound the process of enframing through its *own* contradictions and ruptures.

Colonizing Natures and the Normalization of Nature

In her analysis of "tropical nature as a way of writing," Stepan (1991) reminds us that "nature is not 'natural' but is created *as* natural." But the converse is equally true. In rendering temperate nature as 'normal' nature, colonial discourse simultaneously constructed nontemperate nature as radically other and thereby established an essential distance between 'normal' nature and its excesses. This distance was essential because it was a gap that was *necessary* for the formation of metropolitan-colonial identity and for the privileges colonialism accrued to itself. 'Nature' was enrolled as another register within which colonial discourse could map the space between colonizer and colonized as a surface of difference. Writing tropical nature as 'other' thus conveyed "its discursive differentiation from home and the familiar," and in doing so helped to establish the 'superiority' of the domestic over the exotic (Stepan, 1991: 496–7). That distance was always precarious, however, for if those 'unnatural natures' remained *un*domesticated there was then the ever-present possibility of transgression: the hideous threat that these monstrosities would break out from the 'place' that colonial discourse had assigned to them.

In response to these ideas I want to consider two questions. How did colonial discourse represent these other natures *as* 'other,' as in some sense *pathological* natures? And if these distinctions simultaneously shored up *and undermined* the foundational divide between the space of the colonizer and the space of the colonized, how were these instabilities inscribed in the practices and performances of colonizing powers?

The central representational predicament was to find a way of conveying the otherness of other natures (and other cultures), of bringing them within a European project of a universal 'earth-writing' that would make them intelligible to metropolitan audiences without at the same time destroying the very signs that marked them *as* other. Europeans embarked on the early modern voyages of discovery found the (multiple) terms for this dilemma in the problematic of 'wonder,' a sort of radical passion that careened between ravishment and repulsion and which effected what Greenblatt (1991: 135) sees as "the crucial break" with an-other world that could only be described "in the language of sameness." There were several ways to traverse this paradoxical space of rupture and connection. One was to search for affinities and parallels that would recognize and validate the presence of each in the other. There were thus European representations of North America in the sixteenth and seventeenth centuries that portrayed it as "an Old World in the rough," producing an uncanny sense of "strange familiarity" through an imaginative ordering of the land as an almost-but-not-quite European landscape (Dickenson, 1998: 127). Another strategy was to refine and heighten the sense of radical difference, to develop the reflex of estrangements, so that the distance from the other would be accentuated in ways that could license its colonial appropriation and transformation on quite other terms. But this distance did not remain an uncharted abyss: it was artfully and imaginatively mapped so that, over time, the discursive production of other natures established its own protocols and conventions. Explorers and travelers underwrote their observations through a whirlwind spiral of citation and cross-reference that installed and naturalized imaginative geographies whose canonical forms were reproduced and elaborated in successive accounts. By these means, through a colonial discourse that gradually widened its horizons of meaning and thickened its contours, the strangeness of other natures eventually became *familiar in its very strangeness*.

Pathologizing nature

By the middle of the nineteenth century European natural historians and travelers could draw on a deeply sedimented imaginative geography of 'the tropics,' for example, and those who failed to satisfy the expectations of their audience usually met with little popular success. The dominant discourse of 'tropicality' was structured by two major thematics (Arnold, 1996: 141–68). The first represented the tropics as an Acadia, a sort of Garden of Eden before the Fall. This rhetorical space was most closely associated with the islands of the Caribbean and the South Pacific. In the eighteenth and on into the nineteenth centuries the production and reproduction of such an emphatically *exuberant* nature was sustained by an intimate cross-fertilization between luxuriance and sexuality. Although there was nothing new in engendering 'nature' as feminine, the production of a distinctively tropical nature as sultry and seductive had a genealogy of its own. This cultural formation derived in part from what Livingstone (1991) calls a 'moral climatology' that asserted a causal connection between the heat and humidity of the 'torrid zones' and the supposed moral lassitude and intemperance of their indigenous populations. But it also derived from a botanical discourse whose taxonomies fastened on the reproductive anatomy of plants, and from the subterranean diversion of those classifications into a vernacular discourse of elite eroticism (Bewell, 1996; Browne, 1996). And it owed much to philosophical and aesthetic discourses of primitivism that were preoccupied with 'nature' as much as 'culture' and which were eventually modulated in complex ways by a *fin-de-siècle* modernism that continued to remark the object-lessons to be learned from contemplating both 'noble savages' *and* the lush garden of delights that they enjoyed (Barkan and Bush, 1995). It was through *all* of these routes, through the constitution of what I prefer to think of as a more general 'moral economy of nature,' that somewhere like Tahiti became such a complex mythical symbol that intermingled "pastoral innocence and threatening libertinism" in powerfully unsettling ways (Bewell, 1996: 184).

In the course of the late eighteenth and nineteenth centuries these imaginative geographies were overwritten by a second thematic, inscribed most vividly in South Asia and Africa, that constructed the tropics as pestilential rather than paradisaical. Here abundance became excess and, at the limit, *excrescence*: tropical nature was produced as a brooding, duplicitous, and enervating monster. Moral climatology played a central role in this "pathologization of space" too, but its rhetorical atlas was dramatized by a biomedical discourse that constructed the tropics as "the pathological site par excellence" (Naraindas, 1996). By the early nineteenth century it had become common for European writers to identify the tropics with putrefaction, decay, and decomposition, and with fevers produced by 'bad air' ('malaria') that supposedly spread in a particularly acute form as a 'miasma.' The baseline for mapping South Asia as part of this tropical zone was laid down by the British East India Company in Bengal, where the tripartite regime of heat, humidity, and overabundant nature was assumed to be symptomatic of the subcontinent as a whole, and to flag it as a distinctive and dangerous space. These diagnostics were projected onto local populations whose bodies were folded into this pathologized tropical nature by the racialized and sexualized discourses of environmental determinism. In the early nineteenth century, India was thus constructed as "the kind of place, subject at once to indolence and passion, where disease and sexuality alike flourished," and its indigenous inhabitants were elaborately feminized by a masculinism that identified the people of the humid and marshy plains with "physical and moral weakness" (Metcalf, 1995: 171–3; Arnold, 1998: 7). Even when environmental theories of disease yielded to bacteriological theories in the late nineteenth century, the connective imperative between tropical nature and tropical culture was retained; "One now sought to avoid not 'miasmatic fluxes' but Indian bodies, the filthy carries of contagious disease" (Metcalf, 1995: 177).

By the end of the nineteenth century these two versions of tropicality had become entangled with one another. Consider the two views of the city of Chandrapore with which E. M. Forster opens *A Passage to India*:

> Edged rather than washed by the river Ganges, it trails for a couple of miles along the bank, scarcely distinguishable from the rubbish it deposits so freely . . . The very wood [of the houses] seems made of mud, the inhabitants of mud moving. So abased, so monotonous is everything that meets the eye, that when the Ganges comes down it might be expected to wash the excrescence back into the soil. Houses do fall, people are drowned and left rotting, but the general outline of the town persists, swelling here, shrinking there, like some low but indestructible form of life. (Forster, 1971: 9)

Inland, however, "the prospect alters." Viewed from the rise beyond the railway, where the European civil station is laid out,

> Chandrapore appears to be a totally different place. It is a city of gardens. It is no city, but a forest sparsely scattered with huts. It is a tropical pleasaunce washed by a noble river. The toddy palms and neem trees and mangoes and pepul that were hidden behind the bazaars now become visible and in their turn hide the bazaars. They rise from the gardens where ancient tanks nourish them, they burst out of stifling purlieus and unconsidered temples. Seeking light and air, and endowed with more strength than man or his works, they soar above the lower deposit to greet one another with branches and beckoning leaves, and to build a city for the birds. (Forster, 1971: 10)

These two views are common motifs of the later colonial imaginary; they construct three sights/sites. In the first place, they set up two exhibitions of nature. One presents tropical nature as fallen, wretched, and rotting – a nature of excrescence – while the other presents tropical nature as a heterotopia, a prospect of delight and desire – a nature of abundance. In the second place, these views enable Forster to assimilate colonized culture *to* tropical nature. Seen from within, accordingly, the city of Chandrapore is part of a hideous, disfigured nature of excrescence. Seen from without, where the distance between the native city and the civil station is scrupulously established, the city can be recomposed as part of a nature of abundance. But Forster (1971: 10) makes it clear that this is a powerful yet precarious fantasy: "Newcomers cannot believe it to be as meagre as it is described, and have to be driven down to acquire disillusionment." In the third place, therefore, moving from one view to the other establishes an opposition between the culture of the colonizers and that of the colonized. The fantasy of a tropical heterotopia is possible only when the point of view is removed from the landscape, only when it is recognized that the civil station, with its regular geometry and its red-brick club on the brow, "shares nothing with the city": which is all another way of saying that the civil station is *apart from* rather than *a part of* tropical nature.

The limits of colonial imaginaries: nature as menace

In these ways tropical nature was enrolled to sustain a colonial geography: "a world cut in two," "a world divided into compartments" (Fanon, 1967: 29), not only by built forms and other architectures of colonial power, as Fanon emphasized, but also by colonial productions of nature. If 'seeing the tropics' required them to be made visible in the 'right' way, and if these imaginative geographies circulated through metropolitan audiences and were re-exported to travelers in the field in an endless spiral, then it is easy enough to understand Gide's (1929: 25) relief as he ventured deeper into the Congo to find that "the scenery is beginning to be more what I expected; it is becoming *like*." And yet: in becoming 'like,' tropical nature was simultaneously required to become *un*like. Gide marked this transition when, "homeward bound," he wrote that "the landscape is less vast and less vague; it is growing more temperate and more organized" (p. 207). That sense of other natures as *dis*organized was a goad to the ordering projects of natural history and natural science, but it also marked the perimeter of their powers, which explains the undertow of menace running through my characterizations of tropicality.

To fix this more precisely, consider this passage in which Alexander von Humboldt recalls his arrival in South America in 1799:

> When a traveller recently arrived from Europe steps into South American jungle for the first time he sees nature in a completely unexpected guise . . . With each step he feels not at the frontiers of the torrid zone but in its midst; not on one of the West Indian Islands but in a vast continent where everything is gigantic; mountains, rivers, and the masses of plants. If he is able to feel the beauty of landscape, he will find it hard to analyse his many impressions. He does not know what shocks him more: whether the calm silence of the solitude, or the beauty of the diverse, contrasting objects, or that fullness and freshness of plant life in the Tropics. It could be said that the earth, overloaded with plants, does not have sufficient space to develop . . . The same lianas that trail along the ground climb up to the tree-tops, swinging from one tree to another 100 feet up in the air. As these parasitical plants form a real tangle, a botanist often confuses flowers, fruit and leaves belonging to different species. (Humboldt, 1995: 83–4)

This is not the colonial picturesque but the *tropical sublime*, forcibly reminding its European viewers of their inability to distinguish, differentiate, and identify. The superfluity of the tropics threatened to overwhelm the space of its representation, and to mock, even challenge the sovereignty of the 'monarch-of-all-I-survey.' Tropical nature seemed to demand a different mode of traveling: episodic, tactical, improvisational; a different way of seeing: sensual, corporeal, 'haptic'; even a different form of writing: overwrought, palpitating, ambivalent. Colonial discourse thus produced a sort of 'tropical Gothic' which, even as it sought to *confirm* that necessary distance between the tropical and the temperate, simultaneously threatened to *collapse* metropolitan-colonial culture into tropical nature.

Deserts, too, confounded Europeans abroad. When Florence Nightingale traveled through Egypt in 1849–50 she saw the western desert fringing the Nile as "a great dragon, putting out his fiery tongue, and licking up the green, fertile plain, biting into it, and threatening to encroach still more" (Nightingale, 1987: 63). The desert not only exceeded its proper place but it appeared to this young Englishwoman as nature *in extremis*, exhausted and hollowed out, a space of inversion that mocked the harmonies of a temperate nature: "A lifeless desert would be far less frightful than this dead desert, the idea perpetually recurring of an awful evil at work, making this kingdom his own, overwhelming everything by some monstrous convulsion" (Nightingale, 1987: 49). The desert was not only an unfamiliar nature but, as she said herself, an "unnatural nature" that lay outside the space of Reason itself.

These textual gestures were more than the field responses of an amateur; they were part of a much more pervasive normalization of nature that affected the culture of science too. When the American physical geographer W. M. Davis proposed his 'ideal' cycle of erosion at the very end of the nineteenth century, he described it as the 'normal' cycle and modeled it on temperate regimes. Moving towards the poles or the tropics, he noted "significant departures from normal geographical development" and these prompted him to propose "special" cycles of erosion to accommodate them (Davis, 1899, 1904). Likewise, in *The Physics of Blown Sand and Desert Dunes*, Ralph Bagnold (1941: xix) attempted "to explain on a basis of experimental physics some of the many strange phenomena produced by the natural movement of sand over the dry land of the Earth." In deserts, he continued,

> Instead of finding chaos and disorder, the observer never fails to be amazed at a simplicity of form, an exactitude of repetition and a geometric order unknown in nature on a scale larger than that of crystalline structure. In places vast accumulations of sand weighing millions of tons move inexorably, in regular formation, over the surface of the country, growing, retaining their shape, even breeding, in a manner which, by its grotesque imitation of life, is vaguely disturbing to an imaginative mind. (Bagnold, 1941: xxi)

Bagnold's mind was doubly imaginative. He sought to bring its formations within the calibrated spaces of Reason by disclosing a "geometric order" to their strange topographies. But, as his image of the dunes "breeding" in a "grotesque imagination of life" suggests, Bagnold was also fascinated by the topologies of the monstrous and the uncanny.

In fact, in his travel writings Bagnold had transformed the regular geometries of Egypt's seemingly lifeless Western Desert into a trickster landscape imbued with stealth, cunning, and even agency. At first, he wrote, the dunes "had seemed quite friendly, without evil intent, too big to bother about such a tiny invasion of their empire. They had let us crawl over them without much hindrance once we had got to know them." But as Bagnold and his companions traveled south into the Great Sand Sea, the dunes became "hostile, resenting our presence" (Bagnold, 1935: 155–6). Undeterred, Bagnold and his party pressed on, driving between two sand ridges which became steadily higher until – the horror! – they began to close in. The next morning all three cars sank to their axles in the sand, and the party was trapped. "The dunes had selected this of all places for their second attack." Bagnold recalled, "the exact centre of a lifeless circle of country 360 miles across." The group retraced its tracks for 12 miles and finally broke through, cresting the ridge "as fast as the going would allow, intent on nothing but escape from the fiery dunes" which at last began to break up "amongst groups of friendly solid hills." "But for many miles farther," Bagnold continued, "we could see them still pursuing us in long persistent tongues of gold, dodging between the purple hills, keeping abreast of us like a pack of wolves." Bagnold did not feel safe until he had reached "real rocks that breathed a restful permanence" with no sign of "the monstrous elusive organism of the dunes" (Bagnold, 1935: 160–4).

If colonial discourse required the land to submit to the demand that its language offer what Carter (1987: 63) calls "a more coherent rhetorical eqivalent, a more logical arrangement of what was to be seen" than any local language, then in moments like these the project of "replacing local difference with universal intelligibility" seems to have been underwritten by something approaching panic. For example, deserts could be seen as landscapes of redemption or as landscapes of retribution, but common to these discordant thematics was a chronic loss of words, a failure of language itself. Florence Nightingale (1987: 89) had fretted that it was "useless to try to describe these things, for European language has no words for them." "How should it," she demanded, "when there is no such thing in Europe? All other nature raises one's thoughts to heaven: this sends them to hell." Other travelers resorted to Arabic transliterations: *barchan, seif, wadi*. Yet to most of their audience these strange sound-shapes must have been utterly unintelligible, marking the desert as at once exotic *and* obdurately unyielding to European language. If the limits of our language mark the limits of our world, then recourse to these alien words confirmed that such forms were beyond the limits of any European language – that they were literally 'un-worldly' – and, if Nightingale is any indication, their recuperation often involved a language of fantasy, monstrosity, and inversion (see Greogry, 2001).

Finally, the tropical rainforest could effect its own paralysis of colonialism's imaginative geographies. The British and French derived the word 'jungle' from the Hindi *jangla* to produce "a metaphorical contrast between the orderliness of temperate woodlands and the tangled, menacing, malarial vegetation that constituted tropical nature" (Arnold, 1998: 8). But this very contrast was so unstable that it could undo itself: as the distance between 'there' and 'here' was torqued, so the metaphor slipped and meaning itself became dis-placed. The anthropologist Michael Taussig captures what I have in mind when he described the efforts of the German film-maker Werner Herzog to represent the Amazon rainforest as "a nature conceived as pitting extremes of meaning, a deconstructing tropicality *that implodes oppositions* in the profusion of their rank decay and proliferating disordered growth" (Taussig, 1987: 79; my emphasis). For Herzog, for the colonizing powers that he represents in *Aguirre* and *Fitzcarraldo*, the jungle appears as "a text that frustrates all hermeneutic efforts from the outside," all attempts at translation and interpretation, and its seemingly "chaotic diversity" exposes with extraordinary force what Koepnick (1993) calls "the systematic inappropriateness of Western routines of cognition and ordering."

> The jungle rejects any attempt to be read, mastered or even represented. As it reduces human beings to insignificant receptacles of what will always escape their grasp. Herzog's rainforest delineates a unique training ground for sentiments of sublime terror. (Koepnick, 1993: 136)

Gandy (1996) complains that Herzog's imaginary eviscerates 'culture' and hypostatizes the agency of 'nature'; yet, for colonial discourse, that was all too often precisely the point. As I've repeatedly emphasized, colonial cultures, with their fears of miscegenation and creolization, were riven by fears of a different sort of hybridization too. The colonial project required European culture to penetrate another nature, but there was also the unspeakable possibility of inversion, of another nature penetrating what Duncan (2000) calls the 'moral masculinity' of colonial culture.

In the Amazon rainforest, the usual signals were indeed reversed; the green of the rainforest stood for danger:

> It is out of this green that hostile Indians, wild animals, insects and diseases emerge. It is this green which prevents the eye from finding easy riches to plunder. It is this green which fills the sites reserved for the sugar-cane plantations. It is this green which hides and protects a population whose fate it is to serve. Relief comes in the form of a red signal: fire in the forests, to

open up the horizon as far as the eye can see, and when it gets there, fire
again. (Sevcenko, in Martins, 2000: 20)

There were certainly sites where the horizon was opened up, where 'nature' was
beaten back by the colonial economy and its political and military apparatus:
the construction of roads and railways, mines and plantations, barracks and
towns. By the end of the nineteenth century, Manaus had become the nerve-
center of the Amazonian rubber economy, shipping 20,000 tons downriver
each year. It was also the shock city of the province of Amazonas, a site where
the excesses of unrestrained capitalism and its production of a social nature – a
'normal nature' – were revealed with unusual clarity. A vast new harbor was
completed, and there was a regular steamship service across the Atlantic to
Liverpool. A gridiron of cobbled streets had been blazed across the rainforest,
paved in Portuguese stone. Boulevards were bordered with serried ranks of
exotic fig trees, jacarandas, and eucalyptus, punctuated by electric lamp
standards and festooned with a canopy of telephone wires. Trolley-buses
clattered through the streets, and high over the city rose the ornate dome of
the Opera House (Collier, 1988). Here, surely, colonialism's 'culture' had
visibly triumphed over 'nature.'
      Upriver, however, these polarities were reversed. Agents of the Peruvian
Amazon Rubber Company, backed by British capital and a board of directors
in London, worked out of trading-posts and encampments in the high Amazon
to collect wild rubber through the enforced employment of indigenous people.
In this 'Devil's Paradise' what Taussig (1987: 40) calls "a massive staging of
punishment in a theatre of cruelty" took place, "a spectacle in the proscenium
of the open space cleared in the forest." Thousands of Huitotos – men, women,
and children – were systematically tortured, violated, and killed. A subsequent
British committee of inquiry put the burden of these atrocities on the back of
political economy: on the capitalist logic of extracting low-grade rubber using
scarce labor. There is no doubt that the wild rubber industry involved high
transactions costs and risks; no doubt too that indigenous people were trapped
in a system of debt-peonage whose bonds of credit and debt wound round
their bodies "like the vines of the forest around the great rubber trees" (Taussig,
1987: 68). And yet: can any of this explain the ferocity, the sadism – the
savagery – of the company's agents? Taussig suggests that this "theatre of
cruelty" was intimately related to colonialism's staging of a 'wild,' tropical
nature. He argues that the rubber traders and their Barbadian militiamen feared
a 'brute' and 'animal' nature which they saw surrounding them, advancing,
threatening to engulf them; and that they identified this 'unnatural nature'
with the indigenous people who inhabited the rainforest (Taussig, 1987: 97).
Colonial discourse constructed a space of terror, therefore, in which 'wild
Indians' were figured as deviant creatures of a deviant Nature: "hostile elonga-
tions of the disorganized natural environment" (Koepnick, 1993: 141). As these

traders and militiamen constructed a landscape of wildness and savagery, so they *themselves* became wild and savage: the violence of their actions mirrored the violence of their fears. "The only way they could live in such a terrifying environment," Taussig (1987: 122) concludes, was "to inspire terror themselves."

I doubt that this really was "the only way." Other responses were possible, at least thinkable, because agency is always conditional and contingent. In postwar Malaysia, for example, the 'jungle' was assigned its own agency, its own code of violence ('the law of the jungle'), and constructed by the state and its military apparatus as "an uncontrollable space providing refuge to an uncontrollable population." But the response there was large-scale deforestation, not genocide (Sioh, 1998). Still, the salience of Taussig's argument does not lie in the particular circumstances that he describes – which were surely exceptional – but precisely in the way in which such an extreme case establishes much more general *limits*.

For if his explanation is difficult to comprehend, Taussig believes that this is because we insist on clinging to the distinction between 'reality' and 'representation.' On his contrary reading, and conforming to the arguments I have been developing throughout this essay, the dilemmas of representation – revealed here through the monstrous deformations brought about by the discourse of normalization – are never 'merely' philosophical: they also constitute a powerfully charged means of domination. In trying to make sense of the insensible, the extraordinary brutality of the agents of the Peruvian Amazon Company, Taussig claims that "the terrors and tortures they devised mirrored the horror of the savagery they both feared *and fictionalized*" (Taussig, 1987: 121, 133). My added emphasis underscores what I said at the very start: imaginative geographies are never 'merely' representations because they have *practical, performative force*. More than this, Taussig's reading also shows that the discourses of domination and normalization are duals of one another. In their connectivity – in their contradictory combination – it becomes clear that separations between 'culture' and 'nature' are fabrications too, and that they come undone precisely because they have always been conjoined.

Acknowledgments

I owe a particular debt to Cindi Katz for insisting so patiently and with such critical intelligence that I take the politics of nature seriously. Many thanks also to Bruce Braun and Noel Castree for their exemplary patience.

Notes

1   It should be clear by now that I do not use the term 'the production of nature' in the economistic sense of several Marxist theorists (see Castree's chapter 10, this volume). Rather, I want to focus attention on the 'productivities' of discourse and culture in, quite literally, making 'nature' visible and available for transformation within colonizing societies.

Further Reading

Arnold's (1996) *The Problem of Nature* is an excellent introduction to productions of nature under colonialism. A special issue of the *Singapore Journal of Tropical Geography* (vol. 21, March 2000) is devoted to 'Constructing the Tropics' and contains a number of useful (and brief) essays. Sawyer and Agrawal (2000) address many of the themes discussed in this chapter and illustrate their importance for a contemporary cultural politics of nature. Blaut (1999) shows how assumptions about European nature continue to inform present-day polemics about modernity. For useful case studies see Gilmartin (1994) and Braun (1997).

References

Adas, M. (1989). *Machines as the Measure of Men: Science, Technology and Ideologies of Western Dominance*. Ithaca: Cornell University Press.

Albanese, D. (1996). *New Science, New World*. Durham: Duke University Press.

Arnold, D. (1996). *The Problem of Nature: Environment, Culture and European Expansion*. Oxford: Blackwell.

Arnold, D. (1998). India's Place in the Tropical World. *Journal of Imperial and Commonwealth History* 26: 1–21.

Arnold, D. (2000). "Illusory Riches": Representations of the Tropical World 1840–1950. *Singapore Journal of Tropical Geography* 21: 6–18.

Bagnold, R. (1935). *Libyan Sands: Travels in a Dead World*. London: Hodder and Stoughton.

Bagnold, R. (1941). *The Physics of Blown Sand and Desert Dunes*. London: Methuen.

Barkan, E. and Bush, R. (1995). *Prehistories of the Future: The Primitivist Project and the Culture of Modernism*. Stanford: Stanford University Press.

Bewell, A. (1996). "On the Banks of the South Sea": Botany and Sexual Controversy in the Late Eighteenth Century. In D. Miller and H. Reill (eds.), *Visions of Empire: Voyages, Botany and Representations of Nature*. Cambridge: Cambridge University Press, 173–93.

Blaut, J. (1999). Environmentalism and Eurocentrism. *Geographical Review* 89: 391–408.

Braun, B. (1997). Buried Epistemologies: The Politics of Nature in (Post)colonial British Columbia. *Annals of the Association of American Geographers* 87: 3–31.

Braun, B. (2000). Producing Vertical Territory: Geology and Governmentality in Late Victorian Canada. *Ecumene* 7: 7–46.

Browne, J. (1996). Botany in the Boudoir and Garden: The Banksian Context. In D. Miller and H. Reill (eds.), *Visions of Empire: Voyages, Botany and Representations of Nature*. Cambridge: Cambridge University Press, 153–72.

Carter, P. (1987). *The Road to Botany Bay*. London: Faber.

Collier, R. (1988). *The River That God Forgot: The Story of the Amazon Rubber Boom*. London: Collins.

Conrad, J. (1985). *Heart of Darkness*. London: Penguin.

Conrad, J. (1991). An Outpost of Progress. In *The Complete Short Fiction of Joseph Conrad*, vol. 1. New York: Ecco Press.

Cronon, W. (1983). *Changes in the Land: Indians, Colonists and the Ecology of New England*. New York: Hill & Wang.

Davis, W. M. (1899). The Geographical Cycle. *Geographical Journal*, 14: 481–504.

Davis, W. M. (1904). Complications of the Geographical Cycle. In *Report of the Eighth International Geographical Congress*, Washington, DC.

Davis, W. M. (1909). *Geographical Essays*. Boston: Ginn (contains Davis 1899 and 1904).

Duncan, J. (2000). The Struggle to be Temperate: Climate and "Moral Masculinity" in Mid-Nineteenth Century Ceylon. *Singapore Journal of Tropical Geography* 21: 34–47.

Fanon, F. (1967). *The Wretched of the Earth*. London: Penguin.

Forster, E. M. (1971). *A Passage to* India. London: Penguin.

Gandhi, L. (1998). *Postcolonial Theory: A Critical Introduction*. Edinburgh: Edinburgh University Press.

Gandy, M. (1996). Visions of Darkness: The Representation of Nature in the Films of Werner Herzog. *Ecumene* 3: 1–21.

Gide, A. (1929). *Travels in the Congo*. New York: Knopf.

Gilmartin, D. (1994). Scientific Empire and Imperial Science: Colonialism and Irrigation Technology in the Indus Basin. *Journal of Asian Studies* 53: 1127–49.

Gilmartin, D. (1995). Models of the Hydralic Environment: Colonial Irrigation, State Power and Community in the Indus Basin. In D. Arnold and R. Guha (eds.), *Nature, Culture, Imperialism: Essays on the Environmental History of South Asia*. New Delhi: Oxford University Press, 210–36.

Greenblatt, S. (1991). *Marvellous Possessions: The Wonder of the New World*. Chicago: University of Chicago Press.

Gregory, D. (2001). Orientalism and the Cultural Politics of Nature. In *The Colonial Present*. Oxford: Blackwell.

Grove, R. (1988). *Green Imperialism: Colonial Expansion, Tropical Island Edens and the Origins of Environmentalism 1600–1860*. Cambridge: Cambridge University Press.

Guha, R. (1989). *The Unquiet Woods: Ecological Change and Peasant Resistance in the Himalayas*. Delhi: Oxford University Press.

Headrick, D. (1988). *The Tentacles of Progress: Technology Transfer in the Age of Imperialism 1850–1940*. New York: Oxford University Press.

von Humbold, A. (1995). *Personal Narrative of a Journey to the Equinoctial Regions of the New Continent*. London: Penguin.

Johns, A. (ed.) (1999). *Dreadful Visitations: Confronting Natural Catastrophe in the Age of Enlightenment.* London and New York: Routledge.

Jones, R. (1997). "The Sight of Creatures Strange to our Clime": London Zoo and the Consumption of the Exotic. *Journal of Victorian Culture* 2: 1–26.

Koepnick, L. (1993). Colonial Forestry: Sylvan Politics in Werner Herzog's *Aguirre* and *Fitzcarraldo. New German Critique* 60: 133–59.

Lévi-Strauss, C. (1992). *Tristes Tropiques*, trans. J. and D. Weightman. London: Penguin.

Livingstone, D. (1991). The Moral Discourse of Climate: Historical Considerations on Race, Place and Virtue. *Journal of Historical Geography* 17: 413–34.

Martins, L. (2000). A Naturalist's Vision of the Tropics: Charles Darwin and the Brazilian Landscape. *Singapore Journal of Tropical Geography* 21: 19–23.

McClintock, A. (1995). *Imperial Leather: Race, Gender and Sexuality in the Colonial Encounter.* London and New York: Routledge.

Merchant, C. (1980). *The Death of Nature: Women, Ecology and the Scientific Revolution.* New York: Harper & Row.

Metcalf, T. (1995). *Ideologies of the Raj.* Cambridge: Cambridge University Press.

Mitchell, T. (2000). The Stage of Modernity. In T. Mitchell (ed.), *Questions of Modernity.* Minneapolis: University of Minnesota Press, 1–34.

Mitchell, W. J. T. (1994). Imperial Landscape. In W. J. T. Mitchell (ed.), *Landscape and Power.* Chicago: University of Chicago Press, 5–34.

Moore, D. (1997). Remapping Resistance: "Ground for Struggle" and the Politics of Place. In S. Pile and M. Keith (eds.), *Geographies of Resistance.* London and New York: Routledge, 87–106.

Naraindas, H. (1996). Poisons, Putrescence and the Weather: A Genealogy of Tropical Medicine. *Contributions to Indian Sociology* 30: 1–35.

Nightingale, F. (1987). *Letters from Egypt: A Journey on the Nile, 1849–50*, ed. A Sattin. New York: Grove Press.

Pagden, A. (1993). *European Encounters with the New World.* New Haven: Yale University Press.

Prakash, G. (1995). Orientalism Now. *History and Theory* 34: 199–212.

Prakash, G. (1999). *Another Reason: Science and the Imagination of Modern India.* Princeton: Princeton University Press.

Pratt, M. L. (1992). *Imperial Eyes: Travel-Writing and Transculturation.* London and New York: Routledge.

Ryan, S. (1996). *The Cartographic Eye: How Explorers Saw Australia.* Cambridge: Cambridge University Press.

Said, E. (1978). *Orientalism.* London: Penguin.

Sawyer, S. and Agrawal, A. (2000) Environmental Orientalisms. *Cultural Critique* 45: 71–108.

Sioh, M. (1998). Authorizing the Malaysian Rainforest: Configuring Space, Contesting Claims and Conquering Imaginaries. *Ecumene* 5: 144–66.

Smith, N. (1984). *Uneven Development: Nature, Capital and the Production of Space.* Oxford: Blackwell.

Stepan, N. (1991). Tropical Nature as a Way of Writing. In A. Lafluente, A. Elena, and M. L. Ortega (eds.), *Mundialización de la Ciencia y Cultural National.* Madrid: Doce Calles, 495–504.

Taussig, M. (1987). *Shamanism, Colonialism and the Wild Man.* Chicago: University of Chicago Press.
Watts, M. (1997). Black Gold, White Heat: State Violence, Local Resistance and the National Question in Nigeria. In S. Pile and M. Keith (eds.), *Geographies of Resistance.* London and New York: Routledge, 33–67.

Chapter 6

Gendered Natures: Feminism, Politics, and Social Nature

Jane Moeckli and Bruce Braun

In recent years connections between women and nature have received a great deal of attention, both in popular culture and academic scholarship. Indeed, for some readers this connection may seem commonsense. After all, Western culture is replete with metaphors that link women and nature, or that figure human transformations of nature in terms of sexual violence – 'mother' earth, 'virgin' forests, 'raping' wild nature. There are also countless examples where women have stood in the forefront of political struggles over the environment – the Greenham Common peace camp in England, working-class women combating toxic pollution at Love Canal in New York state, ecofeminists leading protests against logging in Clayoquot Sound on Canada's west coast, or the much discussed Chipko ('tree-hugging') movement in Uttar Pradesh, northern India. How these connections are understood, however, has varied widely, and has often been a matter of intense debate. In this chapter we examine competing approaches to understanding the relationship between gender and nature developed by scholars and activists who have sought to articulate a specifically feminist politics.

Before proceeding, it is important to note that although nature has long been *gendered* in Western culture (and others too), and although attention has recently been directed toward understanding the connection between gender and nature, this does not mean that issues surrounding gender and nature have always been taken seriously by academics and environmental activists. Indeed the opposite has often been the case. One needs to go no further than the reception of Rachel Carson's *Silent Spring* (1962), a book often touted as the beginning of the contemporary environmental movement in the United States, to find an example. Carson's exegesis of the harmful effects of pesticides, particularly DDT, called attention to the toxic landscapes produced by industrial capitalism and the military. Concurrent with the emergence of ecosystem ecology and its view of nature as an interconnected system, her cautionary tale of a small rural village poisoned by unseen and unnamed toxins taught Americans to see their environments in a new light, and to understand human practices in terms of far-reaching environmental effects, both through time and across space. This clearly threatened a postwar order in which massive transformations of nature by industry, capital, and the state had been justified through ideologies of progress, and in which science and technology had become privileged sites. Not surprisingly, Carson came under sustained attack, and often it was her standing as a 'woman' that was the target of critics. Dismissed as 'biased,' 'incompetent,' 'ignorant,' 'hysterical,' a 'communist sympathizer,' and a 'lesbian,' she shouldered a barrage of criticism from other scientists, captains of industry and the mainstream press, even as her book went on to become a best-seller (Gottlieb, 1993). Women, after all, were 'emotional' rather than 'rational' – only (white) men could qualify as properly objective.

Equally as important as these attempts to dismiss Carson's work, however, was the *gendering* of the mainstream environmental movement that occurred in the following decades. Carson's book raised a number of key issues: the interconnections of humans and nature; public participation in science; public health, toxicity, and children's safety. Perhaps above all else, she called for Americans to understand nature as 'home,' rather than something external, emphasizing people's *lived relationship* to their environments (Norwood, 1993). For a variety of reasons, including divisions of labor within the US economy, these were issues that were important to women. Paradoxically, mainstream environmentalism in the decades after Carson's pathbreaking book moved in quite different directions. Its rapid professionalization in the 1970s led to a predominantly white, affluent, male leadership. In turn, this leadership emphasized issues like wilderness preservation, wildlife conservation, and pollution control rather than issues surrounding health and home (Seager, 1993). This did not put an end to women's environmental activism – women continued to be prominent in the antitoxics movement (Pardo, 1990; Krauss, 1993; Newman, 1994), the antinuclear movement (Unity Statement of the Women's Pentagon Action, 1980/3; Caldecott and Leland, 1983; Sturgeon 1997), and in issues around workplace, home, and environment (as well as more mainstream issues like wilderness preservation) – but it meant that mainstream environmental groups often failed to understand the complex ways in which gender, nature, and power were intertwined in the construction of social natures, not only in the United States, but elsewhere too.

Although Rachel Carson did not consider herself a feminist, it is not surprising that many claim her as an 'ecofeminist foremother' (Sturgeon, 1997: 200n.4), echoing the introduction to a prominent ecofeminist anthology: "many would argue that it was not coincidental that a woman was the first to respond both emotionally and scientifically to the wanton human domination of the natural world" (Diamond and Orenstein, 1990: ix). This recalling of Carson, as well as a now well-established tradition of environmental activism by women, raises a number of important questions. How are we to understand the relationship between gender and nature? Is gender an essential part of environmental issues? Are women somehow closer to the natural world? Is this connection to be understood in terms of biology? As a product of ideology? Or a result of everyday material practices? Is 'woman' a universal category, or do we need to attend to the ways in which gender, race, class, and nature are constructed in and through each other?

As we will see, these questions have been answered in very different ways. For analytical purposes, we will group these under four labels: ecofeminism, feminist environmentalism, feminist political ecology, and poststructural feminisms. These are labels of convenience. In reality feminist work on nature is streamed in more complex and cross-braiding ways. Moreover, the temptation is always present to understand these positions through a *progressivist* narrative that sees each as a stage that leads to and is superseded by the next. This is particularly true in intellectual debates and in the academy, in which there are often institutional incentives to dislodge established ideas and replace them with new ones. It is therefore perhaps best to see these approaches as a somewhat unstable and shifting constellation of ideas that exceed whatever typology is used to understand them. Indeed, many feminist scholars and activists have questioned the demand for 'purity' in theory or the demand for theoretical fidelity, making room for political and theoretical positions that allow for, and are open to, flexibility, fluidity, and coalition-building (see Haraway, 1991; 1997). This is captured well in what Chéla Sandoval (1991) calls 'differential consciousness' – a way of weaving between and among oppositional ideologies, not as an end in itself, but as a means for changing relations of power. By attending to competing viewpoints, we wish to develop the sort of 'differential consciousness' advocated by Sandoval, which moves between positions in nonreductive, but also non-innocent, ways in order to achieve the sort of political consciousness needed for specific, historically and geographically situated, contests over nature, gender, and power. Why this matters will become clear as we proceed.

Ecofeminism: Women, Nature, and an Ethics of Care

Ecofeminism provides a convenient point of departure for this journey into questions of gender and nature, in part because it has gained a certain currency in popular culture through its use in art, poetry, and nature writing, its presence in mainstream feminist publications (like *Ms.*), and its association – rightly or wrongly – with alternative cultural and spirtual movements like Wicca. For our purposes, ecofeminism refers to both a movement and a set of ideas positioned at the intersection between feminism and radical environmentalism. As a movement ecofeminism emerged in part as a response to the ways in which women and nature were marginalized in modern, patriarchal societies, as well as in reaction to the patriarchal values embedded in mainstream environmental organizations like the Sierra Club and more radical groups such as the US Green Party and Earth First! As a set of ideas ecofeminism is most closely associated with the notion that the subjugation of women and the domination of nature are *connected*, and that the oppression of one cannot be eliminated without also eliminating the oppression of the other (Warren, 1993). Most ecofeminists operate within this definition. How they theorize the connection between nature and gender, however, can differ dramatically, and has been the source of considerable conflict and misunderstanding.

Feminist scholars and environmental activists commonly group ecofeminism into two opposing 'camps.' *Cultural ecofeminism* encompasses those who argue that women and nature are mutually associated, and that in patriarchal society both are devalued. Within this view, the emancipation of women and nature must come through women celebrating their connections with nature, thereby inverting patriarchy's hierarchical structure of power. Carolyn Merchant (1992) claims that this branch of ecofeminism is based on the assumption that women have a *biological* connection to nature (often termed an 'essentialist' position). Accordingly, women are seen as inherently *closer* to nature than men, on account of their 'natural' role as nurturers, or due to their bodily cycles, such as menstruation. Merchant further suggests that this belief in women's connection to nature has led cultural ecofeminists to look to earth-based spiritualities, premodern rituals, and the idea of a living, nurturing earth taken from Renaissance organicism, in order to locate resources for their efforts to revalue women's experience and to reestablish women's connection with nature. The appeal of these sites stems from their location in a time and place 'outside' of, or predating, patriarchy (and religious and cultural traditions – like Christianity – that are thought to reinforce patriarchal relations). Many populist ecofeminist movements in the US draw upon cultural ecofeminist positions (see Diamond and Orenstein, 1990; Plant, 1989; Caldecott and Leland, 1983).

Socialist ecofeminism, in contrast, encompasses ecofeminisms that are at least in part defined *against* cultural ecofeminism. Drawing again on Merchant's typology, socialist ecofeminism rejects the notion of women's *biological* connection with nature, and instead locates women's and nature's oppression as an effect of *capitalist patriarchy*. Within this view, patriarchal relations of production and reproduction subordinate women, while capitalist relations of production exploit nature for human 'need.' Capitalist market economies use both women and nature as resources to be exploited; therefore, the emancipation of nature and women can come about only with a restructuring of society to a economy not based on profit, but rather on sustainable development.

Typologies like these have an initial appeal, since they sharpen our sense of some of the analytical and political stakes involved. But they can also be misleading. Noel Sturgeon (1997) suggests that they lead to the dividing and ranking of different feminisms, whereby certain feminists find themselves the 'losers' in the competition for the 'best' feminism. They can also give the impression that the distinctions between opposing 'camps' are clear, when in reality the boundaries between them are often blurred. Still, it is not difficult to see why some feminists have sought to draw these sharp divisions – many are uneasy with claims that there are important connections between women and nature, especially if the basis for these connections is posited as *biological*. The worry most often expressed is that this may inadvertently give support to the same biological determinist arguments that have historically been used within patriarchal societies to *justify* women's oppression (i.e. that women are, *by nature*, inferior). For critics of cultural ecofeminism, then, biology is decidedly *not* destiny, and to suggest otherwise is to posit antifeminist ideas (see Biehl, 1991; King, 1993).

In reality, few ecofeminists hold such a strong biological or 'essentialist' position. It is important to stress this, because at times this assumed link between ecofeminism and biological determinism has been used as a justification for disregarding the usefulness of ecofeminism for radical environmentalism, feminist theorizing, or political activism. As a challenge to this tendency to essentialize ecofeminism, Sturgeon (1997: 28–9) has suggested an alternative characterization of woman–nature connections in ecofeminist work, based on five key conceptualizations:

a)   Because patriarchy connects women and nature, a feminist analysis is needed to understand environmental degradation;
b)   Because women are associated with nature, and Western culture is steeped in a belief system that assumes culture's superiority over nature, women's oppression cannot be fully understood without an environmentalist analysis;
c)   Because of pervasive gendered divisions of labor, women are more likely to understand and more severely experience the impact of environmental degradation, therefore the woman–nature connection is best understood through a historical-materialist analysis of women's work;
d)   Because of their reproductive characteristics, women are closer to nature than men and therefore they are more in tune with nature's needs; and
e)   Because earth-based spiritualities often honor women, some feminists involved in creating feminist spiritualities turn to these traditions for resources.

Although there is a core difference between those conceptualizations that identify the connection between women and nature as oppressive (a, b, and c) and those who are empowered through their connection with nature (d and e), multiple and contradictory conceptualizations are often incorporated into a single work.

Ecofeminism has also had an important impact on, and drawn from, feminist philosophy. Feminist philosophers seek to dismantle the 'phallocentrism' of Western philosophical traditions (i.e. forms of logic that are masculinist or that provide ideological support for male privilege), in order to make room for alternate forms of reason not wedded to patriarchal norms. This has included challenges to conceptual frameworks that feminize nature and naturalize women. According to Karen Warren (1993), traditional philosophy constructs and connects women and nature through forms of *dualistic* and *hierarchical* thought whereby women are opposed to men, and nature to culture. In turn, these pairs are arranged hierarchically, where one term (i.e. men, culture) is elevated over the other (i.e. women, nature). These dualisms are then interlinked, such that men come to be associated with culture and women with nature, or, as we saw in the example of Rachel Carson, men with reason and women with emotion.

Gendered dualisms in Western thought

Culture / Nature
Masculine / Feminine
Human / non-Human
Reason / Emotion
Mind / Body
Autonomous / Dependent
Order / Chaos
Objective / Subjective
Production / Reproduction
Rationality / Intuition
Active / Passive
Competition / Cooperation
Subject / Object

Like Warren, Val Plumwood (1993) critiques the dualistic structure of ethics. As she notes, the definition of 'human' within modern philosophy rests upon Descartes's initial separation of mind from matter, and the privileging of the former over the latter. Plumwood explains that this leads to a 'divided-self theory' whereby human-as-biological (matter) is separate from and subordinate to human-as-rational (mind), and where that which is 'authentically' human is viewed as external to, or outside, nature (or the body). Not only does this disqualify women from being 'authentically' human (they are too closely associated with the body not the mind), it also provides support to forms of *instrumental rationality* that value matter only in terms of its usefulness for the mind. In other words, modern ethics presupposes that humanity and nature are separate spheres, values the former over the latter, and thereby serves to justify the 'control' or 'mastery' of nature and women.

These are important insights and have been enormously influential. The value of this critique is that it helps us see the masculinist and anthropocentric underpinnings of a system of ethical thought that accords intrinsic value based on rationality. The solution proposed by ecofeminists, however, has not been to merely *extend* value to nature and women, but instead to challenge the structure of thought that gives rise to notions of humans (and other entities) as discrete, autonomous beings. In other words, to merely extend intrinsic value (as many mainstream environmental philosophers advocate), does not address the core problem of the hierarchical dualistic frameworks that provide support for existing ethical systems. Rather, as the geographer Sarah Whatmore (1997) argues, ethics needs to provide a model that accounts for humans as social, connected, relational beings. Along these lines, ecofeminist philosophers have argued for an *ethics of care* that focuses on an experience of, and relationship with, nature in the place of the abstractions, universals, and disconnects associated with traditional (masculine) ethics (Plumwood, 1993: 288). Ynestra King (1993: 115) expands this argument to address not only anthropocentrism and sexism, but also racism and classism: "I contend that the systematic denigration of working-class people and people of color, women and animals are *all connected* to the basic dualism that lies at the root of western civilization" (emphasis added).

Historicizing Women and Nature: Feminist Environmentalism

Like Ynestra King, Val Plumwood, and Karen Warren, many ecofeminists are committed to critiquing modern dualisms, demonstrating their porousness, and creating alternative conceptualizations of human–environment interactions. However, not all feminists have embraced ecofeminism. One of ecofeminism's sharpest critics has been Bina Agarwal (1992), who faults ecofeminism for locating feminist ecopolitics in the realm of *ideology* (ideas) instead of in the historical, material *conditions* that shape women's everyday interactions with their environments. Agarwal calls instead for a *feminist environmentalism* that focuses on three themes: (1) understanding women's relationships with the environment through a political-economic lens, thereby producing explanations centered on the material conditions of production, reproduction, and distribution, and how these are in turn gendered;[1] (2) tracing how these gendered relations mediate people's interaction with their environment and in turn lead to the production of different gendered environmental knowledges; and (3) understanding and accounting for how environmental conflicts and environmental social movements come to have gendered components. In short, Agarwal argues that we need to understand the relation between women and nature in terms of its *historical-geographical specificity*.

Agarwal illustrates the importance of a political-economic analysis through her examination of resource scarcity in rural India. Here she positions herself directly against a body of influential work by ecofeminist Vandana Shiva (1988), who had explained the subordination of women and nature in India in terms of the ideological effects of Western interventions into India. While acknowledging Shiva's contribution to ecofeminism and her powerful critique of colonialism, patriarchy, and Western development projects, Agarwal finds fault with several aspects of her account. Most problematic, she argues, is that Shiva romanticizes precolonial India, with the result that she identifies Western reductionist science and development policies as the *root* of women's and nature's oppression, thereby missing the historical and local forces of power, privilege, and property rights that intermingle with outside (Western) interventions in the colonial and postcolonial periods. A focus on the historical and material conditions shaping competing ideologies, Agarwal suggests, provides a better explanation of how nature, culture, and gender come to be interwoven.

For our objective of developing politically savvy skills in negotiating theories of nature and gender, Agarwal's arguments merit further discussion. In India, village commons (land that is managed by the community for the community's use) and forests provide important communal sources of food, fodder, fuel, water, and other resources. Over a number of years the availability of these resources has declined. Agarwal suggests two reasons: (1) increasing degradation of the quality of natural resources in village commons due to environmental stresses, and (2) growing decline in the quantity of village commons due to statization (state control) and/or privatization of land and resources. The effects of this socially-produced resource scarcity, Agarwal argues, were felt differently according to class and gender. However, in contrast to ecofeminists, she insists that this must be understood in terms of a set of historical developments, not simply through ideology. For instance, while statization of land and resources began during British colonial rule (in order to extract products from forests for commercial use), the impact of these developments intersected with economic, social, and gender inequalities and environmental degradation that predated colonialism and Western development. As Agarwal notes, pre-British India was stratified by caste, class, and gender, and it is this history of local social structure – more than 'ideas' about woman and nature – that affected future patterns of access to and use of natural resources through each agrarian transition.

Here the details of agrarian change in India matter. Originally promoted by the colonial state, and later a mainstay of 'development' by the postcolonial Indian state, scientific management of natural resources was implemented by governmental and individual landholders in order to promote commercial development of land. This had several negative effects to local rural communities. The logic behind scientific management of agriculture is to maximize productivity by increasing inputs, such as genetically designed seeds, pesticides, herbicides, and harvesting machinery. As Noel Castree notes in this volume (see his chapter below), this logic of increased productivity and profitability changes how land and natural resources are viewed. For instance, it encourages the cultivation of commercially profitable species, often to the detriment of indigenous species used by local populations. This results not only in the loss of easily accessible community resources, including land, but also undermines local knowledge systems about species varieties, environmental processes, and sustainable forms of interaction between people and nature (Agarwal, 1992: 134–5). Scientific management also promotes monocropping, which is thought to raise efficiency and producitivity (and is also amenable to technologically-dependent agricultural practices). However, since such crops are more vulnerable to pests, they require increased use of pesticides that deteriorate soil and water quality. Finally, these forms of 'development' can also damage existing community resource management systems, since they are forced to shift from traditional, often communal, institutional arrangements of resource use and management to state or private ownership and management.

These agrarian transitions and their effects are *gendered* in part because divisions of labor that preexisted colonial and capitalist development placed the responsibility for subsistence agriculture and household provision on women. As common property dwindled (either through decreased acreage or declining quality of land), women were forced to travel greater distances to secure resources for their household. This limited the time women could spend on their own crop production, and led to reductions in personal income. Further, as common property became less accessible and less productive, women's and children's health was compromised due to declining nutrition and increased exposure to waterborne diseases and agricultural chemicals. Social support networks also suffered as daily patterns of interaction among women were disrupted and as families were forced to move due to lack of food and resources. Finally, with the privatization and statization of the village commons, women's knowledge about local species and natural processes was devalued and potentially lost (Agarwal, 1992: 136–43).

The importance of Agarwal's work goes far beyond the Indian context – it also challenges and broadens the frameworks through which we understand the relationship of gender and nature. A political-economic analysis, for instance, draws attention to the relationship between nature, gender, and class, something that has often been overlooked by ecofeminists, who have been criticized for universalizing the experience of white, middle-class women (see Sturgeon, 1997). Further, to the extent that the economy is often *racialized*, as it is in the United States, political-economic approaches can also help explain differentiation among women that extends beyond class alone. It also places the focus of analysis and politics on the specific, place-based forms that gender–environment interactions take in response to a broad set of economic, cultural, political, and technological relations. Ultimately, this places in question notions of an 'essential' relation between women and nature, and insists instead on the historical contingency of such relations. It also undermines the tendency to construct an essentialized and romanticized image of the 'Third World Woman' who, perhaps even more than Western women, come to be seen as inherently 'closer' to nature (Mohanty, 1991).

Many of the issues raised by Agarwal and other critics have been thoughtfully integrated within ecofeminism (see Sturgeon, 1997), although not without some reservations. One of the most significant concerns is that historical-materialist approaches like Agarwal's remain trapped within the *instrumental* approach to nature that ecofeminists have struggled so hard to displace. As Karen Warren (1993) notes, the primary value of nature for Marxist-informed feminisms is its value as a resource for the production of commodities. Ecofeminism, by contrast, seeks to extend value to other, nonhuman entities, beyond their 'use-value' for humans.

Feminist Political Ecology: Gender, Environment, Politics

Feminist political ecologists and geographers have extended Agarwal's insights into the materiality of women's experiences of, and connections with, the environment. *Political ecology* – a research field that has grown tremendously in the 1990s – is concerned primarily with economic and environmental decision-making processes, the social, political, and economic contexts and scales of interaction that regulate human–environment practices (how 'global' institutions influence 'national' and 'local' environmental policies), and the uneven distribution of, access to, and control over resources on the basis of class and ethnicity. *Feminist* political ecologists depart from other political ecologists in their insistence that *gender* is a critical variable (in relation with class, caste, race, culture, and ethnicity) that shapes institutional practices, household-level politics that influence decision-making strategies, and how resources are distributed and controlled (see Bryant, this volume).

We can explore what is gained through a political ecology approach by turning to the work of the geographer Richard Schroeder (1997), who illustrates many of these concepts in a fascinating study of gender, nature, and politics in rural Gambia (for our purposes he also illustrates that men can do *feminist* research too). In it, he shows how gender politics infuse struggles over land tenure systems in the context of shifting funding agendas and development paradigms of NGOs, large donor agencies, and organizations such as the World Bank. The traditional land tenure system in the area Schroeder studied relegated upland regions to groundnut production by men, with land inherited through patrilineal lines. Swampland regions were used for rice production by women and were passed from mother to daughter. The low-lying regions that separated the two were owned by male landholders, but were not usually farmed due to poor growing conditions. During a significant decline in both rice and groundnut production in the 1980s, three competing development projects were initiated in the nonproductive low-lying land in order to ease economic burdens and provide subsistence crops: small-scale market gardens, primarily tended by women; fruit tree orchards, primarily owned by male landholders but tended by women; and rice production by women for family consumption.

What interests us in this tale of swamps, gardens, and orchards, is what we can learn about how gender–environment relations become a site of political struggle where outcomes are not known in advance, but instead shaped by a variety of different actors and events. Schroeder shows how through Women in Development (WID) grants, women were able to obtain usufruct rights to garden the low-lying land, destabilizing the existing tenure system.[2] Previously, senior males had issued usufruct land rights to these lands, while maintaining ownership rights such as decision-making control. Their degree of control diminished over the duration of women's gardening, in large part due to women directly transferring land to other women without the knowledge of male landholders. As defined by traditional land tenure rules, the original exchange was accompanied by a one-time claim payment and any transfer thereafter was expected to happen through the male landholders with the exchange of another payment. What Schroeder discovered, however, was that 70 percent of transfers between women happened surreptitiously, resulting in a loss of male privilege, power, and wealth.

Schroeder documents the process by which male landholders over time reclaimed control of low-lying lands. This occurred within a complex set of local–global relations and actors and eventually resulted in considerable hardship for women. Again, the details are important. Responding to the recent history of famine, drought, and economic problems in the region, international donor agencies in the mid-1980s shifted their focus from gender equality initiatives, which had supported women's gardens, to environmental rehabilitation. Monies poured into sustainable ecological and economic development schemes, but this also put pressure on granting agencies to create results. In this context, there was considerable pressure to transform women's garden plots to (male-owned) orchards, despite the fact that it had been women's labor and initiative that had rehabilitated this land. Over time, women's use rights of garden plots were increasingly restricted, and in many cases they became tied to women's management of the men's orchards. Adding to these changes, a government-planned, USAID-funded soil and water management program was initiated, resulting in the development of an expansive dike system in low-lying areas to control salination and soil erosion. This allowed for the reintroduction of rice production in the region. Although celebrated among community members as a good source of family sustenance, Schroeder shows how the reintroduction of rice production had dire consequences for women due to traditional divisions of labor dictating women as harvesters of the rice. The overlapping growing seasons for rice, a crop for communal good, and for vegetables, a crop for women's individual profit, increased the burden on women. When women eventually challenged men to share in the household obligation of rice harvesting, men declined, leaving women in the predicament of balancing both gardening and rice production.

This case study illustrates many of the key themes found in feminist political ecology, and adds to the conceptual tools available for feminist scholars to understand the relation between gender and nature. By explicitly addressing livelihood *strategies* and the (limited) control, status, and power that accompanies gendered *shifts* in primary household providers, feminist geographers and political ecologists have brought to light the ways in which these occur within complex and shifting social, political, and institutional fields. To fully understand gender–environment relations, it becomes necessary to understand land tenure systems, legal structures, international NGOs, state agencies, development discourses, and cultural norms and ideologies. Within this complex nexus of actors and institutions, people (men and women) *struggle* over issues of environmental health and economic well-being, as well as over who has authority to define how this will occur. This is not determined in advance either by ideology or economic conditions.

What feminist political ecologists have put on the agenda for political ecology more generally is how these struggles often reflect gendered relations of power, resulting in outcomes that are experienced differently by men and women. Although not directly addressed in this example, feminist political ecologists have also focused attention on two other key issues: the gendering of science and the role of women's collective activism around environmental issues. Here important points of intersection can be found with our earlier discussion of ecofeminism. Drawing upon ecofeminist insights into the professionalized, fragmented nature of Western scientific knowledge and methodologies, feminist political ecologists have sought to locate and articulate an alternative 'science of survival' that takes a more holistic and integrated approach to environment and health issues, and that takes seriously women's knowledges (Rocheleau et al., 1996). The study of women's collective activism has also led feminist political ecologists to examine how 'gender' itself is being reconfigured in these struggles, consistent with attempts by ecofeminist philosophers to challenge the way gender has been constructed in Western philosophical traditions. And, like the ecofeminists we examined earlier, they are also concerned with bringing women's experience and knowledge back into how environmental issues are understood and addressed. As Rocheleau et al. (1996: 15) state: "women are beginning to redefine their identities, and the meaning of gender, through expressions of human agency and collective action emphasizing struggle, resistance, and cooperation. In so doing, they have also begun to redefine environmental issues to include women's knowledge, experience, and interests."

Poststructural Feminist Interventions: Gender/Discourse/Power

This 'redefining' of gender and identity brings us to yet another, increasingly important, resource for conceptualizing gender and nature: poststructuralist feminism. The key contribution of poststructural feminism to the study of gendered nature is its vigilant attention to how categories like 'gender,' 'sex,' 'race,' or 'nature' come to be *constructed* and *stabilized* within intellectual, political, and ecological projects. Or, to say this differently, poststructuralist thought questions the self-evidence of the categories that we use to understand ourselves and the world. Disrupting the coherence of such categories and identities is not simply an academic exercise, but a political one, since it shows these to be the effect of power rather than ahistorical essences (see Braun and Wainwright, this volume). In other words, how social identities and categories are constructed – or fixed – is never innocent, but instead part of how relations of power and domination are set in place to begin with.

In its understanding of 'gender' and 'nature' as constructed rather than fixed categories, poststructuralism is resolutely *antiessentialist*. As we hinted at in our discussion of ecofeminism, *essentialist* positions are those that take as fixed, static, and natural, categories that are actually mutable, cultural, and historical. In other words, they understand categories to have some sort of unified, universal, inherent quality consistent over time and space. Poststructuralist feminist philosopher Judith Butler (1990) argues that essentialist positions mistake cultural processes for natural ones, and instead she defines the processes that lead us to think that there is an essential character to any concept or identity as 'regulatory fictions.' According to Butler, gender categories have no ontological foundation; instead, they are created – and stabilized – through repeated acts which have the effect of congealing over time to produce the appearance of something substantial, real, and natural (Butler, 1990: 33). When we speak of gender as an ontological category – something found in nature – these processes fall from view. Indeed, in our everyday lives we tend to live as though these identities are really 'out there,' prior to, and apart from, their articulation in cultural practices, and thus we participate in making them seem 'real.' Butler speaks of this as a non-articulated (i.e. unconscious) agreement to "perform, produce, and sustain discrete and polar genders as cultural fictions" where "the construction 'compels' our belief in its necessity and naturalness" (Butler, 1990: 140). This is a difficult, and at times counter–intuitive argument, precisely because Western culture is predicated on patriarchal and heterosexual norms that compel us to understand ourselves *through* these terms, although not without also producing a certain ambivalence, especially among those who do not quite 'fit' the prescribed categories. It is perhaps appropriate, then, to let RuPaul – North America's most famous drag queen – express poststructuralism's antiessentialist position: "We are born naked. From then on we're all in drag" (RuPaul, 2000).

What is at stake in poststructuralist interventions? Why insist that 'gender,' 'sex,' 'race,' and 'nature' are socially constructed rather than pregiven? And how does this contribute to how we understand 'gender' and 'nature'? To begin, it is worth noting that poststructuralist feminists share with ecofeminists a concern with the dualistic conceptual frameworks of modern, Western thought. However, in contrast to some ecofeminists who understand the goal of feminist politics to be the inverting of hierarchical relations between 'male' and 'female,' poststructuralists seek to place the very category of 'woman' in question. In other words, they criticize ecofeminists for taking as an ontological given something that is in reality an ideological or cultural construct. As we saw earlier, the essentializing of gender by some ecofeminists can actually hide the operation of power, since it is precisely by constructing women in opposition to (and inferior to) men, and then naturalizing this difference (rendering it ontological and ahistorical), that patriarchy works to marginalize women. Rather than understand society–environment issues in terms of political struggles between 'men' and 'women,' poststructuralists argue that it is necessary to also analyze how constructions of 'gender' are part of what is at stake and negotiated in these struggles. In other words, gender is always 'up for grabs.' Thus, as we saw in the case analyzed by Schroeder, what is of interest was not merely that men and women were situated differently *vis-à-vis* land and resources, but that gendered identities were being reworked and redefined as these struggles proceeded.

Poststructural feminists have also called attention to a number of other problematic assumptions in the existing literature on gendered nature. As we showed earlier, many ecofeminists privilege meaning and ideology in their explanations of women's domination. On the other hand, feminist environmentalism and feminist political ecology tend to focus solely on material conditions. Poststructural feminist perspectives recognize this common tendency to separate meaning and materiality – and to privilege one over the other – as another expression of modern dualistic thinking. Writers like Donna Haraway (1997) instead point to how material and discursive practices are always implicated in each other, such that environmental struggles are never simply about 'nature' or about 'meanings,' but about how the material world is rendered legible in and through ideas and concepts (and these are themselves constructed within particular historical and material conditions). For example, Haraway (1989) examines the history of science and technology from a feminist and antiracist position in order to craft a view of nature as it is (re)constructed in the bodies and lives of apes. Her exploration of the Carl Akeley African Hall in the American Museum of Natural History in New York City unearths the implicit social relations built into representations of natural history in postcolonial United States. Haraway argues that artefacts such as mounted animals, dioramas, and pictures supposedly depicting Africa's wildlife and landscapes instead author a story about race, sex, gender, and class relations in twentieth-century North America. In the context of the African exhibit, the bodies of apes reinforce social structures, including the male–female dichotomy, heterosexual family structures, and race and colonial relations.

Haraway's (1991) work has also been central to attempts by poststructural feminists to deconstruct the category of biological 'sex' in order to disrupt a sex–gender dualism that emerged in earlier feminist writings (this earlier work is often referred to as 'second-wave' feminism). Although this can be a difficult discussion, it is worth reviewing, since it has become central to recent attempts to move beyond the mind/matter, culture/nature dualisms that organize Western thought. As we saw in the case of ecofeminism, feminists have long battled biologically determinist justifications for women's oppression. Most feminists today argue that differences between men and women are primarily social, advocating a social constructivist rather than a biological determinist argument. Implied in this division, however, is a separation between 'gender' (which is taken to be socially constructed) and 'sex' (which is assumed to be biological and therefore grounded in nature). It is easy to understand why feminists have made this move: by understanding 'gender' as cultural, rather than biological, it became possible to combat the justifications for patriarchal relations of domination that rested upon women as biologically inferior to men. However, this leaves intact a culture–nature dualism, such that sex now becomes the 'core' of gender. Still caught within a hierarchical and dualistic structure of thought, 'sex' and 'nature' were constituted as a 'reality' *against which* social constructions of gender and culture were defined, thus allowing 'sex' (nature) to continue to serve as a resource or foundation for all manner of political projects, including what many would consider reactionary movements – like antigay activists who ground a normative sexuality in biology. Haraway (1992: 298) counters this move with a simple, but consequential statement: "biology is a discourse, not the world itself."

This gender–sex divide may be partially responsible for limits to feminist interrogations of gender and nature. For the most part, studies have limited their attention to the relation between gender and (external) nature. Perhaps because feminists have found the gender–sex divide so useful politically, the question of the 'body' has been left off the agenda. Yet, how 'bodies' come to matter within discursive and material practices (such as technoscience) is no *less* important to theories of gender and nature than how women come to have roles defined in relation to their surrounding environment. It is only recently – mostly in the past decade – that sustained efforts have begun to understand how the body has been 'sexed' in Western medical discourse (see Oudshoorn, 1994). For example, Emily Martin (1991) has examined the use of economic metaphors in science textbooks that characterize women's reproductive proc- esses as wasteful and unproductive. These representations shape medical instruction, influence medical practices, and help construct popular (mis)perceptions about male and female reproductive roles, as can be seen in the complex arena of reproductive technologies eloquently described by Rapp (1999). This production of the 'sexed' body is not unimportant, for it can authorize particular practices *on* the body.

Rather than ask what is gained through poststructural feminist interventions, it might be better to ask what is politically at stake in *not* incorporating a poststructural feminist approach. As we have sought to show, ignoring poststructuralist interventions runs the risk that categories become reified, erasing the complex processes by which social identities come to be fixed within specific bounds. That which falls *outside* of such bounded identities is not acknowledged. Queer theory – at times closely aligned with poststructuralist feminist theory – has focused attention precisely on the manner in which a whole set of social identities and actors – gays, lesbians, bisexuals, transsexuals, and transgendered people – are left 'outside' conventional understandings of society, nature, and politics. It is in this context that we should understand Haraway's (1994) claim that her intellectual and political project is to 'queer nature.' It is also why Haraway (1991) takes the 'cyborg' as her privileged metaphor for 'nature' at the end of the twentieth century. Not only does this draw attention to how nature, culture, and technology are intricately interwoven in technoscientific cultures, with its new, and powerful, biotechnological capacities, it also draws attention to the fact that the boundaries that we establish to differentiate between entities – human/nonhuman, organism/machine, nature/culture – are porous (or, more to the point, ideological rather than ontological). The cyborg is a politically potent metaphor precisely because it refuses to accept closure around 'nature,' 'culture,' 'human,' 'machine,' and 'animal,' but instead shows each to be fluid. As Haraway notes, it is only when we understand the dualisms of Western patriarchal thought to have 'leaky boundaries' that we can begin to imagine alternatives.

While it should be clear that we find poststructuralist feminist interventions not only provocative, but productive, there have been a number of important concerns raised about its potential political implications. Among some feminists there is a fear that poststructuralism's emphasis on destabilizing 'gender' and 'nature' undercuts the foundation of political movements. If the meaning of 'woman' is called into question, then what political subject can ground a women's movement? In turn, can we have a feminist ecopolitics if what counts as 'nature' is historically contingent? Further, although most poststructuralists insist on the simultaneity of materiality and meaning, critics argue that poststructuralism focuses almost entirely on questions of representation (how meanings are produced). This brings us back full circle to Agarwal's (1992) initial critique of ecofeminism, in which she faults its focus on the realm of 'ideas' rather than historical-material conditions. The worry expressed by poststructuralism's critics is that if the focus rests only on meaning, political activism can be undercut. Finally, antiessentialist critiques can also fall into the same epistemological traps that they critique others for reproducing. The obvious problem is that the essentialism/antiessentialism debate may simply produce another dualism. One way out of this impasse may be to reframe *anti*essentialist accounts as *non*-essentialist, thereby allowing for accounts that focus on the processes that continually decenter or interrupt seemingly fixed identities, without implying that the resulting identities are polar opposites to 'essences' (Reynolds, 1999). Yet another issue with antiessentialism centers on how antiessentialist critiques are employed. Critics have asked whether the sole focus of antiessentialist work should be to disrupt coherent identities and categories, or whether there is in fact a way to expand antiessentialist pursuits. Can we strive for the conceptual disruptions that antiessentialism advocates as well as acknowledge that much of our experiences and the way we understand them function through essentialisms? This suggests that we refocus our attention on interrogating *how* and *why* essentialisms are employed, explaining why at certain moments making a link between 'women' and 'nature' based on biology may indeed be a reasonable, strategic decision (Sturgeon, 1997).

Shifting Fields: Gender, Nature, Politics, and Theory

Gendered nature is clearly a complex field of analysis with many competing perspectives. Because environmental conflicts unfold in and through social, political, economic, and cultural contexts, 'gender' is necessarily part of social nature. Here we have brought together four perspectives – ecofeminism, feminist environmentalism, feminist political ecology, and poststructural feminisms – in order to stage a debate about how the connections between gender and nature should be conceptualized. The points of contention between these approaches are important, as are their points of convergence. Attending to these brings us to a number of key themes and questions that any future ecopolitics will need to consider. What is at stake for environmental and feminist politics when essentialist positions positing women as closer to nature than men are employed, and can 'strategic essentialisms' avoid these political pitfalls? How do examinations of social change differ according to idealist or materialist perspectives, and does poststructuralism adequately bridge the divide between the two positions? By employing Sandoval's 'differential consciousness' we are able to shift between approaches, not *transcending* the differences but rather *engaging* with the boundaries between them in a non-innocent and nonreductive manner. This is especially important for feminists traversing the muddy terrain of social natures – we need theoretical and political flexibility in order to account for the potentially dangerous margins between the constructions and 'reality' of nature, gender, sex, race, class, and the body.

We have focused on feminist contributions to gendered nature, in large part because feminism offers the most developed critique of 'gender' as a specific power relation. But what of masculinity or critical theories of sexuality? Can a feminist gender analysis stretch to address these social relations? We would argue that a future ecopolitics would need to expand its boundaries to consider these perspectives too. Critical theories of masculinity (Connell, 1997) and queer theories of sexuality, 'sex,' and 'gender' (Gaard, 1997) both overlap with feminist concepts of gender while charting new territory for gendered analyses of nature. This allows us to ask why it is that Rachel Carson was labeled a lesbian for challenging pesticide use, or how motherist claims in antitoxics conflicts reinforce and/or challenge heterosexist notions of family or construction of fatherhood based on a biologically defined masculinity. Feminist conceptualizations of the body and embodiment also open up gender analyses of nature. As genetic information is mapped and monitored, bodies are reshaped through liposuction, skin is smoothed through antiwrinkle technologies, and embryos are preselected for certain traits through reproductive technologies, the connections between the body and science and technology are intensified. Further, as sexuality, masculinity, embodiment, and issues of ableism and ageism are further defined and developed both within and outside of feminist theory and politics, we will have a more textured understanding of how these interwoven categories enable particular 'natures' to emerge. Such expansions of feminist analysis will undoubtedly result in a rich terrain for thinking about the specificities of gendered environments and environmentalisms, something as necessary today as it was when ecofeminism took shape in the 1970s. Perhaps today we need a feminist ecopolitics that turns on the figure of the cyborg – an ecopolitics that is resolutely about *connections* yet without recourse to 'essences' that assume a preexisting natural order outside history, a politics about imagining survivable futures, but without a transcendental blueprint. It would be, above all else, about a sort of vigilance to account for what has been left out of our futures/natures.

Acknowledgments

Many thanks to Ken MacDonald and Rebecca Roberts for lending us their excellent syllabi on gender and environment, and to Tad Mutersbaugh for his insights. Claire Pavlik, Kat O'Reilly, and Rebecca Klug read and commented on various drafts.

Notes

1 'Political-economy' emphasizes how people's life chances are bound-up with their access to economic and political resources. Because most societies are characterized

by inequalities between social classes, political-economy accents the role of this inequality in explaining things like poverty, marginalization, and starvation.

2   Usufruct rights refer to the right to use another's property, short of its destruction or waste of its substance.

Further Reading

Within geography Nesmith and Radcliffe (1993) provide a solid exploration of gendered nature, including the influence of cultural geography and landscape literature, and the potential to develop them further to include gender. For an excellent interrogation of 'race,' gender, and nature, see Kobayashi and Peake (1994). Also the edited volume by Rocheleau et al. (1996) on feminist political ecology provides a geographical perspective on a number of important themes in gender–environment studies. This can be further supplemented by the work of Carney (1993), Merchant (1980), Shiva (1988), Agarwal (1992), Plumwood (1993), and Haraway (1989, 1991, 1997).

References

Agarwal, B. (1992). The Gender and Environment Debate: Lessons from India. *Feminist Studies* 18: 119–58.

Biehl, J. (1991). *Rethinking Ecofeminist Politics*. Boston: South End Press.

Butler, J. (1990). *Gender Trouble: Feminism and the Subversion of Identity*. New York: Routledge.

Caldecott, L. and Leland, S. (eds.) (1983). *Reclaim the Earth: Women Speak Out for Life on Earth*. London: The Women's Press Limited.

Carney, J. (1993). Converting the Wetlands, Engendering the Environment: The Intersections of Gender with Agrarian Change in The Gambia. *Economic Geography* 69: 329–48.

Carson, R. (1962). *Silent Spring*. New York: Houghton Mifflin Company.

Connell, R. W. (1997). Gender as a Structure of Social Practice. In L. McDowell and J. Sharp (eds.), *Space, Gender, Knowledge: Feminist Readings*. London: Arnold, 44–53.

Diamond, I. and Orenstein, G. (eds.) (1990). *Reweaving the World: The Emergence of Ecofeminism*. San Francisco: Sierra Club Books.

Gaard, G. (1997). Toward a Queer Ecofeminism. *Hypatia* 12: 114–37.

Gottlieb, R. (1993). *Forcing the Spring*. Washington, DC: Island Press.

Haraway, D. (1989). *Primate Visions*. New York: Routledge.

Haraway, D. (1991). *Simians, Cyborgs, and Women: The Reinvention of Nature*. New York: Routledge.

Haraway, D. (1992). The Promises of Monsters: A Regenerative Politics for Inappropriate/d Others. In L. Grossberg, C. Nelson, and P. Treichler (eds.), *Cultural Studies*. New York: Routledge, 295–337.

Haraway, D. (1994). A Game of Cat's Cradle: Science Studies, Feminist Theory, Cultural Studies. *Configurations: A Journal of Literature and Science* 1: 59–71.

Haraway, D. (1997). *Modest_Witness@Second_Millennium.FemaleMan_Meets_OncoMouse*. New York: Routledge.

King, Y. (1993). Feminism and Ecology. In R. Hofrichter (ed.) *Toxic Struggles: The Theory and Practice of Environmental Justice*. Philadelphia: New Society Publishers, 76–83.

Kobayashi, A. and Peake, L. (1994). Unnatural Discourse: 'Race' and Gender in Geography. *Gender, Place and Culture*, 1(2): 225–43.

Krauss, C. (1993). Blue-collar Women and Toxic-waste Protests. In R. Hofrichter (ed.), *Toxic Struggles: The Theory and Practice of Environmental Justice*. Philadelphia: New Society Publishers, 107–17.

Martin, E. (1991). The Egg and the Sperm: How Science Has Constructed a Romance Based on Stereotypical Male–Female Roles. *Signs* 16: 485–501.

Merchant, C. (1980). *The Death of Nature: Women, Ecology, and the Scientific Revolution*. San Francisco: Harper & Row.

Merchant, C. (1992). *Radical Ecology: The Search for a Livable World*. New York: Routledge.

Mohanty, C. (1991). Under Western Eyes: Feminist Scholarship and Colonial Discourses. In C. Mohanty, A. Russo, and L. Torres (eds.), *Third World Women and the Politics of Feminism*. Bloomington: Indiana University Press, 51–80.

Nesmith, C. and Radcliffe, S. (1993). (Re)mapping Mother Earth: A Geographical Perspective on Environmental Feminisms. *Environment and Planning D: Society and Space* 11: 379–94.

Newman, P. (1994). Killing Legally with Toxic Waste: Women and the Environment in the United States. In V. Shiva (ed.) *Close to Home: Women Reconnect Ecology, Health and Development Worldwide*. Philadelphia: New Society Publishers, 43–59.

Norwood, V. (1993). *Made from this Earth: American Women and Nature*. Chapel Hill: University of North Carolina Press.

Oudshoorn, N. (1994). *Beyond the Natural Body*. London: Routledge.

Pardo, M. (1990). Mexican American Women Grassroots Community Activists: "Mothers of East Los Angeles." *Frontiers* 11: 1–7.

Plant, J. (ed.) (1989). *Healing the Wounds: The Promise of Ecofeminism*. Santa Cruz: New Society Publishers.

Plumwood, V. (1993). Nature, Self, and Gender: Feminism, Environmental Philosophy and the Critique of Rationalism. In M. Zimmerman (ed.) *Environmental Philosophy: From Animal Rights to Radical Ecology*. Englewood Cliffs, NJ: Prentice-Hall, 284–309.

Rapp, R. (1999). *Testing Women, Testing the Fetus: The Social Impact of Amniocentesis in America*. New York: Routledge.

Reynolds, D. (1999). Personal communication.

Rocheleau, D., Thomas-Slayter, B., and Wangari, E. (1996). Gender and Environment: A Feminist Political Ecology Perspective. In D. Rocheleau, B. Thomas-Slayter, and E. Wangari (eds.), *Feminist Political Ecology: Global Issues and Local Experiences*. London: Routledge, 3–26.

RuPaul. (2000). Interview with Terry Gross on Fresh Air(r), National Public Radio, Aug. 10, 2000.

Sandoval, C. (1991). US Third World Feminism: The Theory and Method of Oppositional Consciousness in the Postmodern World. *Genders* 10: 1–24.

Schroeder, R. (1997). "Re-claiming" Land in The Gambia: Gendered Property Rights and Environmental Intervention. *Annals of the Association of American Geographers* 87: 487–508.

Seager, J. (1993). *Earth Follies*. New York: Routledge.

Shiva, V. (1988). *Staying Alive: Women, Ecology and Development*. London: Zed Books.

Sturgeon, N. (1997). *Ecofeminist Natures: Race, Gender, Feminist Theory and Political Action*. New York: Routledge.

Unity Statement of the Women's Pentagon Action. (1980/3). In L. Caldecott and S. Leland (eds.), *Reclaim the Earth: Women Speak Out for Life on Earth*. London: The Women's Press Limited, 15–19.

Warren, K. (1993). Introduction. In M. Zimmerman (ed.), *Environmental Philosophy: From Animal Rights to Radical Ecology*. Englewood Cliffs, NJ: Prentice-Hall, 251–67.

Whatmore, S. (1997). Dissecting the Autonomous Self: Hybrid Cartographies for a Relational Ethics. *Environment and Planning D: Society and Space* 15: 37–53.

Chapter 7

Social Nature and Environmental Policy in the South: Views from Verandah and *Veld*

Piers Blaikie

Envisioning the Environment

This chapter takes a critical look at contemporary environmental management in lesser developed countries (LDCs). It focuses on two main issues. We start with the different ways in which the environment is interpreted and explained by the various people involved in its management. Among others, these people include government officials and policy-makers (hence the allusion to 'the view from the verandah' in the title of this chapter), as well as local civil society (farmers and pastoralists for the most part, who view things 'from the *veld*' or open rangeland). Often their views about what is happening to the environment and its natural and social causes are in direct contradiction. For instance, how is it that a range ecologist in semiarid southern Africa, drawing upon scientific research indicating a 'maximum sustainable stocking density' (number of animals per unit area) for a particular range, sees this density greatly exceeded and can point to evidence of desiccation, land degradation, and the poor condition of cattle, while a pastoralist denies that the range is degraded, continues to exceed notional maximum densities, and manages to extract a livelihood? What is going on here is that two (admittedly stereotypical) pairs of people are looking at the same landscape, but drawing upon completely different cultural and professional repertoires to interpret it. They see, or fail to see, different things and interpret their landscapes in a different way: in short, different people, different nature.

The second main issue explored in this chapter is how, and with what effects, these different views about nature are contested. Specifically, I focus on the ways in which these views inform (or fail to be heard in) environmental policy-making in the developing world. But my arguments about environmental policy – its construction and contestation – have a wider resonance. After all, environmental issues at all levels – global, national, and local – have become increasingly important to all of us. The reasons for this are complex, and any explanation immediately engages some of the more philosophical concerns of this volume. Is it because there are 'real' and objectively verifiable changes in the state of nature, such that the rate and direction of environmental change increasingly threatens humankind? Is it simply that the optic through which we view nature has changed? Or is it possibly the case that the politics of who holds the looking-glass has shifted, privileging some views over others? These are very difficult questions, and the argument here claims that all three answers are persuasive, and can indeed co-exist. Further, it will be argued, they *should* co-exist, and a recognition of their co-existence can improve the prospect of a more just socioenvironmental future. The obvious charge of inconsistency in my argument is, however, a difficult one to counter, and one that invites a degree of humility and caution in this subject area from this – and any – author.

Environmental Change: Real, Subjective, and Political

To return to the example of the pastoralist and the range manager, it is difficult to argue that there have not been real changes in vegetation and livestock numbers in the ranges of subtropical Africa over the past, say, 50 years. For example, it has been suggested that pastoralists face increasing competition for grass and water due to (i) their declining access to these resources as land has been expropriated for commercial ranching and agriculture, and (ii) to the growth of animal and human populations. Thus, the answer to the first question posed at the end of my introductory comments is 'yes': there *are* real changes to range ecology, or at least 'real' in the sense that even diverse observers would agree that environmental changes of some sort have occurred.

Moving to the second question, there is strong historical evidence that views about subtropical African rangelands have also changed. We can start with the colonial administrators (the view from the verandah), who began to intervene in large numbers from the 1920s onwards. Evidence from aerial photography, and later satellite imagery, was sought and provided by the colonial state in order to observe these changes. The colonial state and environmental consultants in the immediate postindependence period in Africa, increasingly made their views heard in the international environmental organizations (like the United Nations Environment Program), which began set the agenda for managing Southern environments from the 1950s. Various explanations for the perceived physical changes in vegetation through time were developed at the time. Three were, and to some extent still are, powerful.

The first of these was the 'neo-Malthusian crisis' explanation, which claimed that populations (in this instance of both people and livestock) always tended to grow unchecked until a shortage of available resources caused malnutrition, famines, and resource-based wars. This was a grim and pessimistic explanation, which tended to (i) ignore or dismiss the possibilities of increased food production through technical and social transformation, and (ii) was blind to how political and economic marginalization led to natural resources (in this example, land for cattle and agriculture) being taken away from pastoralists. (For the reader who wishes to pursue the controversy surrounding the impacts of population growth upon development, Cassen (1994) and Kiessling and Landberg (1994) provide excellent overviews.) The second explanation for 'range degradation' was the so-called 'tragedy of the commons' thesis. This was first proposed by American ecologist Garret Hardin (1968), who argued that the pastoralist will, if 'rational,' always tend to overstock a common pasture, provided that the benefits of the extramarginal animal put onto it accrues to him/her. However, since Hardin assumed that *all other* pastoralists were also individualistically minded profit-seekers, and that collective action to control stocking densities was absent, overstocking and environmental degradation would, for Hardin, result in the inexorable manner of a Greek tragedy – hence the title of his parable. Hardin's view has been vigorously contested for over 30 years, but still survives today in many policy discourses. Finally, the third member of the somewhat unholy trinity of explanations for rangeland degradation in semiarid Africa is a neocolonial view, taken this time from the verandah of the colonial administrator. According to this explanation, the main cause of environmental problems in the South was (and is) so-called 'primitive' and 'unmodernized' attitudes among native pastoralists. Here, the pastoralist (and most other indigenous resources users in the colonies, or 'target groups' as they're called in postcolonial development projects) was seen as essentially 'irrational,' reckless, and ignorant of the longer-term environmental implications of their resource use. Such a view has prompted environmental policies which are either coercive (to prevent pastoralists from destroying the environment through by laws and other restrictions), or paternalistic (by 'educating' pastoralists to adopt more 'rational' and scientifically based resource use habits; see Blaikie and Brookfield, 1987: 100–21).

This very short description of the three leading explanations of rangeland degradation in subtropical Africa caricatures each of them to some extent. In each case, pastoralists are seen to exceed the fixed capacities of rangeland. During the 1980s, these views started to be challenged. In other words, the optic through which pastoralists and their range were viewed started to change. New views of the 'problem,' new evidence, and new facts started to become apparent. The definition of 'land degradation' itself was seen as deeply colored by the choice of scientific models, indicators, and measurement (see Stocking, 1987). Also, a radically different understanding of range ecology was developed which rejected the conventional physical modeling of rangeland processes, which included equilibrium modeling based upon stable relationships between cattle densities, carrying capacities, plant succession, and biomass production. Instead, the relationships between these and other variables were increasingly characterized in disequilibrium terms. Furthermore, it was rainfall, as by far the most powerful independent variable, which was seen to drive other key rangeland variables (such as biomass production, vegetative ground cover, and grass species diversity), not cattle density at all (Behnke et al., 1993). Indeed, the new argument went, range degradation may well have been very much overemphasized, and when a good year of rainfall came along, the range once more bounced back to previous levels of production. Thus, the explanations of what were considered to be the causes of range-degrading cattle densities, such as the tragedy of the commons and neo-Malthusian projections, lost their claim to be explaining a significant problem: since there may be little or no degradation as previously defined, there is now little need to explain it.

If the optics through which academics and policy-makers view rangelands have changed considerably in recent decades, this begs the third of my initial questions, viz. the politics of 'who holds the looking glass?' It is a question which has attracted increasing attention over the past 15 years or so We can elaborate upon the question thus: whose theories and whose reality count?; and why is some knowledge accepted and authoritative while other knowledge is not? Importantly, these questions encourage us to focus not so much on the production of 'truth,' but upon *claims to truth*, which implies a close connection between power, knowledge, and theory.

Three main groups of political interests are built into different knowledges of environment in developing countries. The first group is colonial, wherein environmental policy has been revealed to be shot through with Western values and assumptions, particularly in the fields of nature conservation and preservation (see Anderson and Grove, 1987, and Grove, 1995, for an earlier period of colonial environmental thought, and Grove et al., 1998, for south and southeast Asia specifically). Conservation/preservation implied a set of measures which would reduce perceived land degradation and reckless resource use, mostly by native farmers, pastoralists, and commercial timber merchants (who cleared land for charcoal, and building construction). Ideas of conservation/ preservation drew their inspiration from European notions of a pristine and 'wild' nature, which was seen as being laid to waste by overhunting, deforestation, and agricultural encroachment (see Cronon, 1995 on 'wilderness,' Grove, 1995 on the notion of 'Edenism'). The trouble was that colonial attempts to conserve/preserve nature derived from very particular Euro-American social constructions and practices (such as national parks, reserves, rangeland management, and wildlife policies). The idea of wilderness and the practices designed to conserve/preserve it were exported from the US and Europe to the developing countries where different constructions of and material relations to nature pertained (Guha, 1989a). The conservation/preservation of a very specific historically and culturally constructed nature also led to some particularly unfortunate outcomes for all, involving, among other misfortunes, hardship for local resource users because of their exclusion from their ancestral communal lands.

It is not difficult to guess that for colonial authorities the key culprits of all this perceived environmental mayhem were usually (though not always) the indigenous population. This is why critical-structuralist (and specifically Marxist) explanations of environmental policy-making in the South have tended to focus on the economic interests of the colonial state and its clients (white settlers and the metropolitan political apparatuses in London, Paris, and Brussels). These economic interests were heterogeneous across different colonial empires, but often involved a common legitimation of the seizing of land for agriculture, ranching, and commercial forestry by settlers and the colonial state. There were other important considerations which were not economic but cultural, and symptomatic of 'civilizing' and modernizing intitiatives wherein the colonized were paternalistically dealt with by the colonial state (though in times of resistance by local people, this relationship became highly coercive and violent). Expulsions from state forests, fines, and brutal police actions against squatters were legitimated by the imperative of conservation and protection of nature, and backed by the science of the colonial state, which provided evidence of the degradation of natural resources caused by – the reader will, by now, be able to reproduce the familiar litany – 'reckless,' 'indigent,' and 'primitive' technologies of local resource users. Resistance took many forms, of which fire was one of the most common, involving the torching of state forests (as in Almora and Garhwal Districts, British India in the 1920s (Tucker, 1984)), or in east Africa (Fosbrooke and Young, 1976), illegal hunting, wire-cutting, trespass, and armed rebellion (as in the case of the Mau Mau actions in preindependence Kenya, and, as this chapter is being written, in Zimbabwe too). Thus the colonial state, to different degrees at different times, created a very particular optic, through which nature and natives were viewed. It was strongly value-laden and usually led to coercive, and sometimes strongly resisted, environmental policies.

A second strand of literature on the politics of environmental knowledge and policy addresses a more recent phenomenon. It is the globalization of environmental conservation initiatives, through international institutions such as the United Nations (especially the Food and Agriculture Organization, and the United Nations Environmental Program), the Consultative Group of International Agricultural Research, the larger aid agencies such as USAID, as well as the growing volume of international environmental treaties. In many ways, their programs followed the assumptions of the Belgian, British, and French colonial states. Indeed, many ex-colonial officers joined these international organizations after the waning of European empires during the 1950s and 1960s, and projected their particular view of nature onto the international stage. There developed a new politics in which these international environmental agendas had to traverse new oppositions, in the form of the leaders of the newly independent states of Africa and southeast Asia. Many of these leaders did not have to have very long memories of the history of environmental conservation/preservation under colonialism to have serious misgivings of a neocolonial invasion – not of settlers and administrators in person this time, but of their ideas, backed by powerful international institutions. These leaders also had to appease populist, anticolonial and nationalist sentiments of their political constituencies, and it was (and is) not surprising that global environmental projects (such as watershed management regimes, national parks, bioreserves, and community forestry) have often not been enthusiastically embraced by local people. Many projects have had to resort to all manner of persuasions (e.g. attractive training opportunities for senior government staff and funding of other, more popular infrastructural projects) and coercion (e.g., heavy policing by forest or park rangers at the local level) to make any headway at all. Here again, the view of nature as under threat by direct resource users, still drew much of its legitimacy from powerful and well-tried scientific methods and policies from the colonial period, but it is one which now had to run the political gauntlet of newly independent states and the new thinking in both the natural and social sciences. Now, in the postcolonial period, bureaucratic foot dragging, rhetorical ploys, lip-service in policy statements, and unjustifiably favorable evaluations and reports of international environmental policies and projects were the order of the day. In other instances, a colonial coercive conservation was reproduced by the newly independent state itself (e.g. Guha, 1989b, for India, and Peluso, 1993, for Indonesia).

The third strand of research into different knowledges of nature is yet more recent, and is woven around the rediscovery of indigenous technical knowledge and its (re-)application in environmental management through participatory policies (Brokensha et al., 1980, Chambers et al., 1989, Richards 1985, Warren et al., 1995). In part, this change has been brought about by a grudging admission of the failure of state-led, top-down, and, many would argue, neocolonial interventions. Without the coercive apparatus of the colonial state, there is even less chance that policies which excluded local resource users, and which forced upon them alien notions of land degradation and its causes, would ever succeed. Instead, why not listen to local resource users, and incorporate their technical knowledge of nature? To return to the example of pastoralism at the beginning of this chapter, ethnobotany, folk vetinerary medicine, and local herding strategies are now part of many rangeland management policies, and sit, sometimes uncomfortably, alongside quantitative ecological and economic modeling. A new (and perhaps uneasy) alliance of local and 'scientific' knowledge has also become the new conventional wisdom in forest management, agricultural technology, artisanal fishery, and wildlife management. However, beneath the surface of project and policy rhetoric of participation and 'harnessing' indigenous technical knowledge there exist all manner of contradictions in the policy arena. This new populist rhetoric established originally in the early 1980s, suggests that the hands of marginal and oppressed people now, at least share, even if they have not grasped for themselves, the looking-glass through which nature is viewed. How far this new, or at least 'hybrid' knowledge of nature (which describes a union of both indigenous and exogenous knowledge: Batterbury et al., 1997) actually alters the outcome of any policy is a matter of opinion, but it certainly runs counter to established bureaucratic and scientific routines of formal policy-making (Blaikie, 2000; Chambers, 1993).

In the discussion so far, we have simplified matters by taking only two, rather stereotypical, actors (the "state official" and the local pastoralist or forest user), who make competing representations about nature. However, it is easy to recognize that there is a whole cast of actors, not just our two stereotypes, who all may construct nature in different ways. First, direct resource users in developing countries (as in developed countries too) are highly heterogeneous, and are divided by gender, class, occupation, and culture which, in their engagement with nature, produces a purely local environmental politics. There is competition for water, land, timber, and a wide range of other natural resources. Also, nature itself provides habitat and is a major material and cultural basis of daily life, and is valued to differing degrees and in different ways. Therefore, there arise both material and ideational struggles over nature at all levels (international, national, and local). Locally, different people make competing claims about nature, and in effect, these competing claims constitute a local politics. For example, European commercial farmers in Zimbabwe, who currently own a vast proportion of the best farming land in Zimbabwe, are making the claim that it is they alone, as opposed to the Shona and Ndebele majority, who can manage the land sustainably and combat land degradation. Of course, this can be recognized as a discursive strategy to hang onto their farms in the face of popular demands for redistribution to the black majority.

There are also a large number of other actors, including international financial institutions, individual scientists and activists, conservation groups, nongovernmental organizations, forest contractors, charcoal producers, industrial entrepreneurs, politicians, and urban consumers, all of which have direct or contingent engagements with the environment (see Bryant and Bailey, 1997, for an extended discussion of these actors). They too interpret environment differently from each other, make representations about it, and act in different discursive and material ways. All bring their professional and cultural repertoires to bear upon what is supposed to be happening in nature, and how it should be shaped and managed in the future – in a word, upon policy itself. Thus, our stage on which competing representations of nature are played out, now no longer has two stereotypical actors (the pastoralist and range management expert). It now has a whole cast of actors, and their dialogue, their actions,

sometimes discursive, sometimes violent, constitutes the very stuff of environmental politics.

Nature, Science, and Politics

We now shift our focus onto how all these different and often competing views
of nature enter (or fail to enter) into the environmental policy process. Let us
start with the dominant view, at least in policy-making circles themselves. This
is the 'truth talks to power' model (the phrase being invented by Wildavsky,
1979). Here, the truth about the environment is established by scientists who
convey what is *really* going on in the environment to policy-makers, who
formulate (or adapt existing) policy, and hand it to the bureaucrats and
administrators to get on and implement it. There are really two sub-models
here, but crucially related. The first is the identification of 'truth' and the
second is the exercise of power in environmental policy-making, and in this
chapter they are discussed in the context of LDCs, and their historically specific
– and, as we have seen, usually colonial – experience of how environmental
knowledge and policy are created.

In the first submodel, scientists establish objective 'facts' about nature by
'good' scientific method (accurate measurement, sound experimental and sam-
pling design, and so on). Good scientific method, the argument goes, will
supposedly yield the same facts, whomsoever carries out the experiment, and
these facts may then to be accepted as true. Therefore, in the 'truth talks to
power' model there is not much call for debate about the correctness of these
facts, provided that the scientific method is persuasive, nor about the political
process which allows the 'truth' to emerge and deliver the outcome of public
scrutiny and due political process. Truths about nature arrived at exclusively by
scientists therefore suit a particular style of policy-making, which is top-down,
state-led, and authoritarian. Scientific knowledge is assumed to provide the
objective truth about the environment, and therefore is above politics, and
confers a mantle of political neutrality and rationality to what is clearly a highly
politically charged field.

For example, British colonial policy in Africa and Asia, although differentiated between states (e.g. settler, Protectorate, or indirect rule) and through
time, often relied upon scientific evidence for its conservation policies. Britain
sent scientific officers destined for various colonial governments to be trained
by the United States Department of Agriculture (USDA) in methods of
identifying, measuring, and combating anthropogenic soil erosion. Modeling
soil erosion and developing extension packages which addressed the technical
causes of soil loss in the United States were then exported to the British
colonies, developed sometimes by in-country research stations, and passed on
to colonial policy-makers. In technical terms, soil erosion in many parts of

colonial Africa (and, to a lesser extent parts of imperial India too) was seen to be anthropogenic and, as we have seen, caused by the 'primitive' agricultural techniques of local cultivators and by the increase in their human and livestock populations. Amongst the causal variables explaining accelerated soil erosion, gradient and length of slope were given explanatory prominence, leading to a problem framing which focused on the need for bench terraces (which, by design, reduce both these variables through mechanical means). These scientific 'truths' were accepted with various degrees of conviction by colonial states. 'Truth' had talked to power, and the colonial state could act with confidence, based upon authoritative facts. The state often prescribed the construction of bench terraces and, as a result, a range of onerous regulations to enforce bench terracing were visited upon African cultivators, especially in Kenya and in the Belgian colonies.

The outcome of these soil conservation policies was almost universal resistance throughout eastern and central Africa, which became politicized to the extent of fuelling independence movements (e.g. the Mau Mau movement in Kenya). It also involved less overt resistance such as foot dragging and evasion – it is hard work to dig bench terraces by hand within a regime of limited labor availability that characterizes many African farming systems. The main point here is that scientific truths about natural processes, which claimed that erosion was caused by people's actions and was a significant social and economic problem, were believed to be objective and authoritative. These truths about the environment also resonated with top-down authoritarian policy regimes, particularly when policy-makers themselves worked in a political environment which had paternalist and modernizing attitudes towards the ruled, and which denigrated or disregarded alternative ('native') understandings about nature.

It was only after a passage of 20 years or so, that alternative constructions of nature began to be heard, both from scientific and indigenous quarters. First, it became clearer from scientific research that rain splash was a major factor in causing accelerated erosion in the tropics, and the importance of slope gradient and length (as modeled in the Universal Soil Loss Equation which appeared from the 1950s from the USA) had been overplayed (Seckler, 1987). Thus, new scientific facts supplanted the old. It was not environmental 'truth,' it seemed, that had been talked to power after all – just misplaced scientific conclusions. Secondly, as we have already discussed, the politics of knowledge construction, both within academe and in postcolonial policy-making arenas, has also changed profoundly, and has questioned this type of authoritative knowledge as well as the unaccountable and undemocratic structures that produce and use it. For almost the first time in Africa from the 1970s, local knowledge as an alternative source of truth about nature was heard and acknowledged in international circles, though it usually had to be ventriloquized by native-language speaking Westerners for others to hear (Blaikie et al., 1997).

In the case of soil conservation, it transpired that African farmers in many different agroecological settings had already appreciated the primacy of the rain splash threat, and developed ground-protecting techniques such as intercropping, trashlines, and a variety of modifications of the geometry of agricultural land (other than bench terracing), all of which reduced it. Many other examples of scientifically based constructions of nature, based on the shakiest foundations, were incorporated into environmental policies carried out by colonial states. Examples include wildlife conservation, forest policy, range management, and the deliberate importation of exotic species wherein lie so many admissions of scientific foundations having feet of clay. Many other environmental debates and the policies which drew from them followed similar paths, and often with unpredictable and disastrous outcomes (see two excellent edited books on these subjects in relation to colonial and postcolonial Africa, Anderson and Grove, 1987, and Leach and Mearns, 1996).

What do these example tell us about the underlying objectivist view of environmental knowledge, the scientific methods producing it, and the way in which it relates to policy? Let us define what we mean by 'objectivism' and sum up its central assumptions in the words of Johnson:

> The world consists of objects that have properties and stand in various relationships independent of human understanding. The world is as it is, no matter what any person happens to believe about it, and there is one correct 'God's-Eye-View' about what the world is really like. (Johnson, 1987: x)

The choice of approaching environmental knowledge in policy as *either* science *or* politics, as objective reality *or* representation, is an attractive one but essentially misplaced and not easily resolved. First, formal environmental science itself is only one form of constructed knowledge of nature, but is political both in the production of that knowledge (Latour and Wolgar, 1979) as well as in the impact it may have through policy. Scientific information is produced in a social context with incentives, reward structures, competition, and alliances which may say more about the politics of the research institution than about any truth claim about nature. It is therefore shaped by the institutions which produce it. Indeed, as Thompson et al. (1986) have said about the degree of scientific uncertainty over the state of nature in the Himalayan region, "the institutions *are* the facts." Financial, social, and political circumstances shape the production of environmental knowledge. Some environmental agendas find funding, while others languish in the minds of hopeful academics, environmental activists and others marginal to the political nexus of funding, politics, and policy. Other scientific findings are actively encouraged through purposive funding by government, or sought from ongoing research by those who make policy.

An example is provided by rangeland policy. A number of research stations, notably the Alvord Institute near Fort Victoria (now Masvingo) in Zimbabwe carried out a number of experiments addressing 'the problem,' as framed by the colonial state, namely cattle-carrying capacities and range degradation (for a more general rehearsal of colonial pastoral policy in Zimbabwe, see Scoones, 1995). Range ecologists organized a number of experiments in which different densities of cattle were grazed in paddocks over a number of years. Variations in the dependent variables (cattle condition, ground cover, grass species diversity, etc.) were then measured to provide a guide to the maximum permissible density of cattle. The experiments were predicated upon both theories of equilibrium modeling and climax vegetation as well as upon the institutional practicalities of running experiments by scientists at a research station. Thus, a representation of nature was constructed by a set of experiments, themselves framed by political expedients of the day and the nature of the institutions which carried them out. However, most of the experimental conditions of cattle-rearing at these institutions bore no relation to the way in which cattle are actually herded by pastoralists themselves. As we have already indicated, pastoralists tend to 'flee drought' and move large numbers of cattle to where the grass and rainfall is, and to subject the range to very high cattle densities but for a very short period of time. Thus the experimental conditions of the research station bore little resemblance to the reality of the pastoralists.

Thus, many scientific constructions about the environment are contested within the scientific and policy-making professions themselves and often just turn out to be plain wrong in their own terms. Scientific knowledge is always provisional and is usually acknowledged as such by scientists themselves – even without the benefit of the deconstructive zeal of critical social scientists! To take another example, there are familiar technical problems in the calibration of soil loss. These include among others: problems of extrapolating the results from a spatially restricted experimental domain to larger scales; extrapolating present processes into the past and future; carrying out measures of erosivity for a long enough period to include extreme events which cause most of the erosion; and problems of scale effects when measuring the export of eroded material across experimental grids of different sizes. These problems of scientific method produce widely different and contested results on which claims to conserve soil are based, but their solution quickly meets institutional, practical, and financial constraints. Also, scientific constructions of the environment in the South are often based upon highly selective 'paper chases' through earlier scientific reports and observations of colonial officers, and amount to little more than the confirmation of prejudice, in the authoritative name of science (see Guthman's 1997 historiography which takes a rather antiscience view of the environmental crisis in the Himalaya). Fairhead and Leach (1996: 105–21), for example, trace the reproduction of conventional wisdom concerning deforestation in West Africa, which turns out to be little more than a compilation of hearsay upon hearsay.

Lastly, the way in which scientific information is selectively used in policy-making has attracted considerable attention (Jasonoff, 1990, and Hajer, 1995, both referring to developed country situations). While many scientific papers and reports are usually careful to emphasize uncertainties where they exist and the provisional nature of findings, it is often useful for policy-makers and politicians to select information, often out of context and shorn of original caveats. Scientific information about the environment in policy-making has to be actionable, certain, and simplified so that other players in the policy process can be brought onboard. Some writers have gone further and pointed to a process in which 'trans-science' is produced by the continual interaction between scientists and policy-makers, which further politicizes and shapes a stylized and persuasive construction of nature for bureaucratic and public consumption. Thus nature is often reduced to the production and consumption of images, emblems, logos, and soundbytes, and subjected to an astute culling of selected scientific 'facts,' which may keep the mass media and the public feeling that they really are participating, while reducing scientific uncertainty and complexity to manageable simplicity. But, 'truth'? No.

Facts or Narratives?

Approaches to how nature is represented by different people can be elaborated by using the idea of a 'narrative.' A narrative is a story (in this case about an environmental issue which stabilizes the expectations of tellers and listeners. It helps the teller to, make sense of a complex, uncertain and puzzling world, and also persuades the listener to buy into a particular set of assumptions and, in the area of policy, into a course of action. In the context of the production of nature and policy-making in Africa, Roe (1994, 1995) has introduced the notion of "the environmental narrative," which different people – particularly development experts and policy-makers – tell to each other about the environment and development issues. Hajer (1995) further develops this idea of the environmental narrative in the context of 'acid rain' in the Netherlands and the United Kingdom, in which an emblem (the actual words 'acid rain') with accompanying explanatory narrative, is created, with which various actors of different experiences and expertise can feel in touch and communicate on the issue. Narratives, or what Hajer calls "discursive coalitions," are forged within the global development industry too. The pervasive 'crisis narrative' (which invites the industry to intervene and save its unfortunate 'victims' – though it may well have caused the crisis in the first place!) dominates many current consultancy and multilateral institutional views of nature. Some key social environmental narratives have already been discussed (the 'tragedy of the commons,' the neo-Malthusian crisis, and native ignorance/indolence), but there are many others, such as the woodfuel crisis, desertification, overstocking, soil erosion, and loss of biodiversity (Leach and Mearns, 1995: 1–33). The labeling of these issues as narratives implies that we (outsiders) should greet them with blanket incredulity. They are authoritative, the argument implies, only because powerful voices utter them, and we are invited to challenge all conventional wisdom and all these tired old paradigms which have had their day, and have been left unexamined for far too long. Certainly, the challenging of conventional wisdom is one of the few strategies which intellectuals might offer to the rest of the world, but a careless acceptance of these invitations without reading the small print may well lead to blanket disbelief, disengagement, cynicism, and inaction. Also, some narratives are, perhaps, 'better' than others. Some of these narratives result in environmental policy that actually damages people and belittles the values they attach to nature. Other narratives, by contrast, may do the opposite and serve what may be considered by some to be progressive or ethical ends. The current policy narratives of local or joint environmental management, empowerment, equity and gender issues, the importance of habitat to local people, and diverse cultural interpretations of nature and others, are some which we may think to be 'better' than others. Of course, these too must also be interrogated and recognized for what they are, and taken not as self-evident truths or unchallengeable paragons of political correctness. Thus, interrogation and the acceptance of a broader range of interpretations of nature are certainly called for and, as Roe urges, these narratives may be used and sifted for discursive resources towards a more just and sustainable future.

From Social Nature to Social Justice

At this point in my own narrative, it is apposite to pause and offer some interim self-critique. Much in the above argument, which essentially takes a social constructionist approach to nature, might be accused by those of a more objectivist view, of fiddling in verbal deconstruction while Rome is consumed in some very real flames; of being antiscience and offering no constructive alternative; of being consistently (and tediously) cynical and critical; of being pointlessly relativist; and of reducing important environmental debates and policies to stories told and listened to as entertainment around a campfire. Indeed, the more trenchant deconstructivist, postmodern treatment of nature has attracted a spirited and carefully argued counterattack (e.g. Soule and Lease's book *Reinventing Nature?*). Two contributors to *Reinventing Nature?* make some instructive comments. Environmentalist Paul Shepherd (1995), for example, takes issue with the 'strong' or more extreme constructionist position, which treats all texts, reports, narratives as mere descriptions – focused chatter about an unknowable external world, psychobabble, webs of words that serve as ammunition in struggles over who dominates whom – and finishes by dismissing all this as "subjective and aesthetic dandyism" (1995: 27). Katherine Hayles argues instead for a "weak constructivism," and draws conclusions closer to my own, when she accepts that each of us (and by implication, the whole cast of actors who use and make representations about nature) has a unique and subjective view of reality, but that the notions of "interactivity" and positionality enliven the stakes in contesting for the integrity of the environment. She urges that representations emerging from marginal positions have a special role to play in knowledge construction (1995: 60).

My elaboration of these challenges is to extend Hayles' argument, and to outline a construction of nature that might offer better, more just environmental and social futures (both these adjectives, 'better' and 'just,' themselves being subject to democratic resolution). How might this prospect be encouraged? The direction to be taken owes much to German critical theorist Jürgen Habermas (1987), and envisages that different truths about nature may be *mutually and democratically constructed*, that these 'truths' can be acknowledged to be provisional and political, and that contending social constructions of nature can be negotiated in a playing field which, while not level, is not on a vertiginously sloping gradient! This direction focuses attention on the ways in which policy is made, or could be made, which have a better chance of achieving better social and ecological futures. These two issues of epistemology and policy are related, since, I argue, the approach to constructing nature for policy, wherever it locates itself within a range of realist and social constructionist positions, should be able to suggest where policy is damaging to people and environment, and how it may be improved. Also, the way in which nature and policy is represented must have some chance of being acceptable to key actors in the policy process in the different countries involved. We may now be in a better position to establish the grounds on which we choose one epistemology for nature over another. I have suggested in the previous section that the criterion for choice of an appropriate epistemology for nature should be that which has the best chance of shifting policy towards a particular set of social-environmental goals. In the academic literature, most cases for a particular approach to nature of whatever persuasion have been made on epistemological grounds alone. This chapter takes a different and more pragmatic approach, and uses discussions about social nature, not so much to discover 'truth,' or the most philosophically appealing approach, but instead as a tool which can focus down to the levels where transformations of nature and society can occur. My argument is that we have to talk about the environment to people who will listen and in a language which we share. Otherwise, the more strongly social constructionist approach begins to take on the flavor of the coffee house or, worse, the academic ivory tower. The relevant audiences here are the stakeholders in environmental management and policy-making in LDCs (for example, farmers, pastoralists, commercial forest users, and professional and bureaucratic cadres), as well as those who frame international environmental and social agendas outside these countries altogether. This is no easy task, and requires an understanding of the historical and contemporary context of environment and society in these countries, and the ways in which the environment is interpreted and represented.

This project is not conceived as yet another anodyne utopia, but as a series of often prosaic steps, some overtly political, others formally legal, others procedural and administrative, still others informal and outside the state apparatus altogether. These directions are discussed in the next and final section. A key question links the two concerns of epistemology and policy, and can be phrased: what social construction of nature helps us all towards a better and more just future?

Alternative Approaches to Environmental Policy

It is first necessary to link the social construction of nature to the policy process. The 'rational' policy model, already described, which is based upon objectivist and science-driven assumptions about the 'truth of nature' has the appeal of certainty, authority, and 'actionability' (or the characteristic of suggesting clearly what is to be done). The rational model does not recognize issues of power and knowledge, and tends to depoliticise the environment. However, the rational model must not be abandoned entirely in a surrender to an agendaless subjectivity, where policy is merely an outcome of the strategies of the powerful. Instead, a more appropriate approach to policy might be to specify social ends to environmental policy in a more accountable way, and to incorporate hitherto marginalized voices. If a conventional rationalist approach to the analysis of environmental policy is adopted, then scientific and authoritative evidence will form the cutting edge of truth claims. On the other hand, if a knowledge–power approach is taken, then the deconstruction of authoritative and powerful truth claims about nature becomes the focus. Finally, if a more justice-based approach is taken, then evidence from the economic, cultural, and social impacts of policy will be given prominence. In this chapter I argue it is the latter which should be selected. It combines a 'weak' form of social constructivism of nature with a policy-making process which allows and builds upon a variety of different constructions in a more democratic manner. At the same time, a justice approach to environmental policy will also have to retain elements of a rational approach, to seek evidence, predict outcomes of actions, and build up a composite and democratically negotiated knowledge about the environment and how humans relate to it. It cannot abandon nature to an unresolved relativism, where one view is uncritically accepted alongside many other, often contradictory ones.

Environmental justice therefore might be thought of as being constituted by the answer to a key question: "what do poor and politically marginal resource users want from nature?". Hecht and Cockburn (1989), for example, answer this question in terms of human rights, legal confirmation of property rights, more equitable distribution of access to resources for the landless, women and other oppressed groups, and the utilization of local or indigenous knowledge and values. Others, like Gadgil and Guha (1995), in a discussion of Indian forestry policy and forest users, point to a more eclectic solution which includes village empowerment and political decentralization. Others again suggest directions which owe much to Mahatma Gandhi, who urges moderation in resource use by urban and richer consumers. Such visions, noble as they seem in some arenas (academic and Western), do beg questions about practical ways forward (see Blaikie, 1999 and Bryant, 1999). A more cynically minded response to these vague and high-sounding objectives might be 'so what?' In policy terms, these objectives demand a great deal from policy-makers and other agents of change in civil society. Either these arguments remain in the stratosphere of utopia, or are acted upon in what might seem to some to be rather prosaic ways, and to many geographers, arcane and reformist. A list of such actions may include reform of land and tenure and fishing rights, lending support to, rather than the usual suppression of, local social movements, participatory agricultural research, social forestry, intellectual property rights to locally researched and developed varieties and gene material in plants, microcredit for local resource utilization, local institutional development to facilitate collective action, among many others. Intertwined in this list lies the principle of sharing and negotiating different constructions of nature and the political means to reach agreement about provisional truths – truths locally grounded and negotiated in an accountable manner. Perhaps then, an academic discussion of social nature can have practical and progressive outcomes – of a modest nature – after all.

Further Reading

Items for a shortlist of particularly recommended texts are starred below.

References

Abel, N. O. J. and Blaikie, P. M. (1986). Elephants, People, Parks and Development: The Case of the Luangwa Valley, Zambia. *Environmental Management* 10: 735–51.
Anderson, D. and Grove, R. (eds.) (1987). *Conservation in Africa: People, Policies and Practice.* Cambridge: Cambridge University Press.
* Batterbury, S., Forthsyth, T., and Thomson, K. (1997). Environment Transforma-

tions in Developing Countries: Hybrid Knowledge and Democratic Policy. *Geographical Journal* 163: 126–32.

Behnke, R., Scoones, I. and Kerven, C. (eds.) (1993). *Range Ecology at Disequilibrium.* London: Overseas Development Institute.

* Blaikie, P., Brown, K., Stocking, M., Tang, L., Dixon, P., and Sillitoe, P. (1997). Knowledge in Action: Local Knowledge as a Development Resource. *Agricultural Systems* 55: 217–37.

Blaikie, P. (2000). *Policies in High Places: Environment and Development in the Himalayas.* Kathmandu: International Center for Integrated Mountain Development.

Blaikie, P. and Brookfield, H. (1987). *Land Degradation and Society.* London: Methuen.

* Blaikie, P. (1999). A Review of Political Ecology: Issues, Epistemology and Analytical Narratives. *Zeitschrift fur Wirtschaftgeographie* 43: 131–47.

Brokensha, D., Warren, D., and Werner, O. (eds.) (1980). *Indigenous Knowledge Systems and Development.* Lanham, Md.: University Press of America.

Bryant, R. (1999). A Political Ecology for Developing Countries. *Zeitschrift fur Wirtschaftgeographie,* 43: 148–57.

Bryant, R. and Bailey, S. (1997). *Third World Political Ecology.* London: Routledge.

Cassen, R. (1994). Population and Development: Old Debates, New Conclusions. In R. Cassen (ed.), *Population and Development.* Washington, DC: Overseas Development Council.

Chambers, R. (1993). *Rural Development: Putting the Last First.* London: Longman.

Chambers, R., Pacey, A., and Thrupp, L. (eds.) (1989). *Farmers First: Farmer Innovation and Agricultural Research.* London: Intermediate Technology Publications.

Cronon, W. (ed.) (1995). *Uncommon Ground.* New York: W. W. Norton.

Fairhead, J. and Leach, M. (1996). *Misreading the African Landscape.* Cambridge and New York: Cambridge University Press.

Fosbrooke, H. and Young, R. (1976). *Land and Politics among the Luguru of Tanganyika.* London: Routledge and Kegan Paul.

Gadgil, M. and Guha, R. (1995). *This Fissured Land: An Ecological History of India.* Delhi: Oxford University Press.

Grove, R. H. (1995). *Green Imperialism.* Cambridge: Cambridge University Press.

Grove, R. H., Damodaran, V., and Sangwan, S. (eds.) (1998). *Nature and the Orient.* Delhi: Oxford University Press.

Guha, R. (1989a). Radical American Environmentalism and Wilderness Preservation: A Critique. *Environmental Ethics* 11: 71–83.

Guha, R. (1989b). *The Unquiet Words: Ecological Change and Peasant Resistance in the Himalaya.* Delhi: Oxford Unviersity Press.

Guthman, J. (1997). Representing Crisis: The Theory of Himalaya Degradation and the Project of Development in Post-Rana Nepal. *Development and Change* 28: 45–69.

Habermas, J. (1987). The Public Sphere. In R. Goodin and P. Pettit (eds.), *Contemporary Political Philosophy.* Oxford: Blackwell.

Hajer, M.A (1995). *The Politics of Environmental Discourse: Ecological Modernization and the Policy Process.* Oxford: Clarendon Press.

Hardin, G. (1968). The Tragedy of the Commons. *Science* 162: 1243–8.

Hayles, K. (1995). Searching for Common Ground. In M. Soule and G. Lease (eds.), *Reinventing Nature?* Washington, DC: Island Press, 47–64.

Hecht, S. and Cockburn, A. (1989). *The Fate of the Forest: Developers, Destroyers and Defenders of the Amazon*. London: Verso.

Jasonoff, S. (1990). *The Fifth Branch: Science Advisors as Policy Makers*. Cambridge, Mass.: Harvard University Press.

Johnson, M. (1987). *The Body in the Mind*. Chicago: Chicago University Press.

Kiessling, K. and Landberg, H. (eds.) (1994). *Population, Economic Development and the Environment*. Oxford: Oxford University Press.

Latour, B. and Woolgar, S. (1979). *Laboratory Life: the Construction of Scientific Facts*. Princeton: Princeton University Press.

* Leach, M. and Mearns, R. (eds.) (1996). *The Lie of the Land: Challenging Received Wisdom on the African Environment*. Oxford: James Currey.

* Peluso, N. (1993). Coercing Conservation? In R. Lipschutz and K. Conca (eds.), *The State and Social Power in Global Environmental Politics*. New York: Columbia University Press, 46–70.

Richards, P. (1985). *Indigenous Agriculural Devolution*. London: Hutchinson.

Roe, E. (1994). *Narrative Policy Analysis: Theory and Practice*. Durham, NC: Duke University Press.

Roe, E. M. (1995). Introduction: Development Narratives. *World Development* 23: 1005–6.

Scoones, I. (ed.) (1995). *Living With Uncertainty: New Directions in Pastoral Development in Africa*. London: Intermediate Technology Publications.

Seckler, D. (1987). Issues in the Economic Evaluation of Soil and Water Conservation Programmes. In P. Blaikie and H. Brookfield (eds.), *Land Degradation and Society*. London: Methuen, 84–99.

Shepherd, P. (1995). Virtually Hunting Reality in the Forests of Simulacxa. In M. Soule and G. Lease (eds.) *Reinventing Nature?* Washington, D.C: Island Press, 17–30.

Soule, M. and Lease, G. (eds.) (1995). *Reinventing Nature? Responses to Postmodern Deconstruction*. Washington, DC: Island Press.

Stocking, M. (1987). Measuring Land Degradation. In P. Blaikie and H. Brookfield (eds.), *Land Degradation and Society*. London: Methuen, 49–63.

Thompson, M., Warburton, M., and Hatley, T. (1986). *Uncertainty on a Himalayan Scale*. London: Milton Ash Publications.

Tucker, R. (1984). The Historical Context of Social Forestry in the Kumaon Himalayas. *Journal of Developing Areas* 8: 341–56.

Warren, D. M., Slikkerveet, L. J., and Brokensha, D. (1995). *The Cultural Dimensions of Development*. London: Intermediate Technology Publications.

Wildavsky, A. (1979). *Speaking Truth to Power: The Art and Craft of Policy Analysis*. Boston: Little Brown.

Chapter 8

Political Ecology:
A Critical Agenda for Change?

Raymond L. Bryant

Why is it that the so-called Third World seems to be plagued by environmental crises? Everywhere we turn we are confronted with images of havoc: tropical deforestation, desertification, flooding, drought, air and water pollution, land-slides, or hurricanes. If it's not Hurricane Mitch in Central America, it seems to be flooding in Mozambique. Why, too, does it always seem to be the case that the people most afflicted by these catastrophes are poor people? Indeed, what are the links between social and political processes and environmental change in the Third World?

In the 1970s and 1980s scholars began to explore these questions and the research field of Third World political ecology was born. Subsequently, geographers and fellow-travelers such as Piers Blaikie, Michael Watts, Stephen Bunker, Susanna Hecht, Melissa Leach, Ramachandra Guha, Nancy Peluso, Vandana Shiva, and Karl Zimmerer have provided a wealth of ideas clarifying the nature of political and ecological interaction in Africa, Asia and Latin America (for an overview, see Bryant and Bailey, 1997). What tends to emerge is a picture of a deepening human grip on biophysical processes. But what kind of grip? And who is doing the gripping?

My objective in this chapter is to clarify how political ecologists make sense of this complex story. In order to do so, it is imperative to understand the theoretical frameworks used by these scholars. I begin by examining Third World political ecology's early years. The role of neo-Marxist ideas (drawing on the work of the nineteenth-century social thinker Karl Marx) and their empirical expression is considered. Attention is then directed to the post-Marxist backlash that occurred in the 1990s. More a flag of convenience than a coherent theory, post-Marxism brings together the concerns of feminism and poststructuralism as part of a general movement away from what many saw as a narrow fixation on economic and especially class questions. The concepts and theories of each of these approaches are used to make practical sense of real-world social and environmental situations. Finally, I conclude by speculating briefly about possible new directions in Third World political ecology. By accounting for the evolution of a subfield of critical geography, my intention is to document how scholars struggle with questions of social nature and human causation as they go beyond headline 'news' of environmental havoc and social misery.

Neo-Marxist Origins

Most political ecologists in the 1970s and 1980s believed that radical measures were needed to solve the Third World's social and environmental problems. It is often the case with new research that it arises out of a profound disquiet with existing explanations. Third World political ecology is no exception here. Its origins reflect a reaction by scholars on the political Left to the then influential neo-Malthusian perspective. The latter attributed Third World misfortunes (like famines) to a 'population explosion' that, if left unchecked, threatened the future of humanity itself. As such, there were supposed 'natural limits' to what people could do (Ehrlich, 1968). Political ecologists argued that neo-Malthusianism was extremely disturbing because it advocated politically authoritarian or nondemocratic solutions based on the curtailment of individual and group freedom. This usually took the form of calls for population control in developing countries. Moreover, political ecologists accused neo-Malthusianism of being 'Euro-centric' in outlook, in as much as it reflected 'First World' interests, anxieties, and biases. The preoccupation with 'runaway' Third World population increases was a classic case in point. It arguably diverted attention away from the real problem: uneven economic development and the drain of resources from South to North, which together made communities in the developing world highly vulnerable to phenomena like droughts and floods.

Political ecologists therefore sought to emphasize the role of political and economic – as opposed to demographic – factors in Third World social and environmental change. In so doing, they painted a picture of oppressive action by the politically and economically powerful at the expense of an impoverished peasantry. How to explain this process? Analysis tended to follow radical thinking, as political ecologists drew upon neo-Marxist literature on Third World 'underdevelopment' (Peet, 1991). First, there was the preoccupation with a global capitalist system that was seen to be the cause of many of the world's troubles. Conditions of social and economic inequality, political and cultural oppression, economic exploitation, and natural resource depletion were linked to the 'laws' of capitalism. The best-known early text, which studied the problem of soil erosion, is a case in point. British geographer Piers Blaikie (1985) explored the social and ecological complexities of Third World soil erosion usually ignored in conventional accounts, and showed how capitalist agrarian production was instrumental in the 'mining' of soils. While careful to acknowledge non-economic influences, Blaikie (1985: 147) concluded that soil erosion would not be substantially reduced "unless it seriously threatens the accumulation possibilities of the dominant classes."

Second, there was an attempt to describe the structural (or systemic) subordination of the Third World. Drawing on the work of 'dependency theorists' like Andre Gunder Frank, political ecologists related notions of 'underdevelopment' to questions of resource extraction and environmental degradation. The best account here was by Stephen Bunker (1985), who related dependency analysis to ideas about the flow of energy and matter to explain Amazonian underdevelopment. Readers of this fascinating text were introduced to an Amazonian hinterland literally being drained of energy as forests were felled, and local livelihoods were disrupted, in aid of metropolitan development in southern Brazil and the First World.

Finally, there was an emphasis on class inequalities, as the oppression of Third World peasant farmers was linked to the practices of local landlords who, in turn, were enmeshed in subordinate relations with capitalists based in Europe and North America. Thus, Jay O'Brien's (1985) account of the political economy of agrarian production in the Sudan (in *Review of African Political Economy*, a key journal for this sort of analysis) links famine conditions in the 1970s and 1980s to the expansion of export-oriented cotton and sorghum production in the 1960s. Such production was linked to patterns of economic accumulation coordinated by capitalists living both within and without the Sudan (O'Brien, 1985).

These scholars, who were joined by the likes of Phil O'Keefe, Ben Wisner, Susanna Hecht, and Michael Watts, thus sought to transcend existing approaches through a neo-Marxist 'progressive contextualization' (or the move from looking solely at local biophysical changes to national and global social and economic causes; see Vayda, 1983). The strength of this approach was that it offered scholars a way to make sense of the power of 'non-place-based' forces (such as the practices of transnational corporations) over 'place-based' activities (for instance, agricultural production). By combining an anthropological under-standing of localities with neo-Marxism's concern with class and North–South dependency relations, writers hoped to forge a truly *political* ecology approach to environment and development issues.

Neo-Marxist political ecology also reflected the need to develop analyses which would not only *explain* Third World poverty, but which would also seek to *change* that situation. In this regard, the pioneers were steeped in an Anglo-American radical geographic culture centered on the journal *Antipode*. This journal emerged in the late 1960s as a reaction to prevailing arguments in the subdiscipline of human geography. Among these arguments were those made by mainstream geographers who supported Third World 'modernization' or economic development along Western lines. For the early political ecologists

Table 8.1 From neo-Marxist to post-Marxist political ecology

Qualities	Neo-Marxist political ecology	Post-Marxist political ecology
Theoretical referent	Marxism, dependency theory	neo-Weberian, Feminist, Foucauldian discourse
Central unit of analysis	class	state, household, discourse
Critique	external (neo-Malthusianism)	internal (neo-Marxist political ecology)
Typical references	Blaikie (1985), O'Brien (1985)	Peluso (1992), Rocheleau et al. (1996), Escobar (1996)

such arguments were deemed to be supportive of a status quo in which the Third World suffered exploitation at the hands of the First World. Yet critique did not readily lead to change, for a few political ecologists could not easily alter the real-world situations they studied critically – leading to what Blaikie (1985, p. 154) called "practical pessimism." Yet there was nonetheless a recognition of the need for a "radical revaluation of both nature and community" in order to promote First/Third World relations not based on social exploitation (Bunker, 1985: 254).

However, the ink had barely dried on these works when their theoretical assumptions came under attack. Critics pointed to a serious 'impasse' in neo-Marxism. It was accused of various intellectual crimes that boiled down to the view that its 'narrow' vision was incapable of understanding complex political, economic, or cultural processes. Then, there was the seeming inability of neo-Marxism to say anything meaningful about the biophysical environment. On the one hand, there was a perception that Marxism subordinated environmental concerns to class issues (Redclift, 1984). On the other hand, the collapse of communism after 1989, and a recognition of the scale of the environmental destructiveness of communist rule, persuaded many of the ecological poverty of Marxist economics (Beresford and Fraser, 1992). Diverse post-Marxist theories rushed to fill the void left by neo-Marxism's decline. The end result was a tendency for post-Marxist analysis to become more varied and fragmented, and less economically preoccupied, than its neo-Marxist forebear. The complexities of cultural and political practices were emphasized in explaining human–environment relations in the Third World as part of a movement away from overarching theories (Booth, 1994). Research in political ecology has thus followed a wider shift in research in the social sciences (see table 8.1).

Three things stand out from table 8.1. Firstly, the shift from a neo-Marxist to a post-Marxist phase in political ecology was reflected in a firm rejection of Marxist and neo-Marxist thinking. In turn, a more eclectic theoretical blend was favored encompassing state-oriented thinking (drawing on the work of the German theorist Max Weber), feminist literature, and discourse analysis (inspired by the French philosopher Michel Foucault). Secondly, an equivalent shift in the main unit of analysis occurred as class was replaced by concerns with the state, the household, and environmental knowledge (or ways of understanding the biophysical environment). Finally, the nature of the critique changed from one focused initially on external targets (e.g. as in neo-Marxist political ecology's critique of neo-Malthusianism) to one centered on internal academic targets (e.g. as in the post-Marxist critique of neo-Marxist political ecology). By the early 1990s, then, political ecology's early progressive contextualization of local and nonlocal processes via neo-Marxism looked to be a regressive step that would only link the field to a static class-based view of global political and economic processes.

A Post-Marxist Political Ecology

The 1990s witnessed a remarkable shift in the theoretical and empirical concerns of Third World political ecology. The postmodern critique of Marxist and other 'modernist' theories was absorbed by a new generation of scholars impatient with the economic 'fixation' of neo-Marxist political ecology. It would be wrong to say, however, that political ecology swapped one narrowly focused narrative for another. As noted, Third World political ecology in the 1990s was marked by a theoretical eclecticism or variety that brought a fresh set of debates into the field, even as it led some to complain of a lack of theoretical coherence or unity (e.g., Peet and Watts, 1996).

Theoretical shifts were reflected in changing empirical concerns. There was, in particular, a new stress on taking the 'political' in the field's name more seriously than before. Topics examined thus included the role of the state as reflecting a nonclass-based set of political concerns such as military security or the politics of bureaucratic behavior. Other topics explored were the politics of environmental discourse formation in relation to global governance, deforestation, and community environmental management. The social dynamics pertaining to relations between men and women as well as between different ethnic groups were also a favored theme.

What are we to make of these changes? I will focus in what follows on two approaches in order to convey a sense of the breadth of work undertaken in the 1990s. These do not cover all aspects of Third World political ecology. Nor do they form self-contained units. And yet, each in its way affords insights into how political ecologists have put neo-Marxism behind them. The first study examines the feminist challenge to neo-Marxist political ecology, and I

consider in particular how gender concerns force a reevaluation of theoretical
and empirical arguments. The second study takes up the question of poststructuralism, as I explore the utility of emphasizing social discourses in the
transformation of 'nature.'

Feminist political ecology

Initially, gender questions received little attention in Third World political
ecology for, as we have seen, a concern with class predominated. However,
the rise of a feminist literature in the 1980s sparked a new approach.
Assorted feminist perspectives emerged – for instance, ecological or 'eco'-
feminist and socialist feminist – marking a lively if highly diverse research
agenda. Indeed, by the mid-1990s, a call for a 'feminist political ecology'
sought to install gender concerns at the heart of Third World political ecology (Rocheleau et al., 1996). How are we to account for the rise of these
research concerns? And what has their impact been on the development of
the field? This section explores these questions, firstly by examining general
issues surrounding feminist political ecology, and, secondly, by exploring how
this approach raises new questions for empirical research in the context of a
Kenyan case study.

    If early political ecology sought to expose the plight of the poor, feminist
scholars such as Vandana Shiva and Bina Agarwal argued that women were
disproportionately represented among that group. For ecofeminists like Shiva
(1989), environmental degradation and women's oppression were flipsides of
the same coin. An 'essentialist' view was thereby embraced based on the alleged
biological affinity of women and nature. The feminist environmentalist perspective championed by Agarwal (1992) argued a different case. Here, the social
marginality of women in male-dominated or 'patriarchal' societies was reflected
in a dependency on environmental resources. For example, in poor Third
World communities women were (and are) often responsible for gathering fuel
wood or tending family food plots. Yet, since these resources are often also
exploited by men – for example, through logging activities – the ensuing
degradation only exacerbated the poor status of women. According to Agarwal,
women were no more 'in tune' with nature than men, but their closeness to
nature rather reflected their marginal status in society. This debate's general
outcome was to underscore the importance of gender questions in political
ecology analysis.

    One way in which to grasp how important those questions have become is
to consider the range of topics that now fall under the heading of feminist
political ecology. Rocheleau et al. (1996) emphasize three themes: gendered
science, gendered rights, and gendered political activism. This three-part
framework of gendered processes (or the ways in which social practices reflect

the unequal interaction of men and women) is a useful way to make sense of the feminist 'revolution' in political ecology.

The first theme, the gendered nature of science, involves scholars in a twofold process. On the one hand, there has been a campaign to challenge the 'value-neutrality' of Western science. In contrast to assertions that it is an objective realm of knowledge, a view has emerged that sees environmental knowledge as "a Western, male-oriented and patriarchal projection which necessarily entailed the subjugation of both nature and women" (Mies and Shiva, 1993: 22). This projection is about elite empowerment or advancement whereby the knowledge of 'non-experts' is devalued at the same time as that knowledge possessed by 'experts' is promoted. It is a system that excludes nonsanctioned owners of knowledge and alternative ways of knowing – a process that is especially held to be prejudicial to women. Western science is also self-defeating, it is argued, in that it understands the environment in a fragmentary manner that precludes any form of holistic or comprehensive analysis. By zeroing in on selected aspects of reality only, Western science develops an inevitably limited and distorted picture of biophysical processes.

On the other hand, scholars have pointed to the benefits of local 'indigenous' knowledge as an alternative to Western 'masculinist' (or male-focused) science. While such local knowledge may involve poor men, it is nonetheless argued that women are its main producers and users (Mies and Shiva, 1993). This knowledge is driven by pragmatic questions of everyday survival and health, and stresses integrative environmental and health themes. Assorted benefits are to be derived from a process of privileging local knowledge. First, such knowledge is more targeted in that it emerges from the concerns, interests, and experiences of affected local groups. Second, the promotion of local knowledge enhances the dignity and position of women as they assume a leading place in the production of knowledge. Third, there is the prospect that putting local knowledge first will serve a wider empowering function, as this process supports women's resistance to political and economic oppression.

The second theme feminist political ecologists have focused on, that of gendered rights, examines the institutional arrangements that affect the ability of women to use, own, and manage the environment. Research has provided much evidence as to the ways in which the gendered political and economic structures that favor men are rooted in, and in turn reinforce, unequal rights to environmental resources. Feminist scholars do acknowledge the diversity of situations that exist in the Third World, and thus caution against unwarranted general statements about the status of women. Nonetheless, selected issues recur. To begin with, there is a tendency for resource tenure to be legally allocated to men (reflecting their political power) even as *de facto* control rests with women (reflecting women's responsibility for household maintenance). There is thus often a gendered division in terms of men/ownership and women/

usage that all but guarantees a politics of who within individual households controls resource use and access.

Linked to the question of rights is the matter of resource responsibilities. In many cases, men take charge of lucrative market-linked activities, leaving women in charge of less financially attractive aspects linked to household survival and local environmental maintenance (such as the maintenance of irrigation channels). Thus, women are in charge of, among other things, growing and cooking food, collecting water and fuel, caring for children and the elderly, and helping to protect the local environment which is usually the only resource base. Yet there is here a paradox, for women "carry a disproportionate share of responsibilities for resource procurement and environmental maintenance and yet they have very limited formal rights (and limited political and economic means) to determine the future of resource availability and environmental quality" (Rocheleau et al., 1996: 13).

The third theme developed by feminist political ecologists, gendered political activism, has led to a research focus on how women organize for collective action in aid of local social and environmental well-being. The reasons for such action are to be found in the systematic political, economic, and cultural discrimination against Third World women which has left their knowledge demeaned and their rights unrecognized in law. Yet these women have rarely accepted their subordinate place. Instead, they have often risked life and limb to challenge their oppression through local action and political protest. In some cases, the objective is to stop further degradation of an endangered resource base. Thus, in the case of the Chipko Movement in India's Himalaya, women opposed commercial logging by hugging trees set to be axed (Shiva, 1989). Women went on to play a leading role in this movement. In other cases, the aim is to restore degraded environments so as to enhance women's livelihoods. For instance, in Kenya the National Council of Women initiated the Green Belt Movement in the late 1970s to reforest degraded regions. To this end, an impressive network of tree nurseries and plantations was established within a matter of a few years (Ekins, 1992).

What is striking about this feminist research is that it shows the predominance of women in struggles throughout the Third World for social and ecological justice. Such activism comes in many forms ranging from high-profile struggles (as in the case of the two just noted) to location-specific activities oriented around 'practical' problem-solving and cooperative endeavors. Yet, whatever the type of activism, women tend to play a crucial role in the proceedings, even in cases where men may formally be in charge. This finding is a key point in the wider argument of feminist political ecology: namely, that research into the nature and dynamics of a politicized environment must confront the gendered dimensions to questions of environmental access, use, management, and resistance.

These arguments are best observed in the context of the rich empirical

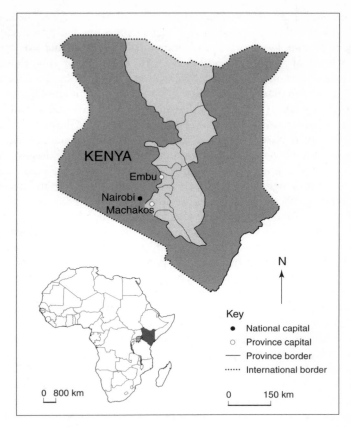

Figure 8.1: Eastern Province, Kenya

accounts which scholars have provided in feminist political ecology. To be sure, different studies emphasize different aspects of the research agenda. The example that follows provides a well-rounded account of gendered science, rights and activism in the context of semiarid regions of Kenya during the 1970s and 1980s (Wangari et al., 1996). As such, it provides useful insights into the empirical utility of feminist political ecology.

What Wangari et al. (1996) term "gendered visions for survival" characterize relations between men and women in the semiarid Embu and Machakos districts of Kenya's Eastern Province (see figure 8.1). The word 'survival' is a vivid reminder of the magnitude of the issues at stake for people living here, and especially for those women who are politically, economically, and culturally at the margins of society. For one thing, this is a region subject to recurrent drought and famine. For another thing, it is an area that has been the subject of political and economic conflict since colonial times, if not before. This combination of linked biophysical and human processes has provided a harsh challenge to women keen to safeguard individual and household livelihoods.

At the heart of that challenge has been the question of land rights. Both colonial and postcolonial regimes in Kenya have modified land tenure in such a way as to systematically reduce the rights of women to the land on which they work. Thus, the 1954 colonial Swynnerton Plan initiated a land 'reform' process in which territory was allocated to male 'heads of household,' thereby undermining customary procedures linked to clan-based management which had provided greater recognition of women's rights. The 1977 Registered Land Act entrenched this arrangement, as title deeds were issued to male household heads. Not surprisingly, then, women are virtually absent from the ranks of landowners, with the Kenya-wide figure sitting at only 5 percent in the 1980s. Without title to land, women have also found it difficult to obtain credit for agricultural production or emergency support, since the land reform process "was predicated upon the use of land as collateral for bank loans" (Wangari et al., 1996: 133). The result has been ubiquitous female hardship and environ-mental degradation, as women are deprived of the funds and support needed to maintain and enhance agricultural productivity and land quality.

Frustrated by these political and economic arrangements, women in the Eastern Province, as elsewhere, have sought to use control over their own labor as a means of survival. Their collective activism has taken the form of what in Machakos is called *mwethya* (a mechanism for local women to exchange labor). These labor exchanges sometimes focus on individual members' farms – helping to repair bench terraces, dig drainage sites, plant trees or undertake weeding. In other cases, the *mwethya* groups tackle common tasks such as building dams and irrigation networks between farms, establishing tree nurseries, horticultural activities, brick-making, or basket-making. As this partial list illustrates, collec-tive action by women in Machakos aims to safeguard environmental conditions as these relate to local livelihoods, as well as to generate new income-earning opportunities for the women in question. How do men react to such practices, though? In general, (male-dominated) government is supportive of such enter-prise because these groups "do not challenge the existing cultural and structural underpinnings of the national government" (Wangari et al., 1996: 139). Indeed, in some cases, local officials will press these groups into providing free labor for general community tasks – that is, tasks of benefit to both men and women. The *mwethya* groups are certainly directed by and for men from time to time. However, they are nonetheless a vital means by which women can acquire power for themselves inasmuch as they build resources and skills upon which women may draw later when outright political activism occurs.

Also integral to the process of local women's empowerment is a greater recognition of their role as custodians of local botanical knowledge. This knowledge – passed down through the generations – has increasingly come to be concentrated with women who, after all, are on the environmental 'frontline' when it comes to family sustenance. Indeed, as many menfolk have migrated elsewhere in search of paid labor, leaving 'their' land in the care of women partners, local knowledge has become increasingly focused on women as male familiarity with local biophysical conditions has declined. During times of great local distress, as with the 1984–5 drought and famine, women's botanical knowledge of local trees and plants proved vital to the survival prospects of individual families. Indeed, an active process of experimentation occurred inasmuch as women sought out new or long-abandoned species in a desperate attempt to fend off starvation. In this way, the shifting division of labor linked, in part, to men's ownership of land, meant that there was a "feminisation of famine and drought response" even as women's skills at the "science of survival" grew (Wangari et al., 1996: 147).

The sort of feminist political ecology that has been outlined in theory and practice here confronts conventional (male-dominated!) political ecology with a gender challenge of its own: namely, that human–environmental interaction cannot be fully appreciated in the absence of an understanding of gender issues. This is the greatest lesson to be learned from a feminist perspective in a post-Marxist political ecology. At the same time, and perhaps inevitably under the circumstances, the rush to point out the many ways in which gender consider-ations influence social interaction with biophysical processes has tended to push to one side other factors which also have a bearing here. Thus, considerations of race, class, or age, for instance, do not always get the coverage that they deserve when the spotlight is focused on gender questions. Further, in the quest to challenge 'Western patriarchal science,' there has perhaps been a tendency to exaggerate the ills of this knowledge system even as local knowledge is generally extolled. Ironically, this process, even if for understandable reasons of social equity and justice, has often replaced one stereotype (i.e. Western science is good, while local knowledge is bad) with another equally untenable equation (i.e. local knowledge is sound, while Western science is distorted by men) (cf. Agrawal, 1995). Thus, while feminist political ecology is undoubtedly here to stay, it will need to nuance its arguments and build bridges to new research themes if it is to continue to be the vital research agenda that it has so swiftly become.

Poststructuralism

The introduction of poststructural thinking (or the effort to move beyond class-based narratives) in Third World political ecology has afforded another opportunity for scholars to move the field onwards from its neo-Marxist past. As with feminist political ecology, the poststructural perspective calls for a rejection of the class-focused assumptions of early political ecology. Further, in its emphasis on the role of language in conditioning human–environmental interactions (see Braun and Wainwright, this volume), poststructuralism offers an alternative research agenda to that which went before in the field (Peet and Watts, 1996). How might poststructuralism provide new insights on the Third World's politically-shaped environment? The following section addresses this question by exploring the general dimensions of poststructural political ecology, before noting its application in a short Colombia case study.

The 'discursive revolution' led notably by Michel Foucault (as noted, one of France's leading social thinkers) made inroads into development studies from the late 1980s as scholars questioned the utility of notions like 'poverty,' 'development,' 'modernization,' and the 'Third World.' Third World political ecology was implicated in this process. The person most associated with the 'poststructural turn' in political ecology is Arturo Escobar, who has sought to map the contours of this new perspective and its implications for the subfield (e.g. Escobar, 1996, 1999). How, then, does Escobar define poststructural political ecology?

An initial assumption is that an appreciation of everyday processes that shape people's practical lives necessitates an analysis of discourse (or ways of repre-senting social realities), since questions of material or lived reality are inseparable from the ways in which that reality is portrayed. Here, the role of language assumes central importance. Rather than mirror reality, language is seen as an active agent in its social construction: discourse is "the process through which social reality inevitably comes into being" (Escobar, 1996: 46). To the extent that this is true, knowledge is inescapably implicated in questions of power, even as power itself is inevitably about the production of knowledge.

A poststructural political ecology applies the insights of discourse analysis to an understanding of the 'social construction' of nature. The argument here is not that the biophysical environment ('nature') does not exist. It is, rather, that ideas about ecology and political economy *actively shape* human perceptions and uses of nature; thus, their contested definition is a matter of great importance. For Escobar, this point becomes clear when the preoccupation with 'sustainable development' is examined. He argues that the promotion of this concept by a First World-led coalition of government, business, and science reflects a series of assumptions about society, science, technology, development, and the environment which are supportive of the social and economic status quo worldwide. The role of Western science is notable here in that its job is to diagnose and treat the 'ailments' of Planet Earth as "[d]isease is housed in nature in a new manner" (Escobar, 1996: 49).

A poststructural political ecology also holds implications for how we understand capitalism. Escobar acknowledges the ongoing role of the modern form of capitalism as it cuts a destructive swathe through the Third World (for instance, the logging of tropical forests). Yet, he makes two important additions to this view. First, he insists that such capitalism can never be fully understood in the absence of an account of the expert, scientific discourses that condition it. Not only how modern capitalism is represented, but also how it actually operates, is influenced by scientific discourses encompassing most aspects of human and nonhuman life. To take the forestry case again, logging practices reflect not only market imperatives of supply and demand. They are also conditioned by scientific knowledge acquired about the properties and incidence of commercially valued trees.

Second, Escobar recognizes a 'postmodern' form of 'ecological capitalism' which runs concurrently with its modernist counterpart. This postmodern form is an attempt by business and science to generate new sources of economic accumulation through penetration of the essence of nature and life itself (Escobar, 1999). Here, we are in the realm of biotechnology, genetic engineering, and biodiversity 'prospecting' – activities which are reshaping basic categories of life as part of the wider quest for profit (on this see Castree's chapter on the production of nature). In the Third World this often involves converting indigenous people living in, or adjacent to, biodiversity 'hotspots' – such as tropical forests or coral reefs – into stewards of these localities, which Escobar (1996: 57) dubs "reservoirs of value." It is also a process whereby new practices of 'sustainable' ecological management are put into action as science and business seek to modify the core of (genetic) life itself.

Finally, a poststructural political ecology calls for a new politics of change in keeping with its reading of the Third World's politicized environment. A struggle by affected local communities against the adverse effects of capitalism on the ground there must be. But also needed is resistance that challenges conventional development 'truths' at the level of discourse itself. It is not enough to challenge exploitative practices. Social movements must also reject notions of 'sustainable development' and 'biodiversity' that underpin these practices. To do otherwise, in effect, would be to weaken the resistance effort insofar as the struggle would be fought in terms of concepts and assumptions (such as the idea that economic growth is inherently good) that are inescapably biased against alternative projects (Escobar, 1996).

I have sought to briefly sketch poststructural political ecology. What does this approach look like empirically, though? A short case study of biological diversity (or biodiversity) conservation efforts in the Pacific coast region of Colombia illustrates the possible utility of poststructuralism to political ecology (Escobar, 1999). This region, which stretches from Panama to Ecuador, contains one of the world's greatest concentrations of biodiversity, and is home to some 800,000 Afro-colombian residents and 50,000 indigenous people (see figure 8.2).

Colombia's Pacific coast has been the focus of national and international attention since the 1980s as modern and postmodern forms of capital leave their imprint. Modern industries such as gold mining, timber, shrimp cultivation, and palm plantations have contributed to social dislocation and ecological

Figure 8.2: Pacific coast, Colombia

degradation. Clearly, a set of practices linked to intensive resource extraction is
at play here. Yet Escobar also stresses the pivotal discursive properties that
surround and enable those practices. Thus, the entry of business to the region
is not only reflected in altered production conditions such as the economic
practices just noted. It is also to be seen in the selective appropriation of local
'traditional' knowledge about social and ecological relations by rival 'scientific'

knowledge touted by outside 'experts'. Such expert knowledge has encompassed such things as health, education, economy, and ecology, and has served the purpose of enhancing outsider understanding of, and control over, local populations and human–environmental dynamics. This dual material and discursive 'invasion' of Colombia's hitherto 'remote' and 'underdeveloped' Pacific coast region culminated in the application of sustainable development thinking to the region in the early 1990s. The publication of Colombia's national Sustainable Development Plan against the backdrop of the 1992 Earth Summit (held in Rio de Janeiro, Brazil), constituted an ideal opportunity for political and economic elites to 'rebrand' conventional development strategies based on natural resource extraction in a new, 'greener' light. Such extraction was thus heralded not only as a source of 'development' that 'rationally' made the most of Colombia's natural heritage. It was also a means of enabling closer and more systematic monitoring of all environmental management practices in the area by the state, with the declared aim of safeguarding the natural environment. The Plan thus pledged to develop the Pacific coast region along 'modernist' lines, of which an integral element was the regulation of local practices by expert discourses on 'sustainable development.'

Yet this region has also become the focus lately of the Pacific Biodiversity Conservation Project (PBP) which symbolizes the arrival of postmodern capitalism in the area, with its associated material and discursive practices. The PBP is a national project whose main objective is to protect the Pacific coast's "almost legendary biodiversity" (Escobar, 1996: 58). It was an outcome of the Global Biodiversity Strategy (part of United Nations deliberations) and was linked from its inception to the World Bank's Global Environmental Facility. As such, the PBP was concerned to recognize the national and global value of protecting the Pacific coast region, and is part of the global push to conserve 'biodiversity hotspots' (for similar cases in Costa Rica and the Philippines, see Meyer, 1996; Bryant, 2000). It has been promoted as an 'alternative' development strategy to conventional development approaches, in that it claims to be more supportive of local biocultural contexts. Specifically, the PBP has four key aspects: 'to know' (knowledge gathering on local biodiversity); 'to valorize' (to create ecologically appropriate economic uses of biodiversity); 'to mobilize' (help to organize and empower local peoples); and 'to formulate and implement' (modify existing local/national institutions to support local decision-making).

The discourse of biodiversity conservation that is manifested through the PBP is a prime example of a wider shift in social and economic life that can be seen in many parts of the globe today. There is, Escobar (1996: 58) argues, "an important transformation in our consciousness of and practices towards nature." With tropical rainforests in mind, this discourse links together issues of 'knowing' (classifying species), 'saving' (protecting from destruction), and 'using' (economic use of genetic properties of local species). But how does this process differ from practices under a 'traditional' capitalist regime? The key difference here is, I think, twofold. First, a premium is placed on the conservation of local natural resources (restyled biodiversity) because long-term commercial prosperity is premised on the ability to 'prospect' for new species and genetic profiles that might lead to new products (for example, a cure for cancer developed by a pharmaceutical firm). In contrast, under a more traditional regime, extraction is focused on known resources (timber, minerals), and little concern is given to safeguarding nondesired species. The differing sets of practices here are reflected in contrasting discursive narratives: development as the extraction of known resources versus development as generic conservation in aid of long-term profitability. Second, a premium is put on the full recognition of local knowledge because such knowledge can provide clues to the discovery of valuable species/genetic combinations. This can be seen to differ from arrangements under conventional capitalism, where local knowledge is firmly subordinated to 'efficient' outsider knowledge. Thus, under postmodern capital, much is made of local 'ethnobotanical' knowledge, as well as the need to recognize local social and economic rights, whereas under conventional or modern capital such concerns are at best marginal, and at worst a hindrance, to capital accumulation.

Despite the apparently greater sensitivity to local concerns, postmodern capital (in the form of the PBP) has met with resistance from local Afro-colombian and indigenous peoples who have mounted a campaign to promote their own version of social and ecological justice. For them, the region is "a fundamental and multidimensional space for the creation and recreation of the ecological, economic and cultural practices of the communities" (Escobar, 1999: 12). Yet, even as postmodern capitalism seeks to tap local 'traditional knowledge,' Afro-colombian and indigenous peoples face an uncertain future as the destructive impact of modern capital is conjoined with the manipulative logic of postmodern capital. The role of discourse in this unequal struggle looms large. Local people thus attempt to redefine 'biodiversity' as 'territory plus culture,' even as they travel to international meetings to make their case for an alternative future (cf. Bryant, 2000). In a struggle that pits politically weak social movements against a (post)modernist approach, these counter discursive strategies are vital to the effort to resist the owners of capital in the area.

A poststructural political ecology thus raises in theory and practice issues inadequately considered before in political ecology. Indeed, its main contribution is to point out that 'discourse matters' not only in attempting to explain complex human–environmental interaction, but also in specifying the cultural politics of resistance. It is still early days, though, for poststructuralism in Third World political ecology and it is not a problem-free approach. For example, the poststructural critique of Western science would appear to suggest, a bit like feminist political ecology, that such science is of limited utility to a struggle for social and ecological well-being (cf. Stott and Sullivan, 2000). But is that the case? Or is there a more constructive role possible if Western science is combined with the 'best' of local knowledge – hybrid science, as it were? The relationship between modern and postmodern forms of ecological capital also requires clarification. How are relations between these two forms of capital regulated? What role do states, international institutions, markets, or scientists play in this process (Bebbington, 2000)? These questions illustrate that a poststructuralism based on discourse analysis has much to explain before it offers the comprehensive account of the politicized environment that it aims to provide.

Conclusion: Political Ecology's Slippery Nature

Third World political ecology has come a long way since its days as a critique of neo-Malthusianism. Its major achievement has been to question simplistic notions about society and nature by exposing the social and ecological ramifications of political, economic, and cultural power in the Third World. Surprisingly, though, the role of nature in this process has been ambiguous. If early work sought to drain some of the 'naturalness' out of nature, it has left political ecologists unsure as to how to treat nonhuman nature in their accounts. For some, this uncertainty is reflected in a desire to restore some of nature's explanatory power even as the human imprint – in all its 'glory' – is also acknowledged (a useful collection of essays here is Zimmerer and Young, 1998). For others, the tightening human grip on life itself indicates that there is little organic nature left in a world of hybrid natures (Escobar, 1999). The difficulty for Third World political ecology, as with other environmental fields of study, is to specify a nature rendered ever more 'slippery' in an increasingly humanized world.

Perhaps a more politically pertinent approach is to consider the question: 'what kind of nature do people want?' If we live in a world undergoing rapid humanization – a world of 'socionature' – then what is the logic that should guide it? And how might that logic be related to issues of social equity and justice? Here is the issue of the radical pretensions of Third World political ecology to be a research agenda supportive of social and ecological justice (Bryant, 1999; Watts, 2000). The objective might be less one of specifying capitalism's assorted natures as it would be about elaborating the multiple natures of capital, ever with an eye to flagging points where capitalist arrangements may be challenged. A return thus to a radical Marxist politics? There is certainly much to be said for a closer engagement with Marxism. But this would be a Marxism that is wiser as a result of the powerful insights of post-Marxist thinking. In this respect, Third World political ecology would do well to 'put the halves together' as it learns from its past and present to move forward into the future.

Acknowledgments

I would like to thank Noel Castree for his many helpful comments on previous drafts of this chapter, as well as Roma Beaumont for drawing the table and figures.

Further Reading

For a general introduction to political ecology see Watts (2000). Hecht (1985) is a good example of 1980s-style political ecology. Agarwal (1992) offers a useful introduction to feminist political ecology and Escobar (1996) to poststructural political ecology. Blaikie (1999) offers a useful assessment of political ecology's current condition.

References

Agarwal, B. (1992). The Gender and Environment Debate: Lessons from India. *Feminist Review* 18: 119–57.

Agrawal, A. (1995). Dismantling the Divide between Indigenous and Scientific Knowledge. *Development and Change* 26: 413–39.

Beresford, M. and Fraser, L. (1992). Political Economy of the Environment in Vietnam. *Journal of Contemporary Asia* 22: 3–19.

Blaikie, P. (1985). *The Political Economy of Soil Erosion in Developing Countries*. Harlow: Longman.

Blaikie, P. (1999). A Review of Political Ecology: Issues, Epistemology and Analytical Narratives. *Zeitschrift fur Wirtschaftsgeographie*, 43 131–47.

Booth, D. (ed.) (1994). *Rethinking Social Development: Theory, Research and Practice*. Harlow: Longman.

Bryant, R. L. (1999). A Political Ecology for Developing Countries? Progress and Paradox in the Evolution of a Research Field. *Zeitschrift fur Wirtschaftsgeographie* 43: 148–57.

Bryant, R. L. (2000). Politicised Moral Geographies: Debating Biodiversity Conservation and Ancestral Domain in the Philippines. *Political Geography* 19: 673–705.

Bryant, R. L. and Bailey, S. (1997). *Third World Political Ecology*. London: Routledge.

Bunker, S. G. (1985). *Underdeveloping the Amazon: Extraction, Unequal Exchange, and the Failure of the Modern State*. Urbana, Ill.: University of Illinois Press.

Ehrlich, P. (1968). *The Population Bomb*. New York: Ballantine Books.

Ekins, P. (1992). *A New World Order: Grassroots Movements for Global Change*. London: Routledge.

Escobar, A. (1996). Constructing Nature: Elements for a Poststructural Political Ecology. In R. Peet and M. Watts (eds.), *Liberation Ecologies: Environment, Development, Social Movements*. London: Routledge, 46–68.

Escobar, A. (1999). Whose Knowledge, Whose Nature? Biodiversity Conservation and

Social Movements Political Ecology. *Journal of Political Ecology* (see http://www.library.arizona.edu/ej/jpe).

Hecht, S. B. (1985). Environment, Development and Politics: Capital Accumulation and the Livestock Sector in Eastern Amazonian. *World Development* 13: 663–84.

Meyer, C. A. (1996). NGOs and Environmental Public Foods. *Development and Change* 27: 453–74.

Mies, M. and Shiva, V. (1993). *Ecofeminism*. London: Zed Books.

Momsen, J. H. (1991). *Women and Development in the Third World*. London: Routledge.

O'Brien, J. (1985). Sowing the Seeds of Famine: The Political Economy of Food Deficits in Sudan. *Review of African Political Economy* 33: 23–32.

Peet, R. (1991). *Global Capitalism: Theories of Societal Development*. London: Routledge.

Peet, R. and Watts, M. (eds.) (1996). *Liberation Ecologies: Environment, Development, Social Movements*. London: Routledge.

Peluso, N. L. (1992). *Rich Forests, Poor People: Resource Control and Resistance in Java*. Berkeley: University of California Press.

Redclift, M. (1984). *Development and the Environmental Crisis: Red or Green Alternatives?* London: Methuen.

Rocheleau, D., Thomas-Slayter, B., and Wangari, E. (1996). Gender and Environment: A Feminist Political Ecology Perspective. In D. Rocheleau, B. Thomas-Slayter, and E. Wangari (eds.), *Feminist Political Ecology: Global Issues and Local Experiences*. London: Routledge, 3–23.

Sachs, W. (ed.) (1992). *The Development Dictionary*. London: Zed Books.

Shiva, V. (1989). *Staying Alive: Women, Ecology and Development*. London: Zed Books.

Stott, P. and Sullivan, S. (eds.) (2000). *Political Ecology: Science, Myth and Power*. London: Arnold.

Vayda, A. P. (1983). Progressive Contextualization: Methods for Research in Human Ecology. *Human Ecology* 11: 265–81.

Wangari, E., Thomas-Slayter, B., and Rocheleau, D. (1996). Gendered Visions for Survival: Semi-arid Regions in Kenya. In D. Rocheleau, B. Thomas-Slayter, and E. Wangari (eds.), *Feminist Political Ecology: Global Issues and Local Experiences*. London: Routledge, 127–54.

Watts, M. (2000). Political Ecology. In E. Sheppard and T. Barnes (eds.), *The Companion of Economic Geography*. Oxford: Blackwell, 257–74.

Zimmerer, K. S. and Young, K. R. (eds.) (1998). *Nature's Geography: New Lessons for Conservation in Developing Countries*. Madison, Wis.: University of Wisconsin Press.

Chapter 9

Natural Disasters?

Mark Pelling

Denaturalizing Disaster

Between September 15 and 28, 1998, Hurricane Georges swept through the Caribbean and the southern states of the USA. More than 500 people were killed and financial losses exceeded US$3 billion. Despite more than four decades of research and concerted effort to reduce the destruction caused by events like Hurricane Georges, the average number of natural disasters reported worldwide per annum continues to double every 10 years (figure 9.1). That this has been taking place, until very recently, with no significant changes in the extent of geological or hydrometeorological risk (Cuny, 1983), suggests that there is a fundamental flaw in the way in which natural disasters have been managed.

Intuitively, one feels that 'natural forces' cause 'natural disasters,' and that the important task of reducing human and economic loss should concentrate on managing physical processes. This physicalist orientation has come to dominate disaster management policy throughout the world. However, somewhat ironically, this approach may itself have contributed to the increased frequency of natural disasters by neglecting the contribution of human factors in disaster origins and outcomes. I want to make an argument in this chapter for the need to integrate both the physical *and* human dimensions of 'natural disaster.' To illustrate the argument let's return briefly to the example of Hurricane Georges. In this case, the distribution of impacts was shaped by physical features, for example the local topography which influenced wind speed and the likelihood of flooding. But it was also shaped decisively by human features, for example the methods and materials used in constructing dwellings and the capability of local and national organizations to respond to the disaster (table 9,1). Similarly, the physical motor for Hurricane Georges was a product of both physical processes (i.e. climatic circulation) *and* human

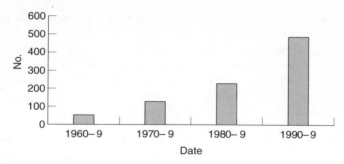

Figure 9.1: Annual average number of reported disasters worldwide
Source: CRED database, University of Louvain, Belgium.

action (i.e. human-induced global climate change). The hurricane was, therefore, not only or simply a 'natural disaster.'

It follows from these observations that successful disaster mitigation policies need to address the human and physical components of natural disasters simultaneously. Technological responses that address physical causes alone can prolong, and even increase, the losses incurred when disaster strikes. This is so for three reasons:

• Technological responses do not engage with deeper human causes and effects of disasters, such as inequality and poverty which determine who is exposed to, and impacted by, hazards.
• The inappropriate use of technology can increase hazardousness by creating

Table 9.1 Distribution of the human and economic costs of Hurrican Georges

Country	Wind speed	Lives lost	Economic damage
USA (Louisiana, Alabama, Mississippi, Florida)	100–120 mph	4	US$750,000,000 in insured losses
Cuba	75 mph	5	Severe damage to crops
Dominican Republic	120 mph	265	US$30,000,000 in insured losses
Puerto Rico	115 mph	3	US$1,750,000,000 in insured losses
Antigua	140 mph	2	No data

Source: PartnerRe, 1998

a false sense of security, for example by encouraging people to live close to sea-walls or on flood plains.

• Technological responses to hazards are associated with scientific decision-making and are often not open to public scrutiny. This can provide an opportunity for business, political, or professional elites to mold technological responses to their advantage at the expense of those in society with little access to economic, political, or social power.

In the 1980s, doubts over the effectiveness of many physical interventions to reduce human suffering from natural disasters prompted academics and activists to support more critical, people-oriented approaches. These critical approaches stressed the importance of underlying inequalities in human access to resources (both locally and globally) – rather than the geographies of physical forces – in shaping where and who natural disaster strikes. This left disaster mitigation at something of an impasse, with physicalist explanations and techno-fixes on the one side, and critical arguments on the other, stressing human causes and social policy responses. But, as already stated, knowledge of both physical and human processes needs to be brought together if we're to understand what happens in a natural disaster. I would argue that the impasse is, in fact, less the product of reasoned argument than of a scientific division of labor, which has not only separated physical and social sciences but placed them in competition with one another for access to research funding and political influence. This is true even in geography, which is supposed to unite both physical and social perspectives, but where the two sides of the discipline often function in isolation. The growing urgency for scientific interaction and for a movement beyond the imagined impasse comes not only from the increasing frequency of catastrophic natural disasters, but also from a range of novel threats to humanity which were first recognized at the end of the twentieth century. These so-called 'manufactured risks' (Giddens, 1998) are the (un)intended results of the scientific and industrial manipulation of nature.

This chapter begins with a question: to what extent are 'natural disasters' products of natural forces? To help think about this question, the chapter looks at the strengths and weaknesses of the physicalist and critical arguments, discusses the implications of recent integrated approaches to understanding disaster, and ends by examining new forms of manufactured risks. First, though, to prepare the way, we need to understand how natural hazard and disaster are categorized.

Categorizing Hazard and Disaster

Despite their differences, both the dominant physicalist and the alternative critical approaches are anthropocentric, categorizing hazard and disaster in relation in human needs. From this anthropocentric perspective, three types of nature/society relation are recognized: *resource, benign*, and *hazard*. A resource relationship is one where a natural element can be made productive use of by humanity (for example: rainwater can be captured and used for irrigation). A benign relationship is one where a natural element offers neither an advantage nor a threat to humanity. A hazardous relationship is one where a natural element is threatening to humanity and where a 'natural disaster' can result.

Natural events and conditions can shift between benign, resource, or hazard status, and can be seen differentially at the same time by different people utilizing different knowledges and values. Thus, to take one example, a forest fire in southern Australia might be seen as a hazard by a settler or agroforester (the fire will reduce the short-term economic value of the forest), as a resource by a forestry ecologist (fire is a catalyst for diversification in forest plant communities, so the medium-term ecological value of the forest will be enhanced), and with benign indifference by a distant urban dweller in Melbourne (who will be more concerned about getting through a traffic jam and arriving at work on time!). Differences in perception and value are often experienced as a conflict between popular or grassroots worldviews and expert knowledge systems (Grove-White, 1996), especially when new hazards are felt, such as those presented by manufactured risks (to be discussed later in the chapter).

So far, we have focused on natural hazards leading to *catastrophic* natural disasters (hurricanes, floods, earthquakes, and droughts). But natural hazards can also generate a second type of natural disaster, called *chronic disaster* (Satterthwaite, 1998). Chronic disasters are more common than catastrophic disasters, but less visible – at first. They become apparent over lifetimes, and include everyday risks to human health and wealth – such as those associated with poor sanitation or a lack of clean drinking water. The combined effect of chronic disasters in terms of loss of life and human hardship is far greater than the combined impact of all catastrophic disasters, yet chronic disasters are rarely acknowledged. This is partly a product of the representation of disaster by the news media, which has raised public awareness about catastrophic disasters but tended to neglect the less visually shocking chronic disasters. An example of the power of media representation to shape popular consciousness about natural disasters was Bob Geldof's Band Aid and Live Aid fundraisers between 1984 and 1986. These events were inspired by powerful television news images of the Ethiopian famine, which shocked many ordinary people worldwide. In many of the worst natural disasters, catastrophic and chronic hazards overlap.

Figure 9.2: Catastrophic and chronic hazards overlapping
Source: Guyana Chronicle, Guyana, Nov. 15, 1996; reproduced by kind permission.

The frustration of living with such a double burden is expressed by another media representation, this time a cartoonist from flood prone Guyana (see figure 9.2).

Evolving Understandings of Disaster

Physicalist origins

The physicalist perspectives on disaster are derived from the first attempts to take an analytical approach to the topic and to find some general guidelines to enhance mitigation efforts. The roots of this perspective lie in human ecology theory of the 1920s. This was first applied to natural hazards by the American geographer Gilbert White (1942). Human ecologists defined natural hazards as "those elements of the physical environment harmful to man [*sic.*] and caused by forces extraneous to him [*sic.*]" (Burton and Kates, 1964, in Smith, 1992: 8). People were seen as contributing in only a limited way to the production of disaster. This bias was rooted in the behavioralist theory from which human ecology at this time drew. Attention was focused on the behavior of individuals rather than society, and the ways in which individuals perceived and responded to natural disaster. This approach was weakened because it ignored the role that wider socioeconomic and political structures play in shaping individual behavior. Moreover, the human ecologists did not address questions of power and inequality – such as the unequal distribution of wealth in society – when seeking answers to why it was that some people were generally more vulnerable to natural disasters than others. Policy recommendations, from this perspective, tended to be narrowly technological, focusing on engineering and the control of the physical environment (for example by building seawalls) instead of wider social change.

Despite the weaknesses of human ecology, the physicalist approach to hazard management it inspired continues to dominate disaster discourse. It can be seen, for example, in early mission statements from the United Nations' International Decade for Natural Disaster Reduction, 1990–2000 (IDNDR). The name alone betrays a naturalistic conception of disasters. The resulting focus displayed an environmentally deterministic worldview that downplayed the human dimension and overemphasized the naturalness of disasters. The IDNDR's goal statement reveals the bias: there is repetitious mention of technological responses – early warning systems, disaster-resistant structures, scientific and technical knowledge, and the like – and little mention of vulnerability reduction or the political and socioeconomic roots of disaster. Such an approach begs the question: were the real target beneficiaries those vulnerable to hazard and disaster, or engineering and disaster management consultants and their employing institutions? Certainly, vulnerable people were largely absent from the discussions that set the agenda.

This said, it would be wrong to suggest that successful technologically based disaster mitigation schemes are not capable of reducing hazard – for example, the application of appropriate construction techniques in earthquake-prone cities has saved many lives. But, as the example of flood hazard in Bihar shows (box 9.1), political and socioeconomic factors need to be considered to prevent the subversion of good intentions and good technology.

Box 9.1: Physical Bias in Responses to Flooding, North Bihar, India

Bihar is perhaps the most vulnerable state to riverine flooding in India, with many large rivers, including the Kosi, Gandak, Ghanghara, Ganga, and Yamuna, passing over its flat plains on route from the Himalayas to the Indian Ocean.

Under British colonial government, and later Indian self-rule, the natural drainage system of North Bihar has been 'improved' by the construction of river dams and embankments to contain monsoon floods. The result after 200 years of work is that, despite some reduction in local flooding, a great deal of money has been spent while the overall flood hazard has increased! Why should this be? And how has a response to flooding, that obviously has serious flaws, been allowed to continue for so long? To get answers to these questions we need to follow the history

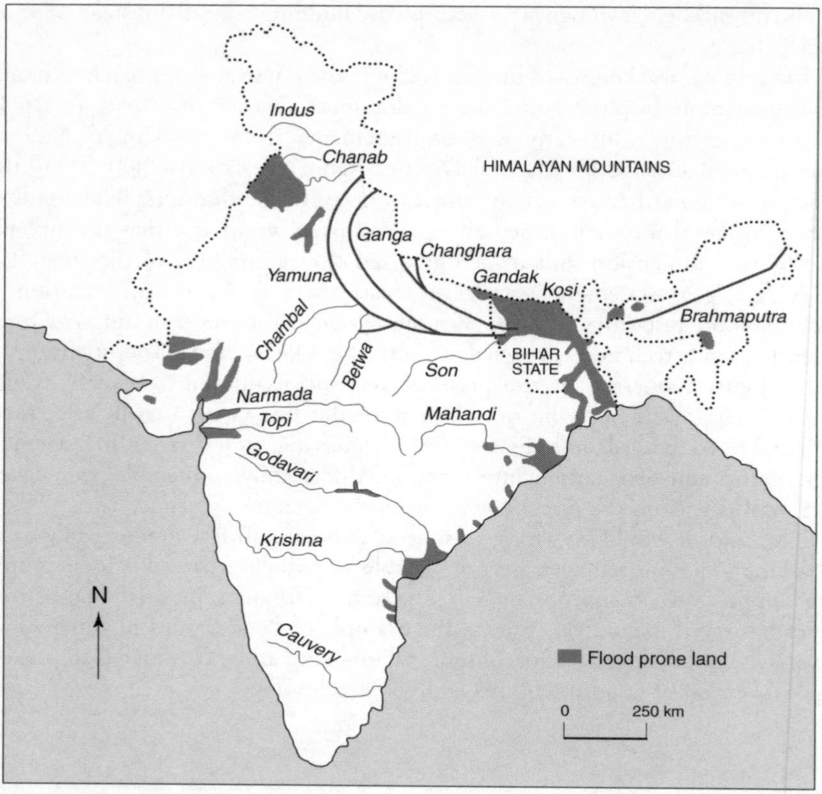

Figure 9.3: India: flood proneness
Source: based on CSE, 1996.

of development in Bihar and examine the motivations of the various actors involved. (See figure 9.3.)

British reports at the turn of the twentieth century say that local semimigratory cultivators welcomed the annual flood, because it left behind a rich deposit of silt, invaluable for the winter crop. During the period of British colonialism the migratory cultivators were forcibly settled in permanent villages, and small dams were built to try and contain floods. A Western, technocentric vision had taken hold. Since independence in 1947, the Indian government has continued to follow a Western development model in Bihar. The first major project undertaken by the Indian government was the Kosi River project in 1954, since when embankments have been built along all the major rivers in the state, with some 3,400 km. of embankments being constructed between the 1960s and 1990s.

There are a number of reasons why building embankments has increased vulnerability to flooding in Bihar:

- Embankments force rivers to deposit their sediment loads within their confines, raising the bed of the river, eventually above the level of the surrounding flood plain.
- Sediment is no longer available to fertilize the surrounding flood plain, thus decreasing soil fertility and agricultural capacity with potential knock-on effects for household economies and regional development.
- Embankments have produced a new hazard phenomenon – the flash-flood – which occurs when there is a sudden breach or collapse in an embankment wall. Flash-floods are more devastating than slow onset floods, for which there is normally more warning time to respond.
- Embankments, and also roads and railway lines, have been built against the drainage gradient, thus impeding the natural drainage of adjacent lands and leading to loss of good agricultural land, this time through waterlogging.
- Vulnerability to flooding has increased as people have increasingly settled next to embankments on what appears to be safe land, creating communities with high exposure to flood hazard.

If the technological approach to flood hazard in Bihar is so clearly adding to the developmental problems of the region, then why has it been pursued for so long? The answer arguably lies in the special interests of elite groups that dominate decision-making in Bihar, and also in the national government of India. The huge sums of money to be made from flood engineering works have produced an entrenched group of engineers, politicians, and contractors who benefit from these projects, and are hostile to the idea of non-engineering responses to floods. Within the schemes themselves profit-hungry contractors often use faulty materials which can increase flood risk. Local political influence can also be seen in embankments that have been placed away from their planned location, usually so that a politician can win the votes of a community.

Local people have not been mute in the face of such corruption and there are many accounts of grassroots protest against flood control schemes. The media has also been critical of the political corruption in Bihar, and been crucial in raising national and international awareness.

Source: CSE, 1996.

Critical reactions

The Bihar case study shows the need to take into account the social aspects of disaster. This is the key argument of the alternative theories of disaster that rose to contest the physicalist approach in the 1980s. These so-called critical approaches concentrated on the role played by the social and spatial distribution of economic and political resources in the production of disaster. For example, whilst the global distribution of earthquake hot spots is environmentally determined, their relationship to human land-use and settlement is less clearly so. Moreover, if a populated area should experience an earthquake, even one of high magnitude, this need not result in a disaster. The extent to which it does, and the type of impacts which result, are argued to be the products of social context – of human processes which interact at local, national, and global scales. Two approaches have been proposed to help understand the social aspects of natural disaster: the *entitlements* approach and the *Marxist* approach.

The entitlements approach was first proposed by an Indian economist, Amartya Sen, in his book *Poverty and Famines* (1981). Sen's argument is useful to us because it provides a framework with which to question the environmental determinism of the physicalist approach to natural disasters. Sen drew from experience of famine in India, China, and Africa to argue that food shortages do not result directly from environmental change (drought), but from changes in the price, or 'market value,' of food resources. During famine the market price of staple foods increases rapidly, at a certain point going beyond the purchasing capacity of many households. In Sen's terminology, hunger results from an individual or household not being able to acquire enough 'entitlements' to obtain or grow food for subsistence. Entitlements are those resources or rights to which a household has access. Entitlements include: labor (which can be exchanged for money to buy food or used to cultivate food crops), tangible assets (land, cattle, consumer goods, housing, savings, jewelry) and rights to social resources (community or family support networks, support form NGOs or state organizations). At times of economic stress (which may be triggered by a natural event such as a drought, but also – and increasingly – by social events such as war), the value of an individual's entitlements are likely to fall relative to the costs of staple foods. This results in reduced access to food and so increased vulnerability to malnutrition and famine. Sen's approach is supported by empirical findings that show not only agricultural wage laborers, but also small-scale service traders, to be the economic groups most vulnerable to exchange failure and hunger in rural society in developing countries.

In light of all this, Sen argued that reducing vulnerability is best achieved by adjusting the mechanisms by which food is allocated in society. Sen's arguments have had a great influence on subsequent government policy in South Asia and sub-Saharan Africa. A favorite strategy has been for governments to stockpile grain in good years, when there is an excess and the price is low, and to sell this off at a cheap price following bad harvests when grain would otherwise be too expensive for many people to buy. By selling-off the stored grain at a cheaper price the market price is lowered so that people with little money can still afford to buy grain, averting hunger and even famine.

Kenneth Hewitt's work, *Interpretations of Calamity* (1983), heralded the arrival of the second major critical perspective on disasters, the Marxist approach. This focused on the socioeconomic structures in which individuals and communities are embedded to pinpoint the root social causes – local and international – of catastrophic natural disasters. Unlike Sen, who concentrated on one type of natural disaster (drought and famine), the Marxist approach considered a wider range of disaster types in order to reveal a generalized class dimension to them. This work is particularly useful to our argument for an integrated approach to natural disaster because it sees disasters not as unique events powered by natural phenomena, but as momentary manifestations of ongoing environmental *and* social interaction, with class inequality being a key consideration. Underlying states of human marginalization are conceived as the principal cause of disaster. Marginalization, or the exclusion of certain individuals and groups from economic, social, or political resources, shapes who in society is vulnerable to risk and whether risk turns into disaster. This introduces questions about the influence of social, economic, and political power and inequality into analyses of natural hazard. Specifically, the Marxist approach linked the production of social inequalities in access to economic resources and secure living environments to exploitative class relationships within and between countries in the global capitalist economy, and prioritized research on vulnerability in the global South, or less-developed countries, where the greatest marginalization exists (see Susman, O'Keefe, and Wisner, 1983).

An idealized version of the relationship between socioeconomic marginalization, development, and disaster in the South is shown in figure 9.4. This is useful to our argument because it shows clearly that a disaster event has its roots in human stress (those groups who have few resources to protect themselves against the effects of, say, a drought) and physical processes (a deteriorating physical environment). The model also suggests that relief and development aid can act to reinforce marginalization. In figure 9.4, broken boxes indicate processes, such as that by which populations become marginalized, and solid boxes indicate events, such as a flood. Both events and processes are complex in the real world, but the model serves to show the way in which disaster – and even disaster relief and aid – can exacerbate marginalization and so deepen a population's susceptibility to future natural disasters (as we saw in Bihar). Developmental activists, academics, Southern governments, and nongovernmental organizations (NGOs) have all been active since the 1980s, lobbying to reform disaster relief and development aid so that this cycle could be broken. There has been some positive unilateral action by

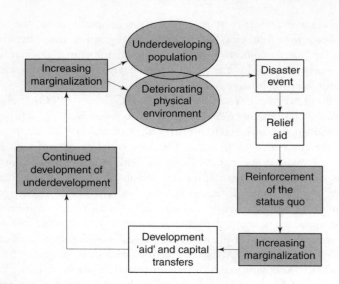

Figure 9.4: The process of marginalization and the production of disaster in the South
Source: P. Susman, P. O'Keefe, and B. Wisner, 'Global Disasters: A Radical Interpretation.' In K. Hewitt (ed.), *Interpretations of Calamity* (London: Allen and Unwin, 1983), fig. 14.3, p. 279. Reproduced by kind permission.

Northern governments in providing limited debt relief, and by NGOs in reforming the aid industry, but inequalities in the terms of trade and weaknesses in the delivery of disaster relief and its distribution persist.

The Marxist approach to disaster, though insightful, was criticized in two ways during the 1980s and 1990s. First, it was seen to focus too much on the capitalist world economy and class as if they were the sole causes of marginalization. Second, some felt that the Marxist approach implied that centrally planned economies were less prone to the social marginalization that prefigures disaster. However, capitalism and class alone cannot be held responsible for social marginalization. Moreover, there's no doubt that centrally planned economies, which did not follow capitalist development paths, were equally susceptible to disaster. For example, the great famine in communist China of 1959–61 led to 26 million premature deaths. Notwithstanding these weaknesses, the structural frame of analysis brought in by the Marxist approach still has much to offer in understanding natural disasters.

The impasse and beyond: interdisciplinarity and vulnerability assessment

In the 1980s and early 1990s, the critical approaches to disaster became popular in the academic world and also amongst nongovernmental organizations in the policy world. For example, Oxfam International shifted emphasis from providing postdisaster emergency relief to facilitating integrated vulnerability reduction within its community development work. This contrasted with the conservative – and dominant – positions of key international and governmental agencies that continued to support a physicalist and engineering-based orientation in disaster policy. The conservatism of dominant national and international actors fits rather too comfortably with the multibillion dollar disasters industry, which is founded on engineering schemes to mitigate the physical causes and consequences of disaster. Most of the engineering companies that benefit from disasters are based in the North, whilst the majority of natural disasters occur in the South. As a result natural disasters contribute to a drain of resources from the South, and are a business opportunity for the North. For key national and international agencies to redeploy resources from engineering solutions towards social change solutions would require Southern leaders who are not only capable of overcoming lobbying from the multinational engineering industry and their powerful host governments, but who are also confident enough to invest in strategies of social change which might easily be overlooked by their own electorate – poverty reduction is a far less visible sign of an active government than dam construction.

The United Nations Conference on Environment and Development held in Rio de Janeiro, 1992, has become symbolic of North/South confrontation over apparently nonpolitical issues such as environmental disasters. The conference stimulated an awareness of the increasing frequency and impact of natural disasters, and through its holistic agenda sanctioned debates that linked this trend to other social/natural issues such as population growth, urbanization, war, and global environmental change. As these issues have become more prominent over time it has become more difficult to deny the need for *integrated* human and physical approaches to hazard management. For example, the human pressures leading to rapid urbanization and inadequate construction standards have been singled out as being of critical importance in the high impact rates of earthquakes in Turkey in 1999.

Figure 9.5 represents the points at which the physical and human elements of disaster connect from a more integrated perspective. From this starting point it becomes clear that it is important to address both elements in programs to reduce the frequency and severity of natural disasters. 'Natural disaster' is shown as a product of human vulnerability and natural hazard. Natural hazard is shaped by the magnitude and frequency of a physical event. However, even the

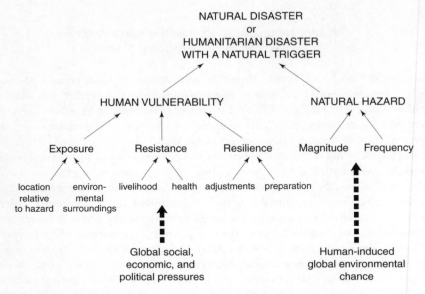

Figure 9.5:   An integrated view of natural disaster.

basic physical triggering forces may not be shaped by the natural world alone. For instance, research into the causes and consequences of global climate change (such as greenhouse gases, deforestation, desertificaion, sea-level rise) indicates that many supposedly 'natural forces' are, in fact, anthropogenic to a significant extent.

The human side of figure 9.5, termed 'human vulnerability,' is similarly a product of the interaction of physical and human elements. I have broken vulnerability down into three components: *exposure*, *resistance*, and *resilience*. Exposure is largely a product of physical location and the character of the surrounding built and natural environment. For example, a family living in ground-level, poorly maintained rental accommodation on a river bank, and adjacent to a sewerage outfall, will be highly exposed to flooding. The exposure component can be reduced by any hazard mitigation investments from individuals or households, such as building a house on stilts, or through public/private social investment policy such as the building of a wall to protect a community from landslides. Resistance reflects economic, psychological, and physical health, and their systems of maintenance, and represents the capacity of an individual or group to withstand the impact of a hazard. If resistance is low then even a small hazard stress can lead to injury, homelessness, or death. There are a plethora of ways to enhance individual or collective resistance to natural hazards. The most important will not directly target vulnerability, but focus on the wider goals of economic, social, and political inclusion. Finally, resilience to natural hazards can be thought of as the ability of an individual or collective actor to cope with or adapt to hazard stress. It is a product of the degree of preparation undertaken in the light of potential hazard, and of adjustments made in response to felt hazard, including relief and rescue. Several policy options are available to enhance resilience, the most important being those that shape formal or informal insurance mechanisms. Insurance is a key tool for use in spreading the economic costs of disasters across society and over time.

Together, exposure, resistance, and resilience are all conditioned by an actor's access to rights, resources, and material assets (Burton et al., 1993; Blaikie et al., 1994). Access profiles are, in turn, rooted in local and global political and socio economic structures. Though the relationship between these components of vulnerability may not always be negatively reinforcing, this is often the case, such that opportunities for resilience tend to be less common when resistance is already low and exposure is high. In this situation, vulnerability increases with each successive disaster event.

From the foregoing discussion we can see that vulnerability is closely linked to the dominant social divisions in a given society, be they class, caste, gender, ethnic, or religious. Cutting across these primary social divisions are secondary factors such as age and physical health. In different circumstances, primary and secondary factors may combine to enhance or reduce vulnerability. For example, elderly people may be made vulnerable through physical fragility but are also more secure because of their command over an extended family and its resources. Vulnerability should not be linked too mechanically with economic poverty, although these two phenomena often seem to operate simultaneously. Poor households often have to play-off poverty and vulnerability in daily life, invariably 'choosing' to invest available resources in day-to day expenditures rather than against a more distant threat, and in so doing accepting greater vulnerability (Chambers, 1995).

It is an everyday situation for most people, but especially those living in the global South, to experience a state of vulnerability. Under these conditions disasters are an almost inevitable future for millions, notably in Africa, south Asia, and parts of Latin America. Without vulnerability, 'natural hazards' loose their hazardousness and become benign or even potential resources for exploitation. Given this relationship between ongoing human vulnerability and natural hazards, it is more accurate to refer to 'natural disasters' as *humanitarian disasters with a natural trigger*. This change of emphasis is important because it stresses the connectivity of the humanness *and* the naturalness of disaster, and acknowledges that the two are deeply interlinked.

A Deepening Human Influence: Manufactured Risk

Until very recently our understanding of natural hazard was limited to the catastrophic and chronic types. However, the increased technical capacity some societies – notably those in the North – now possess to manipulate nature has led to a new range of hazards, against which policy-makers are even less well equipped to respond. Human-induced changes in physical systems have been recognized from the subcellular (genetically modified food) to the global (global warming). The hold that these anthropogenic changes have over developed countries in particular, has led some theorists to describe this contemporary period as that of 'risk societies' (Beck, 1992).

Ulrich Beck – a German sociologist who famously coined the term 'risk society' – argues that a transition can be discerned, in the more economically developed countries especially, from a popular concern with catastrophic or chronic hazard to more novel forms of 'manufactured risk' (Giddens, 1998). Manufactured risk is a product of applied advanced technology acting to change the very substance of nature, natural hazard, and risk. The distinction between what is natural and what is of human origin becomes increasingly blurred under these conditions. Risks associated with the natural world also become harder to identify, and scientific expertise is needed to detect them. These risks stem from the imperatives of industrial production and business culture, which push scientific innovation and its application ahead of a full, or sometimes any more than a cursory, understanding of the environmental consequences. Because of this approach, apparently benign innovations or actions can suddenly be identified as sources of hazard (e.g., eating beef, sunbathing), and, conversely, old risks can be reinterpreted as benign or possibly even resources (e.g., drinking red wine). Thus another element of risk societies is a new dynamism in the hazard/resource/benign trinity of society–nature relations. Box 9.2 takes the example of the so-called 'mad cow' crisis that hit the UK in the 1990s. It demonstrates the difficulty of forming policy and responding to a crisis where there is little straightforward scientific advice and where the stakes are high.

Box 9.2: The UK 'Mad Cow' Crisis

The 'Mad Cow' crisis unfolded in an environment of scientific uncertainty, government indecisiveness, and powerful vested interests. The globalization of the beef industry also gave the crisis an international dimension, which led to the formation of new institutions for the regulation of cattle farming in the European Union as well as in the UK.

Examples of these elements of the crisis can be found by examining the time chart below:

Dec. 1984   First cattle death from bovine spongiform encephalopathy (BSE or 'mad cow' disease) diagnosed.

June 1987   Agriculture ministers told of new disease.

July 1988   Sufficient scientific evidence is accumulated to warrant government action. A feed ban and new slaughter policy is introduced, with 50 percent of the value of slaughtered cattle being paid to farmers as compensation.

June 1989   UK government introduces a ban on the sale of offal, going beyond scientific advice that a ban be limited to its use in baby food.

July 1989   The European Union bans the export from the UK of cattle born before July 18, 1988.

Feb. 1990   UK farmers to receive 100 percent of the value of cattle in compensation.

May 1990   Both the Chief Medical Officer and the Minister of Agriculture claim British beef is safe to eat.

July 1993   The 100,000th confirmed case of BSE in Britain is announced, in response to a parliamentary question.

May 1995   Stephen Churchill, 19, dies. He's the first recorded death from vCJD, the human form of 'mad cow' disease.

Jan. 1996   New scientific report still says there is no direct evidence linking BSE to vCJD.

Aug. 1996   European Parliament sets up a Temporary Committee of Inquiry to investigate alleged contravention of the implementation of Community law in relation to BSE.

Dec. 1997   UK government announces a Public Inquiry into BSE.

June 1998   EU beef export ban lifted from Northern Ireland but remains for mainland Britain.

Jan. 2000   France refuses to lift British beef import ban and UK pursues legal action.

Oct. 2000   The Public (Philips) Inquiry into BSE is published.

Up to October 2000, 85 cases of vCJD had been identified in the UK. Despite the British government spending in excess of £90 million on research into the origins of BSE, and the factors leading to vCJD, its causes remain uncertain. The future size of the vCJD epidemic in the UK has been estimated at between 100 and 100,000.

Sources: MAFF (1999), Institute of Food, Science and Technology (1999), www.bse.org.uk

Beck suggests that sometime in the 1940s or 1950s advanced technology expanded to touch all aspects of the previously natural world. This is why he considers the period since then to have heralded 'the end of nature.' This does not mean that the environment has disappeared, but that it has ceased to be 'natural.' Beck argues that there has been a shift in what people have perceived to be most threatening from the 'natural' world. As sociologist Anthony Giddens (1998: 26) puts it, "for hundreds of years people worried about what nature could do to us – earthquakes, floods, plagues, bad harvests and so on. At a certain point . . . we stopped worrying [about this and] started worrying much more about what we have done to nature." While this perspective fits well with general trends observed in the global North, for the poorer societies of the South, as Beck (1992) acknowledges, people and communities are still having to deal with the old risks of catastrophic and chronic hazard as well as the new manufactured risks associated with imported technology (e.g. agro-chemical poisoning or the effects of imported hazardous waste).

Ways of responding to manufactured risks need to be developed. Given the rate at which new technology is being introduced, and the speed with which the riskiness of established technology is changing, informed decision-making becomes difficult if not impossible. Individuals have to rely on expert advice, but expert opinion is often shown to be inadequate, as the 'mad cow' case demonstrates. This is a particular problem for politicians who have to walk a tightrope between scare-mongering and covering up (the BSE crisis showed how difficult it is to get the balance right). Whereas before risk was something chosen, now, increasingly, people are having it thrust upon them (Beck, 1998).

Can we draw on conventional methods to assess patterns of risk and vulnerability to manufactured risks? Where risks are tangible, conventional methods can still be applied. An example is the work of the 'environmental justice movement' in the USA, which has successfully demonstrated the negative health effects caused by noxious facilities (like waste incinerators) located in close proximity to poor or ethnic minority neighborhoods. But for those risks that are hardest to identify, and which seemingly impact on no one social group alone, new approaches to understading and tackling manufactured hazards are required.

This all makes the management of manufactured risk very problematic. The institutions that have been built to protect people from traditional risks are less useful and may become part of the problem. The ineffectiveness of current institutional arrangements can be seen in the alarming pattern of increasing environmental degradation that appears to be progressing in step with increasing environmental legislation and regulation. Interrupting this negative cycle requires that previously depoliticized areas of decision-making (corporate economic decisions, scientific research agendas, plans for the new application of technology) need to be opened-up to public scrutiny, which requires new legal institutions (Beck, 1998).

Conclusion

Are we any closer to deciding the extent to which disasters are natural? Over the last 20 years theoretical perspectives have matured, with an acceptance of the need to analyze both the physical and social aspects of hazard and risk. However, policy and disaster management practices have been slower to change and continue to be dominated by a technocratic approach favoring engineering-based solutions that conceive of natural disasters as mainly natural events. In the 1990s, academic debates on natural hazard in the North have been deeply influenced by the 'risk society' thesis and the heightened awareness of manufactured risks which call for new ways of managing hazards. At the same time as these risks are becoming increasingly apparent, more traditional environmental hazards are also becoming increasingly frequent. It is the less-developed countries in the global South which experience the greatest losses from humanitarian disasters with natural triggers. It is also in the global South where the traditional hazards and new manufactured risks are most likely to overlap. This can already be seen in local impacts associated with global climate change. This has produced a new geopolitics of hazard, with vulnerable nations (e.g. small island states) pleading for cooperation from the industrialized and oil-producing states to help them cope. Negotiations on climate change have been at the center of this new geopolitics. In the Kyoto Protocol, for example, national governments – under pressure from environmental lobbyists – for the first time negotiated legally binding carbon dioxide emission targets for highly industrialized countries.

As global climate policies are changing so too are patterns of human organization. Since the end of the Cold War, poverty and political marginalization have increased, pushed by the motors of population growth, unequal development, war, environmental degradation, and rapid urban growth. Recognition of the importance of these human processes, and of the (local and global) inequalities, of which they are symptomatic, is a major step along the way towards a more fully integrative approach to natural disasters. But there is still a very long way to go.

Further Reading

For background data on catastrophic disasters and disaster aid worldwide see the World Disasters Report produced annually by the International Federation of the Red Cross and Red Crescent. For more on the entitlements and critical approaches to hazards, see Sen (1981) and Hewitt (1983). The idea of vulnerabilty to hazards is explored by Blaikie et al. (1994) and Cannon (1994). Giddens (1998) offers a useful introduction to the idea of manufactured risks.

References

Beck, U. (1992). *The Risk Society*. London: Sage.

Beck, U. (1998). The Politics of Risk Society. In J. Franklin (ed.), *The Politics of Risk Society*. Cambridge: Polity Press, 9–22.

Blaikie, P., Cannon, T., Davis, I., and Wisner, B. (1994). *At Risk*. London: Routledge.

Burton, I. and Kates, R. (1964). The Perception of Natural Hazards in Resource Management. *Natural Resources Journal* 3: 412–41.

Burton, I., Kates, R., and White, G. (1993). *Environment as Hazard*. London: Guildford Press. First edn. 1978.

Cannon, T. (1994). Vulnerability Analysis and the Explanation of 'Natural' Disasters. In A. Varley (ed.), *Disasters, Development and Environment*. Chichester: John Wiley and Sons, 13–30.

Centre for Science and Environment (CSE). (1996). *Floods, Flood Plains and Environmental Myths*. State of India's Environment: A Citizens Report #3. New Delhi: CSE.

Chambers, R. (1995). Poverty and Livelihoods: Whose Reality Matters? *Environment and Urbanisation* 7: 173–204.

Chronicle Newspaper. (1996). Geede Lowdown. Nov. 15. Georgetown, Guyana.

Cuny, F. (1983). *Disasters and Development*. Oxford: Oxford University Press.

Giddens, A. (1998). Risk Society: The context of British politics. In J. Franklin (ed.), *The Politics of Risk Society*. Cambridge: Polity Press, 23–34.

Grove-White, R. (1996). Environmental Knowledge and Public Policy Needs: On Humanising the Research Agenda. In S. Lash, B. Szerszynski, and B. Wynne (eds.), *Risk, Environment and Modernity*. London: Sage, 269–86.

Hewitt, K. (ed.) (1983). *Interpretations of Calamity*. London: Allen and Unwin.

Institute of Food, Science and Technology (1999). http://www.ifst.org/hottop5

International Federation of the Red Cross and Red Crescent. (Published annually). *World Disasters Report*. Various publishers.

MAFF (UK Ministry of Agriculture Fisheries and Food). (1999). http://www.maff.gov.uk/animalh/bse/index

PartnerRe. (1998). *Hurricane Georges, September 15–29, 1998*. Parter Research Bulletin. Oct. 1998.

Satterthwaite, D. (1998). Meeting the Challenge of Urban Disasters. In Red Cross and Red Crescent, *World Disasters Report 1998*. Oxford: Oxford University Press, 9–19.

Sen, A. (1981). *Poverty and Famines*. Oxford: Oxford University Press.

Smith, K. (1992). *Environmental Hazards*. London: Routledge.

Susman, P., O'Keefe, P. and Wisner, B. (1983). Global Disasters: A Radical Interpretation. In K. Hewitt (ed.), *Interpretations of Calamity*. London: Allen and Unwin, 263–97.

White, G. (1942). *Human Adjustment to Floods*. Research Paper 29, Dept. of Geography, University of Chicago.

www.bse.org.uk: The independent website of the Inquiry into the BSE epidemic.

Chapter 10

Marxism, Capitalism, and the Production of Nature

Noel Castree

Questions and Counterquestions

Until recently, the idea that nature could be 'produced' by humans seemed to be the stuff of science fiction. The Hollywood movies *Jurassic Park* and *Gattaca* offered entertaining morality tales about the perils of animal and human genetic engineering respectively, and audiences could leave the cinema safe in the knowledge that, even had we the technology, no one in their right mind would allow humanity to 'play God' with nature. Or could they? In 1997 British scientists announced that they had successfully cloned a complex organism, Dolly the sheep. The following year it was revealed that, unbeknownst to most ordinary Americans, some 20.5 million hectares of US farmland was being sown with genetically modified (or transgenic) crops. Not long after, the 'life-science' transnational corporation Monsanto unveiled its new 'Terminator seeds,' which are bioengineered to produce crops that are sterile (meaning that farmers who buy the seeds must purchase new ones from Monsanto each time they wish to grow crops, rather than using seeds generated naturally by the crops themselves). More recently, the completion of the Human Genome Project – an international attempt to describe the genetic make-up of *Homo sapiens* – has raised the specter of 'designer humans' in the not-too-distant future. In short, 'the production of nature' is anything but the stuff of science fiction: for our new "biotech century," as critic Jeremy Rifkin (1998) grandiosely calls it, is already proving to be one where humanity has the power to remake nature 'all the way down' (see Mannion, 1992).

This is a profound and unsettling power that dissolves and complicates the taken-for-granted distinction between 'the natural' and 'the social' (for instance, 'Frankenfoods' is a neologism which has become common currency in debates over GM crops). Not surprisingly, the fabrication of new humanly produced 'second natures' – as opposed to the 'first natures' bequeathed by evolution – has led to optimism and anxiety in equal measure. Apologists, including life-science companies and many biotech scientists, argue that the 'limits' of nature can be overcome in ways that will benefit humanity at large. For instance, EuropaBio – a consortium of European biotechnology firms – has consistently maintained that genetically modified crops will be high-yielding compared to 'natural varieties' and thus help tackle world hunger. By contrast, pessimists – including both radical environmental organizations like Earth First! and 'traditionalists' like Britain's Prince Charles – insist that we must 'save' an inviolable and fast-disappearing nature from the human-centered arrogance of science and technology. Sandwiched between these prophets of hope and despair are those with a foot in both camps, including many national governments, independent scientists, and members of the general public. Whatever position one adopts in relation to humanity's heightened power to produce nature, though, the economic and political stakes are clearly very high. The production of new natures through genetic engineering and the like is a multibillion-dollar industry and amounts to an unprecedented biological experiment with major ecological and human implications. For this reason it is absolutely vital to be able to answer a set of fundamental questions about the contemporary production of nature/s: namely, what forces are driving this production?; what effects are new productions of nature likely to have?; and is it right, morally and politically, for humans to reconstruct nature at the deepest level for their own purposes?

In this chapter I propose to answer all three questions as clearly as I can. However, since the way one responds to any question is influenced in part by one's theoretical and political view of the world, my answer is in no way 'neutral.' This brings me to my chapter title: for in the pages which follow I aim to explain and evaluate a specifically *Marxist* approach to the production of nature. This might strike some readers as odd. After all, isn't Marxism dead? Isn't it a discredited doctrine that passed away with the late-1980s collapse of communism in eastern Europe and Russia? The answer is 'yes' only if one takes Marxism to be a single, unified worldview typified by the state socialism of the former communist countries. But this is not – and indeed never has been – the case. In reality Marxism is a highly *diverse* tradition of thought and politics that is continually evolving. Although today few members of the public and still fewer governments adhere to Marxist principles, certain modes of Marxism are in fact alive and well in the twenty-first century – particularly among radical intellectuals and grassroots activists.

In what follows I consider a body of academic Marxism developed in human geography and cognate fields which endeavors to explain and critique the production of nature as it unfolds within what is arguably the dominant economic system worldwide: capitalism (capitalism is not, however, the only economic system to physically 'produce nature'). This body of work, I hope to show, deserves to be taken seriously for several reasons. First, it offers a clear and compelling explanation of the processes driving seemingly diverse productions of nature in our increasingly capitalist 'biotech century.' Second, it shows that present-day productions of nature are not, in fact, new but only the most recent manifestation of a century-old process, the analysis of which can help us understand these contemporary natures. Finally, the Marxist approach I expli-cate in this chapter takes a distinctive political stance towards the contemporary capitalist production of these natures, one which avoids the blithe acceptance of apologists (like Monsanto) and the antimodern intolerance of critics (like Prince Charles), and yet refuses the status-quo reformism of those in the political middle ground. Taken together, these three attributes suggest the continued relevance of a Marxist approach to understanding nature. However, they must also be measured against a set of key weaknesses, and towards the end of the chapter I argue that Marxism is a *necessary* but not *sufficient* approach to understanding and responding politically to the capitalist production of nature/s in the twenty-first century.

The Production of Nature?

The phrase 'the production of nature' was coined by Marxist geographer Neil Smith in his path-breaking book *Uneven Development*, published in 1984. What was so arresting and counterintuitive about Smith's argument was the claim that twentieth-century humanity did not merely 'interact with,' 'interfere with,' or even 'alter' the natural world but materially *produced* it anew. As he put it:

> What jars us so much about this idea of the production of nature is that it defies the conventional, sacrosanct separation of nature and society, and it does so with such abandon and without shame. We are used to conceiving of nature as external to society, pristine and pre-human, or else a grand universal in which human beings are but small and simple cogs. But . . . our concepts have not caught up with reality. It is capitalism which ardently defies the inherited separation of nature and society, and with pride rather than shame. (Smith, 1984: xiv)

For Smith, then, the conventional belief that nature is, by definition, nonsocial – a fixed, unmalleable domain separate from humans – was being rendered obsolete by capitalist development. Indeed, he regarded such a belief as *ideological*, meaning that it served to either conceal or else justify the process whereby nature is made increasingly *internal* to the dynamics of capitalist accumulation.

Almost 20 years on – and notwithstanding our increased awareness of genetic engineering, cloning, and the like – Smith's arguments may still seem outlandish or at least overstated. After all, even today "nature is generally seen as precisely that which cannot be produced" and, presumably, this was even truer in the mid-1980s when Smith was writing. But Smith was no maverick.

In fact, he was just one of several Marxist researchers arguing that nature was no longer an intransigent realm external to society. For instance, just three years after Smith's book appeared, the geographer David Goodman and colleagues published *From Farming to Biotechnology*, followed a year later by agricultural economist Jack Kloppenburg's book *First the Seed*. In turn, these two important books were complemented by *Fashioning Nature* (written by Goodman and sociologist-cum-geographer Michael Redclift) and *Plants, Power and Profit* (by agricultural economists Lawrence Bush et al.), both published in 1991. Together, these books comprise a substantial corpus of theoretical and empirical work on the capitalist production of nature.

In light of this, we should perhaps pose a series of critical questions that will help us better understand the substance and relevance of the production of nature argument. The first question concerns capitalism and nature. Capitalism is a human-made, socioeconomic system, so how can Smith and other Marxists argue that nature – which is the antithesis of society – is 'produced' by this system? The second question concerns capitalism and science. As the new biotechnologies show, the capacity for humans to intentionally and materially reconstitute nature is reliant on scientific research and expertise of the highest order. But isn't science separate from capitalism and capitalist business interests, and how, therefore, can science be harnessed to the economic production of nature? The third and final question concerns the historical applicability of the production of nature argument. For isn't it only in the last few years, with the advent of recombinant genetic engineering, that the production of nature has become a reality? And, if so, doesn't this mean that nature is for the most part still 'natural,' implying that the arguments of Smith, Goodman, and others are vastly overstated, applying only to a small, albeit growing, sector of capitalist economies (the biotechnology sector)? Let me answer each question in turn and, in so doing, suggest why the production of nature argument is a powerful and compelling one of wide applicability.

Capitalism and Nature

Following Karl Marx, Smith and like-minded writers argue that today capitalism is the dominant economic system worldwide. In this system, goods (whether washing machines or paper clips) are produced according to the following logic:

$$M \longrightarrow C \begin{cases} LP \\ \quad\quad P \ldots C' \longrightarrow M + \Delta \\ MP \end{cases}$$

where M (money) is put forward to purchase C (commodities) – namely, MP (means of production; inputs, raw materials, machines) and LP (labor power) – which are combined in the productive process (P) to produce a new commodity (C′), which is then sold for the original money put forward, plus a profit (Δ). The profit is, in turn, reinvested to enable a new round of production. In this system, therefore, commodities are produced not simply for their practical – or use – value, but for their exchange value. And what is striking about this system is that, despite the dazzling *diversity* of capitalist economic activities worldwide, they are mostly organized according to the *same* overarching logic.

After Marx, Smith, Goodman, and others argue that four cardinal features characterize this system. First, it is inherently growth-orientated: profit, rather than, say, social equity or environmental sustainability, is the primary goal. Second, it is based on competition between capitalists within and between industrial sectors as they fight to sell their products to consumers in regional, national, and world markets. Third, growth and competition set up powerful incentives for individual capitalists to maximize their returns in whatever way possible (e.g. through exploiting new locations, developing a new product, or technological innovation). Finally, the origin of profits lies in labor, rather than any other factor of production. The 'surplus value' realized at the end of the production process thus originates with laborers, whose work is exploited in the form of surplus labor time over and above that for which they are paid.

So far so good. But what has any of this got to do with nature? Well, at first sight very little, other than the very general facts that *all* production (capitalist and noncapitalist) is at some level reliant on materials derived from nature. Indeed, it is significant that the most nature-centered of all economic activities – agriculture – has historically been the one sector resistant to being organized along capitalist lines. As Russian Marxist Karl Kautsky (1899) noted a century ago, agriculture – even in the advanced, industrialized countries – was typically characterized by noncapitalist forms of production (often centered around family farms) and remained so well into the twentieth century (Henderson, 1998).

Why is this? According to agricultural analyst Susan Mann (1990), in her germinal book *Agrarian Capitalism in Theory and Practice*, the reason is that nature is not readily amenable to being altered: that is, it poses physical obstacles to capitalist development (Mann and Dickinson, 1978). A good – and in many was typical – example of this concerns seeds for growing crops. On the one hand, because seeds are "the irreducible core of crop production" (Kloppenburg, 1988: xi) they are, in principle, a highly attractive candidate for capitalist investment. After all, all crop farmers need seeds, and thus a capitalist firm devoted to gathering, selling, and improving seeds would, potentially, be enormously profitable. However, on the other hand, there is a natural barrier dissuading capitalist investment in seed production: namely, the fact that seeds are, by nature, self-reproducing. Each new harvest of crops yields seeds for next year's harvest, meaning that farmers always have a ready-made – and free – supply of seeds. A capitalist seed company would thus encounter an immediate loss of its markets because it could not prevent the natural regeneration of the seeds it sells. Consequently, Mann and Dickinson (1978: 467) were led to observe that "Capitalist development appears to stop, as it were, at the farm gate."

In light of this, it may seem very peculiar that Smith, Goodman, and other Marxists insist that nature is, in fact, produced within capialist societies. If Kautsky, Mann, and Dickinson are right that agriculture, the most nature-centered of all economic activities, has been highly resistant to capitalism, then how can Smith et al. take such a bold, contrary position? Is it just that Smith et al. think that writers like Kautsky et al. are wrong? Or is it that Kautsky, Mann, and Dickinson were right and what Smith et al. are arguing is that the natural barriers to capitalist accumulation have been progressively and ingeni-ously *overcome*? The answers to the latter two questions are 'no' and 'yes' respectively. But to understand how capitalism has conquered the obstacles put in its way by nature, we need to say something about how science has been harnessed by capitalist industries.

Capitalism, Science, and Nature

Science is pivotal to present day human–nature relations, and yet the 'nature' of science is widely misunderstood. Without scientific research and new technologies stemming therefrom, humans would not have the capacity to remake nature in the ways they are currently doing (for instance, genetic engineering would not be possible today if scientists had not identified DNA as the building block of all life in the 1950s or figured out how to shuffle genes around (so-called rDNA technology) in the 1970s). Yet despite science's importance, it is surprising just how misunderstood it is. Most people – including, I suspect, many readers of this chapter – tend to think of science "as a special human enterprise, governed by standards that are essentially different from other, ordinary ... [human activities]" (Busch et al., 1991: 34). As Demeritt (1996: 485) rightly observes, "Since the Enlightenment, science has been synonymous with the revelation of truth about the world." Above all, science is taken to be objective and value-free and scientists themselves are presumed to be independent researchers who, when they enter the laboratory, put their personal prejudices to one side. However, this standard view of science has long been subject to criticism from Marxists and other radicals (see Demeritt for a review of these criticisms). Indeed, for several decades now science has been shown *not* to live up to the standards of objectivity and value-freedom.

How, then, does science work? According to Marxists like Busch et al., scientists do not exist in a vacuum, working independently of external influences. Instead, scientists are seen as 'institutionally embedded,' working chiefly for universities, government institutions, and businesses. In all three cases, but particularly the latter, Busch et al. argue that scientists' research activities are indelibly influenced by the aims and objectives of the institutions they work for. This is not to say that scientists' activities and discoveries are wholly determined according to their employer's wishes, but it is to say that a dynamic, two-way (or dialectical) relation exists in which scientific research both conditions and is conditioned by the institutions it is embedded in (see Busch et al., ch. 2; Demeritt (this volume) also makes some important arguments about how scientists help to remake nature both conceptually and physically).

As we will see momentarily, plant and molecular biologists working for agribusiness and life-science companies have, for nearly a century, had their researches into nature (both 'basic' and 'applied') heavily influenced by the capitalist objective of developing profitable products. For now, though, let us add-in the insights gained from this and the previous section and expand Marx's original theory of capital accumulation:

CAPITALISM

$$M \longrightarrow C \begin{cases} MP \\ \\ LP \text{ (inc. SRN)} \downarrow \end{cases} P \ldots C' \longrightarrow M + \Delta$$

NATURE

Nature (e.g. seeds) not humanly changeable and therefore poses an obstacle to capitalist development.

In this expanded theory of how capitalism works, nature has been added-in in two opposing ways which set the stage for understanding what Smith et al. mean when they talk about the production of nature. On the one side, we have a materially resistant nature which seemingly cannot, in and of itself, be altered as a means of realizing profits. But, on the other side, we have scientific research into nature (SRN) in which scientists are employed by capitalist firms to investigate how nature can be physically transformed to become what geograher Cindi Katz (1998: 48) calls an "accumulation strategy."

Back to the Future: A Century of Nature's Production

We are now in a position to understand why and how capitalist firms seek to produce nature. We are also in a position to see that the recent, dramatic innovations in commercial bioengineering – such as Monsanto's 'Terminator' technology – are only the latest developments in what has, in fact, been over a century of the capitalist production of nature. In other words, when Smith, Goodman, and other Marxist critics were writing in the 1980s and early 1990s they were not presciently describing events *about to happen*. Rather, they were theorizing and criticizing an *already existing* process that most people did not realize had been going on for decades.

This can be illustrated best by returning to the earlier-discussed case of seeds. Kloppenburg's remarkable book *First the Seed* puts empirical flesh on the theoretical bones of the argument made so far in this chapter. It examines the development of a capitalist seed industry in the USA from the 1920s onwards. As noted earlier, seeds are naturally self-reproducing and, therefore, not readily sold for profit. Indeed, historically the have been considered a 'public good' which farmers are free to use and which cannot be owned by any one individual or company (in 1915, for instance, some 97 percent of US farm seed was sown on the farm where it was produced). Yet, despite this and as noted earlier, the commercial sale and development of seeds is potentially very lucrative: for not only do all crop farmers use seeds, but if seeds can be improved to yield 'superior' crop then seed firms would have two ways of cornering a large market. How, then, did US capitalists overcome the barriers to accumulation thrown up by seeds' natural reproduction in order to make seed manufacture both possible and profitable? And in what sense can this be considered a process of 'producing' nature?

Kloppenburg's analysis takes off from two facts: first, that the USA possesses very few indigenous crops of commercial importance; and second, that during the nineteenth and early-to-mid twentieth centuries the US needed to feed a very fast-growing population (which increased by 200 million between 1840 and 1960). The first fact will surprise many readers of this chapter: after all, the USA has long been one of the world's major producers of wheat, corn, and other agricultural staples. However, virtually none of these staples are, in fact, indigenous to the US. Instead, they derive from developing countries and were imported into the US in the nineteenth century by federal governments who were worried about America's food security. This links to the second fact stated above. In order to increase crop yields US governments from the nineteenth century realized the importance of identifying particularly high-yielding varieties. Any single crop – like wheat or corn – is made up of a large number of different but related 'strains,' and some (either individually or in combination) tend to be higher-yielding than others. Consequently, from the mid-nineteenth century, successive American governments – again, concerned that the US should be self-sufficient in food – established a system that would ensure farmers got expert advice and agricultural inputs so as to improve and 'freshen-up' the genetic stock of their crops. This system, heavily funded with taxpayers' money, was based around a series of land-grant universities (LGUs) and state agricultural experiment stations (SAESs) scattered across the country and answerable to the US Department of Agriculture (USDA). Both LGUs and SAESs were supplied with seeds gathered in a series of 'germplasm collection expeditions' to naturally biodiverse countries in Africa, South America, and the Far East possessing multiple strains of wheat, corn, and other crops on which the US's agricultural wealth was based. Both kinds of state-funded institution were instructed to distribute seeds to farmers free of charge – particularly seeds which could produce crops with desirable qualities (e.g. be high-yielding or resistant to particular pests) – and to work with them on the farm to improve crop quality.

By the early nineteenth century, as Kloppenburg shows, this new seed distribution system benefited from a major scientific discovery that was the product of 'independent' research but which ultimately was used in the service of private, commercial gain. That discovery was the work of Russian plant biologist Gregor Mendel, whose research on the principles of plant evolution had, inexplicably, been ignored for several decades until its rehabilitation by geneticists in 1900. Prior to Mendel's work, plant breeding was more of an 'art' than a 'science' and one usually undertaken by farmers experimenting with different crop strains. What Mendellian genetics provided for the first time was an understanding of the rules of plant heredity. The implication was that plant breeders could now systematically and precisely interbreed crop strains in order to produce 'crops to order': that is, crops equipped with specific, sought-after traits (relating to yield, size, pest resistance, color, etc.). However, such was the time and expertise required to interbreed crops successfully along Mendellian lines that farmers, it soon became clear, could not continue their traditional role as the US's chief plant breeders.

Consequently, from the early twentieth century, the USDA took the process of plant-breeding 'off-farm' and placed it firmly in the LGUs and SAESs under the auspices of a new generation of professionally trained plant biologists such as E. M. East, Donald Jones, and George Schull. Let us take the case of corn. Unlike most other principal crops, corn is naturally open- or cross-pollinated rather than self-fertilized such that each ear of corn may be fertilized with pollen from a different corn plant. Thus, unlike self-pollinated crops like wheat, most corn plants are the product of a unique cross, and corn crops are "in a constant state of genetic flux" (Kloppenburg, 1988: 95). Clearly, this sexual promiscuity poses a major natural barrier for plant breeders: for 'superior' corn plants are constantly admixing with 'inferior' plants.

As Kloppenburg (1988, ch. 5) shows in fascinating detail, Mendellian genetics offered a solution to this problem. Using Mendel's rules of heredity, what George Schull discovered at his Long Island SAES from 1905 onwards was that *inbred* corn plants were often higher-yielding than open-pollinated varieties, particularly when two inbred plants were crossed with each other (a so-called 'single-cross'). This new process of 'hybridization' is summarized in figure 10.1. What it meant, in the words of US plant scientist William Bateson (speaking in 1902), is that "he [the plant breeder] will [now] be able *to do what he wants to do* instead of what merely turns up" because, as USDA cotton breeder W. A. Orton (1905) put it, "The . . . breeder's new conception of varieties as *plastic groups* must replace the old idea of fixed foms of chance origin which has long been a bar to progress" (cited in Kloppenburg, 1988: 69). There are three crucial things to note about this new hybridization process. First, it was far too complex to be undertaken by the average farmer. Second, seed from corn plants produced by double-cross hybridization were 'naturally' sterile, meaning that farmers who used the seed would suffer major yield reductions the following year. Finally, the scientists and institutions producing hybrid corn seeds could potentially claim property rights in the seed on the argument that they had created a new, innovative product for which they should be financially rewarded.

In other words, US government scientists had – quite by accident – found a way to overcome the corn seed's natural self-reproducibility in their quest to increase corn yields (and, indeed, by the 1960s over 90 percent of US corn was hybrid, because it yielded four times as much as nonhybrid corn). And it is here, at last, that we see how and why capitalist firms penetrated the US seed sector from the 1920s onwards. Shortly after the excitement caused by the rediscovery of Mendel's work, a number of *private* seed companies were set up, sensing a commercial opportunity on the horizon. Many of these commercial companies were set up by former LGU and SAES scientists or at least employed these scientists. Organized in an umbrella group – the American Breeders Association (the ABA, established in 1903) – these firms took a keen interest in hybridization for obvious reasons: for, in the case of corn, it potentially created a seed market where before none had existed. Because hybrid seeds produced high-yielding plants, farmers wanted them; but because hybridization occurred *off-farm* and, additionally, produced crops *unable to successfully reproduce*, farmers *had* to get a new supply of hybrid seeds each year (see figure 10.2).

However, if hybridization broke down the seed's natural barriers, American private seed companies faced two institutional barriers before a capitalist seed industry could be fully developed: namely, the US government and US law. On the one side, the US government was effectively a competitor, blocking private seed companies because it was distributing hybrid seeds to farmers for free. On the other side, because seeds were considered a public good, the law provided no property rights for those who spent time, expertise, and money developing new hybrid varieties. As a result, as Kloppenburg explains, from 1903 the ABA vigorously lobbied successive federal governments. By 1920 it had persuaded Washington to cease free seed disbursements. And by 1930 it secured the passage of the Plant Variety Protection Act which, for the first time in US history, permitted ownership of 'natural' plant varieties so long as they

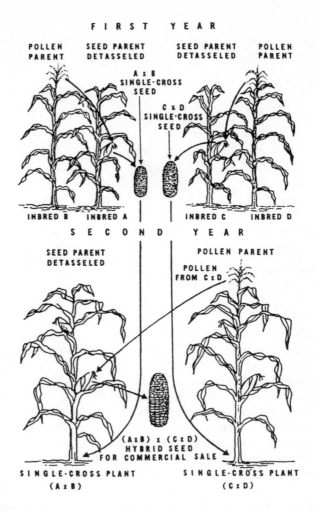

Figure 10.1: Production of double-cross hybrid seed corn using manual detasseling. The process beings with two pairs of homozygous inbred lines (A, B and C, D). Each pair is crossed (A × B, C × D) by planting the two lines in alternating rows and emasculating the female parent by manual removal of the pollen-shedding tassel (this process is known as detasseling). Only seed from the female parents is collected to ensure that no selfed seed is obtained. Plants grown from this single-cross seed are themselves crossed following the same procedure: (A × B) × (C × D). Seed is again collected from the female parent, and it is this germplasm that is the double-cross hybrid seed sold for farm production.
Source: J. R. Kloppenburg, Jr., *First the Seed: The Political Economy of Plant Biotechnology* (Cambridge: Cambridge University Press, 1988), p. 100. Reproduced by kind permission.

Seed Company

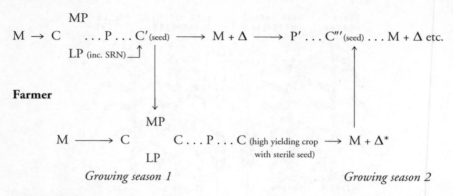

Farmer

Growing season 1   *Growing season 2*

Figure 10.2: Seed firms, farmers, and capitalist accumulation: producing nature. Here the hybrid seeds produced by the capitalist seed firms become a means of production for farmers and must be purchased. Because the seeds produced by hybrid crops are sterile, farmers must, each growing season, give a share of their profits (Δ^*) back to seed firms in order to purchase new seeds

were novel and non-obvious 'inventions.' Some 20 years later, a multibillion-dollar seed industry existed in the US on the basis of hybrid seeds, including now well-known 'agrofoods' firms like Funk Seeds and Cargill Ltd. By the 1970s, the capacity these firms had to literally 'produce' seeds (since hybrids are hardly products of 'nature') meant they dominated US and many other national seed markets across the whole spectrum of commercially important crops.

What Kloppenburg's Marxist analysis shows in compelling detail is the way that capitalism, as long as a century ago, found ways to materially produce that which seemed beyond the power of humanity to alter: nature. The seed – that most fundamental and seemingly natural of all agricultural inputs – became a vehicle for capital accumulation in just two short decades and kick-started a process of producing nature which has culminated in the new plant, animal, and human biotechnologies of the last few years. True, the cut-and-paste technologies of genetic engineering are able to reconsistute nature at an altogether deeper level than techniques like crop hybridization. But according to Marxists like Smith (1984; 1998), Goodman, Sorj, and Wilkinson (1987), and Goodman and Redclift (1991), the basic economic processes underpinning the new biotechnologies are very similar to those animiating capital–nature relations throughout the twentieth century. Monsanto's new Terminator seeds are, perhaps, the best example of this. Although these seeds are the product of gene-splicing rather than cross-breeding, it is arguable that they simply take a stage further the same economic logic driving the product development of the first US seed companies 100 years ago. For Terminator seeds are engineered to be even *more sterile* than the seeds of hybrid crops, thus *biologically guaranteeing* that farmers will have no choice but to buy more seeds from Mansanto in order to sow the next crop.

Social and Environmental Implications

I have now, at some length, fulfilled one of my aims in this chapter: namely, to explain theoretically and illustrate empirically the forces which, from a Marxist perspective, drive capitalism to produce nature. Along the way, I have tried to show that, contrary to popular belief, many of the 'natural' entities (such as corn, tomatoes, and soya) which are now being genetically altered through new recombinant methods have, for a long time, been engineered and reengineered by seed, agrofood, and life-science companies. In other words, far from being 'natural' organisms which are only now being 'denaturalized' by GM techniques, they have been 'second natural' for decades and were part and parcel of twentieth-century capitalism. In this section I want to turn, more briefly, to my second stated aim: to explain the effects of capitalist productions of nature. The recent public furore in the UK over genetically modified crops suggests that these effects are of serious concern to ordinary people as much as to scientists, corporate executives, and politicians. According to critics, biotech giants like Monsanto, DuPont, Ciba-Geigy, Hoescht, Novartis, and Astra-Zeneca are putting profitability before environmental, social, and human health considerations. According to supporters, the new biotechnologies promise a series of unparalleled benefits. More agnostic commentators observe that it is too early to tell. We should, they counsel, 'wait and see.' Who, though, is right?

While it will indeed be several years before we know the full effects of, say, genetically modifying salmon (already there are GM salmon farms in Europe and North America) or injecting pigs with GM growth hormones (already a decade-old practice), previous productions of nature offer clues as to the likely impacts of contemporary ones. Let us return, by way of example, to the hybrid crops grown on a large scale in Northern countries like the US from the 1930s onwards. It is undeniable that hybrids dramatically increased agricultural yields in the US, Canada, Britain and similarly advanced countries during the twentieth century. Given the tripling of world population during that century, this must be considered enormously beneficial. However, there is a darker side to the capitalist production of nature. First, there were the economic and social effects of privatizing seeds. Commercial farmers in the US and beyond now not only have to pay for many agricultural inputs (of which seeds are just one) but are thereby rendered dependent on seed, agrofoods, and life-science companies. Second, in environmental terms, hybrid crop production has led to far more farmland than at any time in human history being monocultural. In other words, because farmers are sowing a relatively limited range of 'superior' seeds purchased from suppliers, their crops lack genetic diversity and are susceptible to pests and disease unless protected by doses of herbicides and pesticides. Finally, rather than diversify the genetic basis of hybrid seed stocks, many capitalist agricltural suppliers developed hybrid varieties that would tolerate these chemical pesticides and herbicides – pesticides and herbicides manufactured by the self-same suppliers! Not only did this lock farmers into further dependence on these companies. It also led to serious environmental pollution and damage, first detected by American biologist Rachel Carson in her classic book *Silent Spring* (1962).

These three problems arose (and continue to arise) not only in the agrarian regions of the North. They have also appeared in large parts of the South, affecting multiple environments and hundreds of millions of farm workers. The reason is because from the 1950s hybrid seeds were exported by Northern multinational seed producers to countries like India and Kenya. As Indian critic and activist Vandana Shiva shows, the so-called 'Green Revolution' which followed, though it increased food output and further enriched Northern seed companies like Funk and Cargill, led to all manner of deleterious ecological and social effects for farmers and rural people (Shiva, 1993). In sum, then, though the production of nature is not an unmitigated evil, from a Marxist perspective it is certainly driven by rather narrow pecuniary interests which displace important nonprofit considerations (e.g. environmental well-being). Indeed, the recent, business-led development of GM technologies seems only to confirm this, since firms like Monsanto do not yet know the long-term ecological or health effects of producing GM foods yet are still prepared to market and sell them (see Anderson, 1999; Teitel and Wilson, 1999).

The Politics of Produced Nature

We've seen, in the previous sections, how Marxist critics explain and evaluate the capitalist production of nature. In this penultimate part of the chapter I want to show how the Marxist perspective adumbrated here translates into a distinctive political stance towards nature. In the introduction, I observed that the startling biotechnical transformations of natural entities witnessed in recent years have, broadly speaking, generated three political responses: enthusiastic acceptance among pro-business and pro-science constituencies; downright opposition among many environmentalists; and guarded acceptance among politicians and members of the public seeking to balance the benefits of technology with other social and environmental considerations. These three positions typify a century-old spectrum of political opinion about nature in many countries worldwide, and can be described as 'technocentric,' 'ecocentric,' and 'liberal-managerial' respectively. The former is a very human-centered position that places faith in science and technology (in alliance with big business) to 'improve' nature in the interests of human well-being. Ecocentrists, by contrast, put nature first and argue that it is being progressively destroyed by an arrogant and careless humanity; they seek a return to ecologically 'friendlier' systems of production and consumption. Straddling the techno-ecocentric divide, those of a 'liberal-managerial' persuasion argue that the demands humanity places upon nature can and must be balanced with those of nature itself.

Despite their differences, from the perspective of Smith, Kloppenburg, and other Marxist critics they have one crucial thing in common. For what the three political rhetorics of 'improve nature,' 'protect nature,' and 'balance nature and society' all have in common is the questionable assumption that nature and humanity *are two separate realms needing to be brought together or held apart in particular ways.* In contrast, what advocates of the production of nature thesis argue is that any politics of nature today has to reckon with the fact that, under capitalism, *nature and society have been indissolubly interlinked for over a century.* The question then arises: what does a politics of nature look like once one dispenses with the nature–society dualism?

Smith (1996: 50) and another Marxist, David Harvey (1996: chs. 8 & 13), provide an answer. First, the 'back to nature' romanticism of ecocentrics – especially 'deep green' organizations like Earth First! – is simply not an option. As Harvey (1996: 187–8) rightly argues, the 'constructed ecosystems' of capitalist countries "cannot be allowed to deteriorate or collapse without courting ecological disaster." In other words, the capitalist production of nature/s is so far-gone that we cannot easily turn back the hands of time. Secondly, however, this does not mean we should embrace the technocentric logic of capitalist businesses and capitalist-led science. On the contrary, as Kloppen-burg's work shows and as the new biotechnologies suggest, the capitalist production often 'improves' nature in questionable ways. Thirdly, though, this does not imply a Marxist politics wherein one 'tinkers' with capitalism in order to yield a more socially and ecologically just economic system. Rather, Marxists like Smith argue that capitalism is incapable of producing nature in progressive ways because the pursuit of profit is its overriding objective. Accordingly, what Smith, Harvey and other Marxists suggest is that, *while we cannot not produce nature in the twenty-first century, we can at least endeavor to produce it in noncapitalist ways.* As Smith (1996) puts it, "The political question becomes this: how, and by what . . . means and through what . . . institutions is the production of nature to be organised?" A Marxist politics of nature thus accepts the fact that today nature and society are totally intertwined but seeks a revolutionary abolition of capitalism in favor of an economic system that is not driven by narrow monetary interests. In short, it accepts the myriad benefits of scientific and technical transformations of nature but it seeks to uncouple science and technology from capitalist imperatives.

Evaluations

Whatever its strengths as a way of understanding human–nature relations, the production of nature approach is hardly beyond criticism. Several practical, theoretical, ontological, and political problems loom large. Practically speaking, technocentrists, ecocentrists, and those sandwiched between them might legitimately complain that in criticizing capitalism, advocates of the production of nature approach fail to offer any viable economic *solutions* to economically produced environmental problems (Dietz and van der Straaten, 1995) – other than the rather unrealistic notion of totally overthrowing capitalism. Theoretically speaking even sympathetic critics complain that the production of nature approach is *productivist*. That is, it overemphasizes production at the expense of other processes which simultaneously socialize nature (Castree and Braun, 1998, ch. 1). After all, production is in reality 'embedded' in a set of non-economic and noncapitalist relations (Thrift and Olds, 1996). Ontological issues also arise (an ontology is a theory of what exists or what is real). Central here is the suggestion that the production of nature approach is overly *anthropocentric* (and thus, ironically, in this respect similar to the technocentrists it criticizes). The charge has two components: first, that the approach causally prioritizes the capital 'side' of the capital–nature dialectic; and second, that it therefore fails to appreciate the 'agency' of produced nature/s. These criticisms have some validity. After all, the production of nature approach was inspired by Marx's economics and Marx has been shown to be more interested in understanding the human consequences of capitalism than its environmental consequences (Castree, 1995: 19). Accordingly, geographers like Smith have looked more at how capitalism produces nature and less at how produced nature affects capitalism. In response, a number of Marxists outside geography have sought, at the theoretical level, to add to Marx's economic concepts a set of ecological concepts that can help us make sense of the material properties of produced nature (e.g. Altvater, 1993).

Finally, the production of nature approach is also subject to political problems. One problem is its *Prometheanism* (Soper, 1991) in which, following the general Western Enlightenment view, nature is seen as but an end to human needs or happiness. For ecocentrists the production of nature approach – like Marxism more generally – cannot ultimately value nature *in its own right* (Hayward, 1995: ch. 3). A second problem, more controversially, is that the production of nature approach is *masculinist*. As several feminist critics have pointed out, Marxism's complicity in the Enlightenment question to 'master' and control nature – albeit in a noncapitalist form – raises questions abouts its gender biases and subtexts. As a concept, nature has long been feminized in Western discourses, as a domain to be 'conquered,' 'tamed,' and 'subdued.' By prioritizing paid (predominantly male?) – as opposed to unpaid, domestic (female?) – labor as the force driving nature's production under capitalism, the production of nature approach may inadvertently perpetuate a social and environmental politics blind to women's unequal place in capitalist societies (Plumwood, 1994).

Production of nature advocates concede many of these criticism (Castree, 1997; Smith, 1998). However – and this is an important point – they would insist that it is necessary and (in principle at least) possible to be *anthropomorphic* without being anthropocentric and Promethean on the one side, or, on the other side, ecocentric. Against 'greens' who wish to value nature 'in its own right,' technocentrists who put humans first, and those somewhere in-between, the production of nature approach implies that it is possible to *balance* human and ecological needs by recognizing that *all* appraisals of nature and what to do with it *are made by humans in the first place* (under capitalism or any other economic system). This anthropomorphic insight avoids the myth of any 'return to nature' in-itself without necessarily lapsing into the human-centered arrogance (anthropocentrism) of the technocentrics, since the argument is that while it is only possible to value nature in human terms – we simply cannot know what a nonhuman valuation of nature would look like since we cannot step outside our humanity – this fact does not preclude a more sustainable production of nature in which the environment is respected.

Criticism and responses aside, what of the future? Marxian theory has, of late, become less popular in human geography and other social sciences. Nonetheless, two notable developments promise to further academic interest in the capitalist production of nature and to sustain the relevance of Marxism into the twenty-first century. The first is the agrofoods and biotechnology industries to which I have referred several times in this chapter. Secondly, and more worrying perhaps, modern science and industry now collude to remake even the human body through genetic engineering, transplantations, and prosthetics. Is the production of *bodily natures* to become a crucial intellectual and political issue for the twenty-first century? (on this see the recent essays in *Society and Space*, 1998). And, if so, will the corporeal become a serious focus of intellectual and political concern for Marxist researchers in the years to come?

Further Reading

Smith (1984: ch. 2) still offers the best theoretical summary of the production of nature argument, while Kloppenburg's (1988) empirical analysis of seed production brilliantly illustrates Smith's basic argument. For Marxian analysis of the new biotechnologies see Goodman et al. (1987). For general, critical introductions to GM technology see Anderson (1999), Kneen (1999), Rifkin (1998), or Teitel and Wilson (1999). This chapter can be read alongside Castree (2000).

References

Altvater, E. (1993). *The Future of the Market*. London: Verso.

Anderson, L. (1999). *Genetic Engineering, Food and Our Environment*. Foxhole: Green Books.

Busch, L., Lacy, W., Burkhardt, J., and Lacy, L. (1991). *Plants, Power and Profit*. Oxford: Blackwell.

Carson, R. (1962). *Silent Spring*. New York: Fawcett Crest.

Castree, N. (1995). The Nature of Produced Nature. *Antipode* 27: 12–47.

Castree, N. (1997). Nature, Economy, and the Cultural Politics of Theory: The 'War against the Seals' in the Bering Sea, 1980–1911. *Geoforum*, 28(1): 1–20.

Castree, N. (2000). The Production of Nature. In E. Sheppard and T. Barnes (eds.), *A Companion to Economic Geography*. Oxford: Blackwell.

Demeritt, D. (1996). Social Theory and the Reconstruction of Science and Geography. In the *Transactions of the Institute of British Geographers* 21: 484–503.

Deitz, F. and van der Straaten. J. (1995). Economic Theories and the Necessary Integration of Ecological Insights. In A. Dobson and P. Lucardie (eds.), *The Politics of Nature*. London: Routledge.

Goodman, D., Sorj, B., and Wilkinson, J. (1987). *From Farming to Biotechnology*. Oxford: Blackwell.

Goodman, D. and Redclift, M. (1991). *Refashioning Nature*. London: Routledge.

Harvey, D. (1996). *Justice, Nature and the Geography of Difference*. Oxford: Blackwell.

Hayward, T. (1995). *Ecological Thought*. Cambridge: Polity Press.

Henderson, G. (1998). Nature and Fictitious Capital. In *Antipode* 30: 73–118.

Katz, C. (1998). Whose Nature, Whose Culture? In B. Braun and N. Castree (eds.), *Remaking Reality*. London: Routledge.

Kautsky, K. (1899) [1989]. *The Agrarian Question*. London: Swan Books.

Kloppenburg, J. (1988). *First The Seed*. Cambridge: Cambridge University Press.

Kneen, B. (1999). *Farmaggedon*. Gabriola Island: New Society Publishers.

Mann, S. (1990) *Agrarian Capitalism in Theory and Practice*. Chapel Hill: University of North Carolina Press.

Mann, S. and Dickinson, J. (1978). Obstacles to the Development of a Capitalist Agriculture. *Journal of Peasant Studies* 5: 466–81.

Mannion, A. M. (1992). Biotechnology and Genetic Engineering: New Environmental Issues. In A. M. Mannion and S. Bowlby (eds.), *Environmental Issues in the 1990s*. Chichester: Wiley.

Plumwood, V. (1994). *Feminism and the Mastery of Nature*. London: Routledge.

Rifkin, J. (1998). *The Biotech Century*. New York: Victor Gollancz.

Shiva, V. (1993). *Monocultures of The Mind*. Penang: Third World Network.

Smith, N. (1984). *Uneven Development: Nature, Capital and the Production of Space*. Oxford: Blackwell.

Smith, N. (1996). The Production of Nature. In G. Robertson et al. (eds.), *Future Natural*. London: Routledge.

Smith, N. (1998). Nature at the Millennium: Production and Re-enchantment. In B. Braun and N. Castree (eds.), *Remaking Reality*. London: Routledge.

Soper, K. (1991). Greening Prometheus: Marxism and Ecology. In P. Osborne (ed.), *Socialism and the Limits of Liberalism*. London: Verso.

Teitel, M. and Wilson, K. (1999). *Genetically Engineered Food*. Rochester: Park Street Press.

Thrift, N. and Olds, K. (1996). Refiguring the Economic in Economic Geography. *Progress in Human Geography* 20: 311–37.

Chapter 11

Dissolving Dualisms: Actor-networks and the Reimagination of Nature

Noel Castree and Tom MacMillan

Thinking Beyond Binaries

The distinction between society and nature is so familiar and fundamental as to seem unquestionable. Profoundly ingrained in Western culture, it is a distinction which not only organizes the imaginations of ordinary people but one which has for decades organized the academic division of labor in schools and universities. Hence, those things which are deemed nonsocial have long been the subject of 'natural science' research and teaching, while putatively nonnatural entities are the preserve of the 'social sciences.' Located in the middle ground between this macrodisciplinary distinction, geography, since its foundation as a subject in the late nineteenth century, has been touted as the 'bridging science' which would study human–nature interactions (Mackinder, 1887). Over the course of the twentieth century, geography as the study of human–nature relations underwent several paradigmatic shifts, from the 'environmental determinism' of the 1910s (e.g. Semple, 1911) through the 'possibilist' positions of the 1930s (e.g. Febvre, 1932) to the post-1950 recognition that humans seemed to be transforming nature more than nature was affecting humans (e.g. Thomas, 1956). Whatever position was taken, though, throughout the twentieth century geography maintained in microcosm the wider academic and lay separation between the human and the natural. 'Physical geographers' were expected to study the natural environment and 'human geographers' were expected to investigate the spatial organization of people's activities. Though several geographers worked on the human–physical 'interface,' few fundamentally challenged the belief that the natural and the social were ontologically different and distinct.

However, in the last few years this has (at least seemingly) started to change. As the essays in this book testify, several 'critical' human geographers and those working in related fields[1] have recently sought to "trespass over . . . the categorical cordon that has marked off 'the non-human world' and the grounds for understanding it" (Whatmore, 1999a: 23). In an exciting and disconcerting set of arguments, these geographers have claimed that nature is not at all – or not simply – 'natural' but in fact *a human construction*. Whereas in the past, geographers and others have imagined a world in which nature was the *antithesis* of society, a newer generation of commentators has argued that nature is social through and through. In the words of Neil Smith (1984: 30), one of the earliest of these commentators, "nature is nothing if it is not social." Crudely speaking, there have been two basic versions of this 'social constructionist' argument (Whatmore, 1999b). The first claims that we can only know nature through culturally specific systems of meaning and signification, such that nature cannot be understood by people 'in-and-of-itself.' This is not at all to deny the reality of the things we routinely call 'natural.' What it is to say, though, is that human representations of those things – in the form of words, concepts, and explanations – are not simply 'mirrors of nature.' Rather, they are seen as cultural products freighted with numerous biases, assumptions, and prejudices (see Braun and Wainwright's chapter in this volume). Moreover, on this argument even the supposed guardians of factually derived truths about nature – the natural sciences (including much physical geography) – cannot step outside culture to comprehend nature 'as it really is' (Demeritt, 1998). The second version of the 'social construction of nature' argument takes a more economic and less cultural focus. In this version the thesis is that nature is increasingly being reconstituted materially, even down to the atomic level (think of genetically modified organisms), as industry-led science and technology exert increasing control over it. Here, then, nature is seen as being physically 'produced' to order in the pursuit of money and profits (see Castree's chapter 10, above, on capitalism and Marxism). In both its cultural and economic permutations, the constructionist line is that nature is not only humanly fabricated at some level but also a tool or effect of power. For the ability to define nature's 'truths' or to alter it physically can, it is argued, help secure relations of cultural and economic dominance in society.

So far so good. The social constructionist arguments, it seems to us, have achieved two important things. First, they have shown the intellectual incoherence of imagining nature as essentially nonsocial. Secondly, they have also provided the political weaponry to attack the dubious invocation of 'nature' as a separate domain to which appeal can be made to legitimate existing or new economic, social, and ecological arrangements. Even today, for instance, much of the environmental movement argues that we need to 'get back to nature' (see, for example, McKibben, 1989), as if nature and society could be separated. Likewise, and despite the apparent differences, 'life-science' companies such as Monsanto justify their ventures in genetic engineering on the grounds that nature (again invoked as ontologically distinct) has 'inherent limitations.' By undermining political projects predicated on this kind of 'separate spheres' logic, the social constructionists have created space for a different kind of nature politics. Not surprisingly, several critics argue that the social constructionists are willfully undermining the truth-claims of natural science or else scuppering green politics with their denial that natural entities have 'intrinsic' value or rights (see, for example, Gross and Levitt, 1994; Soulé and Lease, 1995). However, while a few 'full-blooded' constructionists may indeed be guilty in this regard, most arguably take a moderate line that is not necessarily antithetical to science or the environmental movement.

In light of these comments, it may be thought that our purpose in this chapter is to defend the social constructionist position against the unsupportable versions of 'natural realism' that to this day animate both geographical and everyday imaginations. But that is not, in fact, our aim. While others in this book describe, explain and defend social constructionist arguments in some detail, our intentions here are rather more subversive. For we want to claim that *both* social constructionists and those natural realists they criticize actually have something in common. That common something *is an inability to imagine human–natural relations in a nondichotomous way.* Though social constructionists *seem* to breach the social–natural divide which organizes academic and lay thinking, they arguably go on to *reinstall it* at another level. What we mean is that bringing nature within the domain of the social simply shifts the causal and ontological arrows from one 'side' of the social–natural dichotomy to the other. The dichotomy itself arguably remains intact. This is true even in the most complex of social constructionist positions. Consider, for example, the Marxist position discussed in chapter 10 by Noel Castree. As Castree shows, Marxist geographers such as Neil Smith argue that society and nature exist in a dynamic, two-way relationship (or 'dialectic') in which societies remake nature but nature, in turn, remakes society. Though this argument appears to transcend the human–nature divide, it is arguably just a sophisticated way of making the divide more permeable – swapping the awkward 'either/or' choice for a 'both/and' compromise.

We are thus faced with two key questions. How can we 'think beyond' the nature–society dualism? And why might it be important to do so? In this chapter we offer an answer to both questions by explaining and evaluating a new and exciting body of ideas known as 'actor-network theory' (ANT). ANT has diverse origins, but is particularly associated with a group of sociologists and anthropologists of science (such as Michel Callon, Bruno Latour, and John Law). In geography, it is currently being embraced with enthusiasm by a cohort of researchers dissatisfied with what they see as the impasse between social constructionists and natural realists. This cohort – dominated by UK-based geographers like Nick Bingham, Jonathan Murdoch, Lorraine Thorne, and Sarah Whatmore – is now trying to find conceptual, empirical, and political ways to see the world as hybrid, chimeric, complex, and entangled. In the next section we summarize ANT and show how it reconfigures the geographical imagination. Many readers confronting these ideas for the first time will, we hope, find ANT challenging and disconcerting. In the rest of the chapter we evaluate the logic and usefulness of actor-network thinking. In particular, we seek to follow through the implications of ANT for the kind of social constructionist arguments critically elaborated in the other chapters of this book. We conclude that 'strong' versions of ANT are as problematic as they are useful and suggest the need for a 'weak' version of ANT that does not completely undermine the strengths of existing social constructionist arguments.

Embracing Imbroglios

ANT is a set of overlapping propositions intended to guide thinking and research about human–nature relations (it is what Latour (in Latour and Crawford, 1993: 250) calls an "infralanguage" rather than a 'theory' in the traditional sense). As will be seen later in the chapter, it has major implications for political struggles over those relations. For ANT's geographical advocates, the problems with most past and present disciplinary work on nature – of the constructionist *and* realist kind – are fourfold, revolving around binarism, asymmetry, an impoverished conception of actors/action, and a centered understanding of power. Let's take each in turn.

   i) Binarism refers to the above-mentioned habit of understanding the world in terms of conceptual dichotomies. Against the nature–society dichotomy characteristic of 'modern' geographical thought, ANT argues for an 'amodern' ontology in which we recognize the 'hybrids' or 'quasi-objects' that litter the world we inhabit. As Rebecca Roberts (1995, p. 673) puts it, in a world where pig livers are implanted in humans and plastic may soon grow on trees, "such hybrids are ubiquitous rather than rare – as [the] modern [imagination] . . . would have us believe." This ontology of not-quite-natural, not-quite-social entities rejects the pure transcendences of binarist thinking and urges us to see them as *outcomes* that illicitly compartmentalize a messy, impure, heterogenous world. Secondly, this rejection of ontological binarism is intended as an encouragement to think *relationally* in terms of associations rather than separations. Where conventional, nonrelational ontologies lead us to identify "ontological primitives" (Fuller, 1994: 746), ANT argues that things (including humans) are only definable *in relation to* other things.

   This leads, thirdly, to the *network* as a favored metaphor for conceptualizing socionatural imbrications. Emerging from work by Latour and others on how scientific claims about nature are extended beyond the laboratory, the notion of networks points towards chains of connection between putatively 'social' and 'natural' entities. These networks are multiple and "relentlessly heterogenous" (Murdoch, 1997a: 745), typically involving the unique alignment of humans,

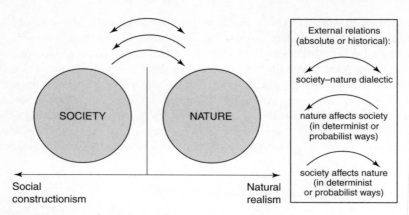

Figure 11.1: Dualistic approaches to nature and society

machines, animals, inscription devices, and other materials in relations which vary in stability, time–space extension and time–space form. For actor-network theorists, they describe a world far richer than the society–nature dichotomy can allow because they stitch back together the socionatural imbroglios that dichotomy has rent asunder.

In turn, this relational, network ontology yields a set of theoretical advantages – and this is the fourth aspect of ANT's rejection of the nature–society binarism. Where dichotomous thinking ultimately resorts to one or other pole (society or nature) as explanatory, ANT refuses to look for causes lying *outside* socionatural networks (an 'ostensive' approach: Latour, 1986). Moreover, it refuses the presumption that *different* networks are driven by the *same* (social or natural) general processes or factors. Instead, the processes determining the constituents, stability and reach of a particular network are deemed to be *internal* to it and, at some level, to involve all the network entities (a 'performative' approach: ibid.). Far from appealing to causal forces separate from and prior to networks (which explain but do not themselves need explaining), it is only *after* each network has been carefully described that explanation can emerge. As Latour (1991: 129) puts it, "the explanation emerges once the description is saturated". Consequently, ANT is suspicious of general theories, supposedly applicable to many different situations, which offer systemic explanations grounded in ostensibly social or natural imperatives. The upshot, in a cheeky and subversive move, is that actor-network theorists see the society–nature dualism as a *post hoc* attempt by analysts to oversimplify complexity by attributing responsibility for network construction to one or other set of entities (see figure 11.1).

ii) In light of this critique of dualism, the actor-network principle of symmetry becomes easy to understand. As ANT advocates in geography are right to point out, binarist thinking ultimately forces the analyst to make a choice: to prioritize one or other domain or actor on ontological, causal, or normative grounds. For instance, we've already seen how the social constructionist desire to resist versions of natural realism has inadvertently led to a certain asymmetry in that the natural is seen as merely a construct of the social – "a substrate for the external imposition of arbitrary . . . [social] form" (Ingold, 1993: 37). The corollary is an anthropocentrism in which, ultimately, nature can only be understood and valued in human (*sic*) terms. Against this, ANT proponents like Whatmore, Thorne, Murdoch, and Bingham argue for a more symmetrical 'greening' of human geography in which nature is re-cognized not on ecocentric grounds (since this is the mirror opposite of anthropocentrism and therefore also asymmetrical) but on a hybrid basis. That is, precisely because the social and the natural are *co-constitutive* within myriad networks, a symmetrical perspective is the only one that is viable. Attending to the ontological, causal, and moral particularities of natural entities is, from this perspective, possible and necessary *without* reverting to the notion that nature is, should or could be a/nonsocial (Whatmore, 1997; Whatmore and Thorne, 1998).

iii) If ANT reveals the binarism and asymmetry of many geographical approaches to nature, it also questions the notions of actors and action which, it is claimed, are built into most of these approaches. According to Bingham (1996: 647) and Whatmore (1999a), these approaches routinely make the following dubious assumptions: that actors' capacities to act are defined by their *intrinsic* powers and liabilities; that the significant actors are *human*; and that action is associated with *intentionality* and *linguistic competence* (logocentrism). Against these impoverished views of actors and action, ANT argues that "every actor is also a network" (Bingham), that actors are social *and* natural (or, more properly, 'socionatural'), and that action – as Callon's (1986) oft-cited study of scallops in St. Brieuc Bay shows – does not necessarily require speech or intentionality (as we normally understand it). As geographers Laurier and Philo (1999: 1060) put it, "The nonhumans are in effect 'levelled up' to the status of humans, and the humans are 'levelled down' to the status of nonhumans." Accordingly, ANT sometimes prefers the term 'actant' to 'actor.' This evokes the idea that "agency is a relational effect generated by . . . interacting components whose activity is constituted in the networks of which they form a part" (Whatmore, 1999a 28) – hence the couplet 'actor-network.' Moreover, it implies that the capacities of an actant will *vary* according to its place within given networks. In short, geography's ANT advocates call for a conception of action and actors which is multiple, contingent, and non-essentialist.

iv) The final main challenge of ANT to existing approaches to society–nature relations in geography and beyond relates to the question of power. Whatever their substantive differences, the various constructionist attempts to bring nature 'back in' to critical human geography are seen to have a conception of power which is anthropomorphic and overly centered. In other words, power is seen to be 'held' and projected by particular social actors or to reside within a distinct social system (like 'capitalism' or 'culture'). As a result, nature is all-too-easily reduced to an *effect* of power in recent green constructionist writings in geography – or so Whatmore and others argue. In challenging this restrictive notion of power (in which the natural is discounted), the champions of ANT insist that power is a *shared* capacity – involving myriad natural actants as much as social ones – which is thoroughly *decentered* in different networks. In Murdoch's (1995: 748) words, "those who are powerful are not those who 'hold' power but . . . those able to enrol, convince, and enlist others on terms which allow the initial actors to 'represent' the others." According to ANT's exponents, to see power as a wholly human attribute which is concentrated rather than dispersed is, therefore, to be deceived. It is also to overstate the power of power. Once power is seen as a relational achievement – not a monopolizable capacity radiating from a single center or social system – then it becomes possible to identify multiple points (neither social nor natural but both simultaneously) at which network stability can be contested.

To summarize, ANT poses a major challenge to existing attempts in geography and elsewhere to theorize human–nature relations. ANT, in effect, encourages us to imagine the unimaginable by doing away with dualistic, categorical thinking (figure 11.2). But how does the nature–society nexus look in practice when one uses ANT to analyze real-life situations? What does a politics of nature look like when one views the world in ANT terms? And how, finally, are we to evaluate ANT's subversive approach to conceptualizing, studying, and agitating politically over social–natural relations? The rest of the chapter addresses each question in turn and, in so doing, seeks to show both the importance and limitations of actor-network ideas about socionatural relations.

Practicing Hybridity

So wide-ranging are the insights of ANT that it can be used to make sense of a vast array of environmental practices. Here we focus on a recent study by the British geographers Sally Eden, Sylvia Tunstall, and Susan Tapsell (2000). Eden et al. use ANT to describe a project to make a stretch of the river Cole, in southern England, 'more natural.' This so-called 'river restoration' project saw a 2km section of the Cole returned to a 'natural,' meandering flow path during the mid-1990s. A group called the River Restoration Project (RRP) orchestrated the funding, planning, and engineering that this entailed. Using Eden et al.'s analysis, we can make sense of the restoration of the Cole under the four headings from the previous section, as follows.

i) At first sight the practice of river restoration is easily explained. A natural

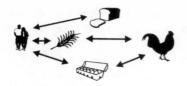

Short network, few actants, e.g. an organic family farm

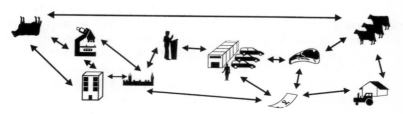

Complex network, many actants, e.g. BSE in the UK

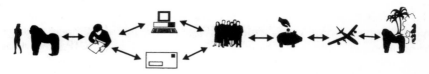

Long network, many actants, e.g. releasing a captive animal into its 'natural' habitat

Key:
Icon - actant
◄──► two-way relationship

N.B.
- 'natural' and 'social' entities are constantly interacting and co-constituting
- causality and power are complex, not reducible to sides of a dualism

Figure 11.2: ANT and the reimagination of nature and society

realist (of a 'deep' or 'shallow' green kind) might approvingly argue, for instance, that river restoration is all about getting 'back to nature,' while a social constructionist might conversely claim that it is about certain social actors changing rivers to conform with their culturally produced image of what nature is supposed to look like (here, then, the claim is that a 'fake nature' is being restored). ANT, by contrast, does not see the practice of river restoration in these dualistic terms. This is why Eden et al. try to elucidate the myriad 'translations' that crosscut the social/natural binary, while highlighting the illicit 'purification' that enables many analysts to incorrectly think that river restoration is either a social *or* natural phenomenon. As before, there are four elements to this.

First, the identity of the river Cole as 'social' or 'natural' is established as an *outcome* of the restoration process, so there can be no question of predetermining whether the restored Cole would be one *or* other in the manner of the environmental realists or social constructionists. The restoration process was predominantly one of *hybridity* involving multiple, indissoluble links between the RRP, the Cole, machinery used to cut new meanders, maps and calculations designed to persuade the National Rivers Authority (the NRA, which regulates river use in the UK) that restoration was feasible, and so on. But successfully enrolling these 'actants' involved coordinating their diverse interests and capacities, which in turn entailed moments of 'strategic purification.' Thus the 'human' actors in the process tended to offer binarist accounts of their actions. For instance, Eden et al. show that the RRP represented the restored river to the NRA as controlled and nonnatural, thus aligning restoration with the NRA's legal responsibility for active flood management.

Second, the river Cole was defined and remade only *in relation* to other actors, such as the RRP, the NRA, or the maps and river flow calculations that passed between them. The restoration project hinged on forging new relationships between these actors, leading, it was hoped, to their eventual transformation – physical for the Cole, institutional for the RRP. The vision plan developed prior to the act of restoration – essentially a map of the proposed changes – was crucial to this process, setting out new associations between the river, the RRP, the construction contractors who would physically alter the Cole, and many others. Third, however, contrary to its name, the plan was much more than just a vision – it was its physical inscription on actual pieces of paper that made it a key actor in building this new *network*. The RRP translated the river Cole, the contractors, vast amounts of computerized data, and distant funding bodies into this single inscription device, which was sufficiently stable and movable to act as a common linkage point for the different actors in the new network. The NRA could thus approve the plan in committee and the contractors could take it with them to the construction site, ensuring that each actant was enrolled in the same project.

According to ANT, it is only by tracing this network that we can explain the restoration process. So, fourth, restoration was not caused by some prior external factor, but by the actual relations between the changing actors *within* the network. This means that there was no unitary cause of the restoration as an event, settling on one or other side of a binary ontology, but many different associations that wove it together as a process. In fact, there is not even a single river or restoration process to be explained, since the processes of translation and purification constantly remake the entire actor-network. To look 'outside' this network for causes, in either 'society' or 'nature,' is to admit that crucial parts of it have escaped analysis.

ii) So far we have focused on the hybridity of the restoration process and of the river that was restored, and how the processes of translation and purification remake them and define them dubiously as social *or* natural. However, ANT's principle of symmetry rules that the same criteria must apply to all actors. We cannot claim that the restored river is hybrid and mutable, *and* assume from the start that the RRP was the social driving force behind the whole network.

On one side, therefore, Eden et al. insist that the RRP was also hybrid: a network as well as an actor. The group was formally launched in 1992, but it was not conjured out of social thin air. It began as a network linking together several delegates who had met at a conference two years earlier. Once the conference had ended, their common interest in alternative river engineering would have vanished had they not been able to act on each other at a distance via documents (e.g. plans) and other devices that translated actual rivers and engineering works into manageable, intelligible forms, culminating in a feasibility study of river restoration. So, just as the river was not asocial prior to restoration, nor was the RRP nonnatural. The RRP was not just an institution or a group of individuals – it was this hybrid network of people, rivers, and other things.

On the other side, like the river Cole, the RRP was also remade during the restoration process. Once the Cole had been selected as a suitable site for restoration, a subcommittee called the Cole Working Group (CWG) was established. As with the river, the CWG/RRP's vision plan was a crucial site of translation and moment of transformation for the group itself. By ascribing the RRP authorship, the plan set out the group's leading part in the proposed project. As the other actors in the network also took on their ascribed roles, the RRP found itself in authoritative new relationships with construction contractors, funding bodies, and of course the river Cole. This success saw it change markedly, with increased offers of funding and a raised budget, a shift to a more advisory role in restoration, and a name-change to the River Restoration Centre.

iii) When it comes to agency, Eden et al.'s account of river restoration seems paradoxical: at one moment it claims that causes are relational and that networks are made up by (and make up) diverse actors; at another, it suggests that the RRP was the prime mover through its network-building 'vision plan.' Two points are important here. First, in ANT, actors only emerge after the event. The RRP only became the key agent as the vision plan, which ascribed it that authorship, enrolled the other actors. The proposal's success and the RRP's agency rested on all the other actors complying with the plan, as opposed to any alternative, and making their envisaged roles reality. Through the plan, the hybrid RRP was remade as a coherent social actor and the driving force in restoration. As we have seen, this purified representation of the RRP as *the* agent played an important part in transforming its subsequent aims, name, and budget.

Second, unsurprisingly, the other actors have only conformed approximately to the 'vision plan'. Most prominently, perhaps, the river itself acted in an unforeseen way, requiring construction contractors to return to the site a year after the main earth-moving work was complete. The plan had instructed the contractors to dig new meander bends with 45-degree slope angles, on the assumption that the river would erode the outer banks into a 'natural' profile. The clay in the banks refused to be eroded, however, so the contractors were re-enrolled to cut a new, vertical profile, in line with the plan's objective. Another unanticipated actor came in the form of a tax recalculation in 1995, allowing the RRB to add an extra set of excavations to the original design. In sum, the RRB's agency rested first on the degree to which other actors also conformed to the plan it had authored, and second, on the persistence of the network after the initial phase of construction, allowing any unruly actants to be re-enrolled.

iv) Finally, just as agency was diffused throughout the changing network of river restoration, so power was shared between the different actants. Of course, some emerge as more powerful than others, via the same processes of translation, enrollment, and purification. The point is not that there is no way to distinguish power differentials, just that we cannot assume what these differentials will be from the start. For ANT, power is an effect of successfully enrolling and representing other actors.

In this case, the RRP was certainly powerful, since it 'spoke for' a large number of other actors. The vision plan and other inscription devices may have been crucial to this process of representation, but insofar as they attributed their authorship to the RRP it was the latter that was powerful. The plan began as a work of fantasy, but gradually came to represent reality. Since the Cole acted more or less as the RRP predicted, for instance, the group became able to speak on the river's behalf to other actors. As Eden et al. (p. 268) point out, this silenced the river itself: "the Cole is represented as 'weak' (having 'low stream power' in terms of energy per cross-sectional area), so that the RRP acts 'for' it by constructing in weeks meanders that the river could only have cut over decades." Similarly, the RRP enrolled organizations such as the NRA and spoke on their behalf to others actors, such as scientists or local residents.

By the same token, though, the RRP was simultaneously represented by other actors, since power is a relational property that cannot be monopolized. The most obvious example is the vision plan itself, which represented the RRP as its author – as *the real* representer (figure 11.3). Similarly the NRA enrolled the RRP into its own projects, justifying its funding expenditures with the RRP's success stories. More subtly, the Cole also spoke for the RRP's success, both directly to the visitors who walked along the new meanders, and through inscription devices such as before-and-after photographs.

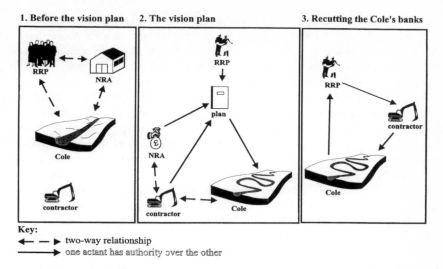

Figure 11.3: How the actants and power relations between them change through the process of 'restoring' the river Cole

The Politics of Impurity

The case of the Cole's restoration demonstrates how ANT's counterintuitive concepts allow us to analyze current environmental practices in a new way. Likewise, ANT offers a fundamental challenge to the assumptions underpinning the broad spectrum of contemporary political views about nature. From an ANT perspective, most shades of political thinking about nature are too 'pure' insofar as they take the side either of nature or society. For instance, despite their seeming political differences, the radical 'deep green' organization Earth First! and the multinational biotechnology company Monsanto actually have something in common: namely, both seek to justify their actions by reference to 'nature in itself.' Though Earth First! opposes the kind of science-led 'tampering' with nature advocated by Monsanto, both organizations are ultimately natural realists: Earth First! wants to reverse current patterns of production and consumption and 'get back to nature,' while Monsanto points to nature's 'inherent flaws' as a way of legitimizing genetic modification. As noted in the introduction to this chapter, the value of the social constructionist argument is to question actions grounded in any appeal to a putatively external, nonsocial nature. But, from an ANT perspective, the problem with a politics of nature founded on social constructionist ideas is that it's as pure or one-sided as the natural realist politics it opposes. For, in the constructionist argument, political programs designed to protect or exploit nature can only ever be justified in human terms – nature politics becomes no more than a process of determining what kind of nature should be fashioned to satisfy whose ends. Consequently, natural entities have no voice: they are erased from the political landscape or, at best, spoken for by social actors.

So much for ANT's critique of the politics of purity – does it have a political agenda of its own? We can examine the political strategy, subjectivity, and geography of impurity by revisiting three of ANT's transgressions. First, and most importantly here, because ANT dissolves any *a priori* division of society from nature it requires a politics attuned to *all* the actors in given socionatural networks. Because the fate of any one actant in a particular network is so intimately bound up with that of others, ANT suggests the necessity for a hybrid politics in which the fate of humans, machines, organisms, plants, animals, and so on are considered *simultaneously* – and on a case by case basis. Moreover, since human and nonhuman actants are considered ontologically equivalent here, a hybrid politics of nature should be neither anthropocentric nor ecocentric: it would refuse to serve the interests of one or other actor in a network.

What or who would be the 'subject' of this impure political strategy? As we have seen, ANT unravels the human–nonhuman, self–other and indeed sub-ject–object binaries that are so crucial to most nature politics. For example, the nature-first politics favored by moderate and deep greens extends liberal conceptions of rights – centered on an autonomous human self – to more or less exclusive groups of nonhumans, embracing so-called 'charismatic mega-fauna' such as elephants, or even all sentient beings. As Whatmore (1997) points out, ANT rejects this individualistic subjectivity altogether, in favor of a relational ethics and politics that does not discriminate on such arbitrary grounds. As we saw in the previous section, the 'individual' agent is a network effect, and therefore cannot be the subject of ANT's politics. Instead of prioritizing one 'actor' or 'group' over another, the politics of impurity highlights their ethical connectivity and the impossibility of discrete political subjects.

Politics is always geographical, and the politics of impurity is no exception. As the river restoration case shows, time and again 'nature' is identified with certain spaces – such as 'rural' spaces (as the River Cole was supposed to be), zones of 'wilderness,' and formally designated 'nature reserves.' Typically, it is these spaces that become foci for environmental politics and action – by governments, nongovernmental organizations, new social movements, and the like. Hence, to offer just one example, Clayoquot Sound in western Canada has recently been designated a World Heritage Site by the United Nations because of its 'special' natural attributes. Natural realists from Greenpeace to the Global Environmental Facility might approve of this and other spatially targeted attempts to 'save nature,' while social constructionists might claim that the nature being saved is but an imaginary ideal (Braun, 1997). But from an ANT perspective, this equation of 'nature' with certain delimited geographical territories where environmental politics can focus many of its energies is problematic: for these spaces are neither wholly natural nor merely zones where certain social actors impose their culturally specific ideas of what nature is supposed to be (see Zimmerer, 2000).

For instance, Clayoquot Sound is not merely home to rare old-growth trees but a social landscape occupied for thousands of years by Nuu-chah-nulth native peoples. A politics of timber preservation thus illicitly purifies and simplifies Clayoquot, rendering the native voice mute and denying the dense imbrications of native practices, trees, berries, salmon, roots, bears, and birds. At the same time, by designating Clayoquot a space of nature, the implication is that *other* spaces – of the city, of heavy industry, of agriculture, of the home, and so on – are 'unnatural' and therefore beyond the point where environmental politics applies. But from an ANT perspective, these spaces are just as hybrid and real as are areas like Clayoquot. Pigeons in London's Trafalgar Square, domestic animals, microbes in hospital petri dishes: all these are also networked with humans, machines, and other actants. Accordingly, for actor-network theorists *all* forms of political thinking and action must have an environmental dimension, for the spaces of nature cannot be confined to a few fast-shrinking areas (Latour, 1998).

Evaluations and Discriminations: Modalities of ANT

Throughout this essay we've shown how actor-network thinking calls into question the seemingly opposed worldviews of natural realism and social constructionism. ANT encourages us to imagine a world where socionatural relations are multiple, messy and complex. Like most of the authors in this book, we're very sympathetic to the actor-network critique of 'nature-in-itself' thought and politics. However, despite being persuaded by the core claims of ANT, we remain uneasy about its implications for social-construction-of-nature arguments. For it seems to us that a 'strong' version of ANT – which is precisely what we've been outlining in this chapter – too readily throws out some of the valuable elements of social constructionist thinking. This is apparent at several levels.

First, ontologically there is "the problem of installing a great *indifference* between the countless things of world . . . which arises when they end up being portrayed as potentially *all the same*" (Laurier and Philo, 1999: 1016). In other words, "the flattening process [of ANT] leads to an obscuring of *differences* between different . . . 'noun chunks' of reality" (p. 1014). Second, there is a further ontological problem arising from the assumption that each actor-network is unique and qualitatively distinct. Though actor-networks are unlikely ever to be similar in every detail, what if the processes constituted by, and constituting, otherwise different actor-networks happen to be the same? Does this possibility not create space for a theory which can abstract from differences in order to identify general processes (economic, cultural, etc.) of 'socio-nature'? Or does inquiry into socionatural networks have to start afresh each and every time? Third, there is a theoretical problem. Arguably, there is, in strong versions of ANT, a potential underemphasis on the explanation of networks. As Murdoch (1997a: 750) asks, "Can . . . we ever do anything more than *describe*, in prosaic fashion, the dangerous imbroglios that enmesh us?" Furthermore, even when explanations are offered – once network description is complete – it is unclear what form it takes. Since full-blooded versions of ANT see networks as 'overdetermined' – such that 'determining' actors/processes and 'determined' actors/processes cannot be readily distinguished – "one can justly ask whether such . . . florescence obviates the need for any theoretical commitment at all, that is to say, the need for any weighting of social forces . . . with systematic logic or causal processes" (Walker, 1997: 273).

Finally, there is a political problem. Though ANT offers a powerful critique of all dualistic forms of nature-society thinking it threatens to remain strangely agnostic about the actor-networks it seeks to describe and explain. Perhaps we should, as Murdoch (1997a: 750) recommends, "ask whether a focus on the performative outcomes of network formation can be brought to bear on the [critical] . . . social scientific concerns of . . . equality and injustice, concerns which have normally been associated with the *responsibilities* of human institutions." Though it may well be liberating to reveal the myriad 'nonhuman' actants obscured by social constructionist arguments, it will count for little if those actants are merely described in their subjugation to others. That is, geographical advocates of a strong ANT agenda risk ignoring the possibility that some actants 'marshall' the power of many others and, in so doing, limit the latter's agency and circumscribe their existence (something Eden et al., to their credit, try to show).

In light of these several problems, it is possible to conceive of a 'weaker' version of ANT which can learn something from social constructionist approaches to nature even as it censures those approaches in the four ways discussed earlier in the chapter. This weaker version of ANT would thus remain critical of binarist thinking, of asymmetry, of limited conceptions of agency and of centered conceptions of power. However, at the same time, it would concede the following points: namely, that many actor-networks are driven by similar processes, notwithstanding their other differences; that these processes are social and natural but not in equal measure, since it is the 'social' relations that are often disproportionately directive; that agents, while social, natural, and relational, vary greatly in their powers to influence others; that power, while dispersed, can be directed by some (namely, specific 'social' actors) more than others; and that a politics of nature attuned to the needs and rights of both human and natural entities must ultimately be orchestrated through putatively 'social' actors. By splitting the difference between ANT and social constructionism in this way, geographers would not just describe existing networks, but could also refresh their own struggles to build a more imaginative, just and inclusive socioecological future.

Note

1   In particular, environmental anthropology, history and sociology, and critical science studies: see Milton (1993), Worster (1988), Hannigan (1995), and Hess (1997) respectively.

Further Reading

Whatmore (1999b) provides an elementary introduction to social construction of nature arguments and to ANT, while Whatmore (1999b) offers a more advanced discussion. Murdoch's (1997a; 1997b) essays on ANT are a particularly lucid but challenging read. For more critical discussions of ANT read Laurier and Philo (1999) and Lee and Brown (1994).

References

Bingham, N. (1996). Object-ions: From Technological Determinism Towards Geographies of Relations. *Environment and Planning D: Society and Space*, 14: 635–57.
Braun, B. (1997). Buried Epistemologies: The Politics of Nature in (Post)Colonial British Columbia. *Annals of the Association of American Geographers*, 87: 3–31.
Callon, M. (1986). Some Elements in a Sociology of Translation. In J. Law (ed.), *Power, Action, Belief.* London: Routledge, 19–34.
Demeritt, D. (1998). Science, Social Constructivism and Nature. In B. Braun and N. Castree (eds.), *Remaking Reality*. London: Routledge, 173–93.
Eden, S., Tunstall, S., and Tapsell, S. (2000). Translating Nature: River Restoration as Nature-Culture. *Environment and Planning D: Society and Space*, 18: 257–73.
Febvre, L. (1932). *A Geographical Introduction to History*. London: Keegan Paul.
Fuller, S. (1994). Making Agency Count. *American Behavioral Scientist*, 37: 741–53.
Hannigan, J. (1995). *Environmental Sociology*. London: Routledge.
Ingold, T. (1993). Globes and Spheres. In K. Milton (ed.), *Environmentalism: The View from Anthropology*. London: Routledge, 3–42.
Latour, B. (1986). Visualisation and Cognition: Thinking with Eyes and Hands. In H. Kuklick and E. Long (eds.) *Knowledge and Society*. London: JAI Press, 1–41.

Latour, B. (1991). Technology is Society Made Durable. In J. Law (ed.), *A Sociology of Monsters*. London: Routledge, 103–32.

Latour, B. (1998). To Modernise or Ecologise? In B. Braun and N. Castree (eds.), *Remaking Reality*. London: Routledge: 221–42.

Latour, B. and Crawford, T. (1993). An Interview with Latour. *Configurations*, 2: 247–69.

Laurier, E. and Philo, C. (1999). X-morphizing: A Review Essay of *Aramis*. *Environment and Planning A*,31: 1047–73

Lee, N. and Brown, S. (1994). Otherness and the Actor-Network. *American Behavioral Scientist*, 37: 762–90.

Mackinder, H. (1887). On the Scope and Methods of Geography. *Proceedings of the Royal Geographical Society*, 9: 141–60.

McKibben, R. (1989). *The End of Nature*. New York: Anchor Books.

Milton, K. (ed.) (1993). *Environmentalism: The View From Anthropology*. London: Routledge.

Murdoch, J. (1995). Actor-networks and the Evolution of Economic Forms. *Environment and Planning A*, 27: 731–57.

Murdoch, J. (1997a). Inhuman/Nonhuman/Human. *Environment and Planning D: Society and Space*, 15: 731–56.

Murdoch, J. (1997b). Towards a Geography of Heterogenous Associations. *Progress in Human Geography*, 21: 321–37.

Roberts, R. (1995). Taking Nature–Culture Hybrids Seriously. *Environment and Planning A*, 27: 673–82.

Semple, E. (1911). *Influences of Geographic Environment*. New York: H. Hold.

Smith, N. (1984). *Uneven Development*. Oxford: Blackwell.

Soulé, M. and Lease, G. (eds.) (1995). *Reinventing Nature?* Washington, DC: Island Press.

Thomas, R. (ed.) (1956). *Man's Role in Changing the Face of the Earth*. Chicago: Chicago University Press.

Walker, R. (1997). Fields of Dreams. In D. Goodman and M. Watts (eds.), *Globalising Food*. London and New York: Routledge, 273–86

Whatmore, S. (1997). Dissecting the Autonomous Self. *Environment and Planning D: Society and Space*, 15: 37–53.

Whatmore, S. (1999a). Hybrid Geographies. In D. Massey et al. (eds.), *Human Geography Today*. Cambridge: Polity, 22–40.

Whatmore, S. (1999b). Culture-Nature. In P. Cloke et al. (eds.), *Introducing Human Geography*. London: Arnold, 4–11.

Whatmore, S. and Thorne, L. (1998). Wild(er)ness: Reconfiguring the Geographies of Wildlife. *Transactions of the Institute of British Geographers*, 23: 435–54.

Worster, D. (ed.) (1988). *The Ends of the Earth: Perspectives on Modern Environmental History*. Cambridge: Cambridge University Press.

Zimmerer, K. (2000). The Reworking of Conservation Geographies: Nonequilibrium Landscapes and Nature–Society Hybrids. *Annals of the Association of American Geographers*, 90: 356–69.

Chapter 12

Solid Rock and Shifting Sands: The Moral Paradox of Saving a Socially Constructed Nature

James D. Proctor

I am strong, I am frail
I am love, I am fear
I'm emotion, I'm a wall
I belong, I don't fit
I am clumsy, I am grace,
I'm a paradox; aren't we all?
　　　　　Song lyrics © 1999,
　　　　　Jeannie Wolff-Gagné

This morning I got up and – creature of the Internet that I am – pointed my web browser to the Environmental News Network online (www.enn.com). Their headline daily news story (see figure 12.1), based on a paper just published in *Conservation Biology* (Ricciardi and Rasmussen, 1999), is titled 'Freshwater Species in Peril, Study Finds.' The first paragraph reads, "Some freshwater species in North America are becoming extinct at a rate as fast or faster than rain forest species, but their plight is largely ignored, according to a recent study out of Canada." This particular ENN story is but one of countless examples of the environmentalist call to action based on the compelling evidence of scientific fact and shared values.

Yet some interpretations of the social construction of nature thesis cast serious doubt on the moral logic – the rationale for why we should care – underlying this and similar environmental concerns. I agree and disagree, and hope to suggest why in this essay. I believe that taking social constructivism seriously necessitates a fundamental and radical philosophical revision of environmental ethics as it has generally been construed. Yet I would be gravely concerned if this revision were to rob the authors of the *Conservation Biology* article of their ability to speak about freshwater species extinction in North

Freshwater species in peril, study finds
Saturday, October 16, 1999
By Margot Higgins

Some freshwater species in North America are becoming extinct at a rate as fast or faster than rain forest species, but their plight is largely ignored, according to a recent study out of Canada.

"A silent mass extinction is occurring in our lakes and rivers," said Anthony Ricciardi of Dalhousie University in Halifax, lead author of the study. Nevertheless, few people are aware of the crisis.

Courtesy Illinois Natural History Survey

Freshwater species, like this endangered mussel, may be dying out as fast as rain forest species.

The study found that common freshwater species — from snails to fish to amphibians — are dying out five times faster than terrestrial animals and three times faster than marine mammals. Moreover, freshwater animals are dying out as fast as rain forest species, which are generally considered to be the most imperiled on species on Earth.

"Freshwater species have received little conservation attention," said Ricciardi. "Conservation campaigns tend to cater to the public fixation on furry, feathery critters. No one would think of using a mussel or crayfish as a conservation . . .

Figure 12.1:   Environmental News Network article, Oct. 16, 1999

America. As with perhaps most contributors to this volume, I am both convinced that people with environmental concerns must embrace social constructivism, and worried that this implies they must flip-flop from moral certainty to moral aphasia.

My argument will be that taking social constructivism seriously leads not so much to some moral flip-flop as a willingness to accept the paradoxical truths that nature is, so to speak, *both* autonomous and socially constructed, that our knowledge of nature speaks to *both* secure objectivity and slippery subjectivity, that our caring for nature is based on values fully arising from our particular and hence limited perspectives yet also fully aspiring to some claim of universality – that, in short, we must all found our environmental ethics in a dual spirit of confidence and humility, with one leg standing surely on solid rock and the other perched tentatively on shifting sands. Though these oppositional categories are themselves problematic (Proctor 1998a), they speak to certain inescapable tensions and ambiguities social constructivism poses for environmental ethics, which must be embraced if our environmental concerns are to be well grounded philosophically.

Environmental Ethics on Solid Rock

What is ethics? Formally, ethics involves analyzing the basis and justification of morality, that full assortment of significant should/should not, right/wrong, better/worse, and similar value-based distinctions we make as a part of living our lives. Another way to think of ethics is that it involves thinking about caring. We all care deeply about some things and not others, and we care or don't care about these things in particular ways and for particular reasons. Ethics involves sorting out why people care as they do and to what extent these ways of caring are philosophically justified. To me, thinking-about-caring does not privilege thinking over caring, because one must care about thinking-about-caring in order to even bother doing so! Caring is an exemplary gesture, and even those of us who wriggle at the word morality nonetheless care about something. The perspective of ethics simply reminds us to care carefully.

The history of humankind is strewn with examples – some merely unfortunate, others utterly cataclysmic for particular humans or nonhumans – of how dangerous unreflective morality can be. To believe that one is right, that one fights the good fight or the noble cause, puts one in a very dangerous position of potentially doing great harm in the name of good. Ethics, as I see it, is the way we stand on guard against such atrocities, knowing that the only way to do so is to care carefully; such is the spirit in which I here approach ethics. I will also in this essay use the term in the singular as a descriptive summary of a particular moral approach. To me, then, environmental ethics can imply analysis of the ways in which we care about nonhuman nature (and here and throughout I will roughly conflate environment with nonhuman nature, though their meanings can legitimately diverge), and it can also imply some attempt to encapsulate the prevailing moral bases upon which people care about nonhuman nature.

Environmental ethics is a relatively recent field of philosophical study, though it has grown by leaps and bounds from its humble origins dating roughly back to the 1970s; there are numerous anthologies one can consult to get a sense of the field (e.g., Botzler and Armstrong, 1998; Pojman, 1998). My focus here, however, will be less on the principal philosophical academic discussions in environmental ethics than on what we could call popular or conventional environmental ethics, the often implicit moral justifications invoked in contemporary environmental concern. What I propose to do in this essay, then, is focus on our taken-for-granted ways of caring about nature that surface in the context of these contemporary concerns.

Let us return, then, to the story that appeared on my screen this morning.

The story points out a number of facts underscoring the plight of freshwater snails, fish, and amphibians in North America; for instance, "Common freshwater species . . . are dying out five times faster than terrestrial animals and three times faster than marine mammals," and "Since 1900, at least 123 species have been lost from fresh water habitat in North America, and hundreds of additional species of fish, crayfish and amphibians are considered imperiled." It also presents an analysis of principal causes of freshwater species extinction, focusing on habitat modification (e.g., dams) and introduction of exotic species (e.g., zebra mussels) as the main culprits. The story notes that these extinctions will "greatly impact global biodiversity" due to the sheer abundance of North American freshwater species. The newswriter, however, concludes by emphasizing that "Ricciardi is confident that humans can modify their behavior to reverse the downward trend of freshwater species, 'without ruining the economy,'" and provides several examples of how people could improve the situation with relatively painless changes.

A brief ethical analysis of the story notes, as a point of departure, that its moral is clear: people should strive to halt the rapid extinction of North American freshwater species. How is this moral justified? Certainly, the facts presented on the alarming rates of extinction, and the ways these facts are contextualized by comparing them to rain forest extinctions and noting their impact on global biodiversity, play a major role in buttressing concern. Also, the analysis of causes of these extinctions points to humans as the responsible agent; the lead author's informed opinion that action can be taken without dire adverse economic impacts suggests that reasonable policies can be implemented to address these driving forces underlying extinctions. Further, this argument assumes that certain important values are reliably in place among the readers of the story and need not be defended here. For instance, the mere fact of extinction would not justify action unless biodiversity in general or freshwater species in particular were seen as valuable, whether for instrumental services to humans, for their own sake, or some combination of both. This story, then, assumes and builds on the great value many North Americans would presumably place on conserving biodiversity.

Which of these moral foundations are presented as controversial or uncertain in the story? None of them. There is only one possible reading: biodiversity is important, people have drastically reduced biodiversity in North American freshwater ecosystems, and thus something can and must be done soon. In short, this story stands on the solid rock of apparently clear incontrovertible facts and shared values in prescribing corrective environmental policy. Surely, one would assume, such a clear case is morally indisputable. What I argue, however, is that this is not so, even when there seems to be little controversy over the facts and values that justify a moral imperative to protect the environment.

The Environmental News Network example I found on my screen this morning is in these respects quite typical of popular environmental ethics. It admittedly contains elements that would make some philosophers squirm. Perhaps the most significant of these is the almost-too-quick leap from description to prescription in citing rates of extinction to justify normative action: the is–ought distinction – that one cannot derive an 'ought' exclusively from an 'is' – serves as a basic premise in much moral philosophy, but ENN's ought-based-on-is storyline is perhaps the most common in contemporary environmental rhetoric, testifying both to the powerful role of science in justifying concern and to the artificiality of separating facts from values in understanding environmental concern. Though these philosophical problems are important, I will not so much focus on them here as consider the challenges posed by a social constructivist perspective.

Enter Social Constructivism: Shifting Sands?

The social construction of nature thesis has been so horribly maligned by its opponents (based in part on relatively few clear defenses of the thesis) that I must try to correct some misinterpretations before I discuss its implications for environmental ethics. It is more than the relatively obvious notion that people have transformed nature in ways we often do not recognize: social constructivism does entail biophysical components in arguing that nature is often less "natural" than we would think, but its primary argument to me is an ideological epistemological one, concerning the knowledge propositions and related meanings we attribute to nature. It is decidedly not, however, simply a rehashing of classical idealism – the notion that nature does not exist except in our individual or collective minds – nor is social constructivism some notion that privileges ideas over action. Rather, social constructivism reminds us that any descriptive or normative pronouncement people make on nature is never innocent of its human origins. There certainly is a nature "out there," but we cannot say anything more about it without relying on human modes of perception, invoking human conceptual apparatus, involving human needs and desires – in short, when we speak of nature we speak of culture as well (Williams, 1980), of the meanings we attribute to nature.

The social constructivist perspective can enrich environmental ethics by reminding us that any human pronouncement on nature entails social as well as biophysical considerations, that there are, so to speak, important truths about the truths we invoke in our defense of certain normative positions. Thus, alarming biophysical facts and seemingly self-evident values concerning nature do not stand outside of a social context, and that context itself must be interrogated, even in what appears to be an incontrovertible case such as that we are considering here.

It is important to know, for instance, whether or not it is indeed true that freshwater species are going extinct at a rate five times greater than terrestrial animals, and that is what scientists like Dr. Ricciardi and others are for. It is also important to know whether or not the values people place on freshwater animals are philosophically robust. But each of the facts and values invoked to buttress the ENN story's position has further, social dimensions as well. As some examples: why is this story appearing at this time and why did it make ENN headlines? Have other studies on freshwater species gotten similar attention, or does the note of alarm the authors raise make it more appropriate to ENN's objectives? Why is the full range of potential social impacts connected with reducing human driving forces of freshwater species loss not treated in any greater detail in the story? Are we simply to trust Dr. Ricciardi's judgment that few adverse economic impacts would result? And what of the value assumption that freshwater species are worthy of our concern? In addition to the philosophical complexities of arguing the general value of biodiversity, isn't it a bit presumptuous to assume that the readers of this story will agree that all freshwater species are valuable? Indeed, whose values are being advanced as *the* values underscoring the story's moral argument? I am sure you can think of many more questions of this sort; they do not so much challenge head-on the integrity of these facts and values as critically situate them in a social context, and scrutinize that context in which meaning – in this case, the compelling case to reduce extinction of freshwater species – is socially produced and consumed.

Indeed, Ricciardi himself is engaged in a debate over meaning when he argues in the ENN story, "Conservation campaigns tend to cater to the public fixation on furry, feathery critters. No one would think of using a mussel or crayfish as a conservation poster child." Ricciardi is challenging the "warm fuzzy" notion of biodiversity conservation that spotlights animals most people are drawn to: my own work, for instance, has considered the northern spotted owl of the Pacific Northwest, surely an important icon of the environmental movement in the late 1980s and early 1990s (Proctor, 1998c). Ricciardi's statement does not challenge whether or not species such as the spotted owl are indeed imperiled, but rather questions the overemphasis on charismatic species in biodiversity conservation efforts, which unintentionally leaves less charming species unnoticed.

If the above were all there were to social constructivism, then the space for conflict between nonconstructivist and constructivist views would be minimal, as they address different domains, different questions. Yet social constructivism is more than just a way to examine the social context of facts and values; it also challenges, given their social origins, whether these facts and values are as solid and unassailable as they are portrayed by many environmentalists. Some terminology is necessary at this point (for fuller discussion see Proctor, 1998a, 1998b). The solid rock upon which conventional environmental ethics is commonly built involves particular philosophical stances about the facts and values used to justify environmental concern; collectively I will call the conventional position *realism*, to distinguish it from constructivism. Realism is the position that the world is real and knowable. Facts are not just made-up things that legitimately differ from person to person, but rather are claims about the real world that are true to the extent that they correspond to this reality. Though realism is primarily a position about facts, it also can be invoked to suggest a similar spirit toward values in that they are not just a matter of preference or context. Realism is thus antirelativistic to the core. What is critical in this realist moral justification of environmental concern is its decided tone of *universalism*: that these concerns are based on facts and values that hold true universally. Universalism is what affords conventional environmental ethics the security of standing on solid rock in its pronouncements, as they are based on what is true, not just true for environmentalists but true for – and hence morally binding upon – everyone.

Social constructivism, however, challenges the universalistic tone of this realist stance on facts and values. The constructivist challenge to value-universalism is probably the less controversial of the two, as most people are willing to admit at least to some extent that ways of valuing nature are of human origin and thus may legitimately differ from person to person or culture to culture. The challenge to facts may, however, be less intuitive and thus require further clarification, especially since facts play such a pivotal moral role in the ENN and similar stories. If one views assertions of scientific fact from a constructivist perspective as primarily a human creation, then a serious measure of doubt enters our consideration of whether or not these assertions map faithfully onto reality and are thus true irrespective of who is making or believing the truth-statement. We may wonder, for instance, how exactly Dr. Ricciardi and his co-investigators assembled the reams of data necessary to come to the conclusion that freshwater species are declining at an alarming rate. Clearly they had to *construct* (note the verb) this conclusion out of a vast quantity of other studies and observations, or if not, they had to do so based on extrapolations from certain limited studies. How detailed a model did they *construct* (here's that verb again) to estimate near-future trends in extinction? Given, for instance, their argument that extinctions have been primarily due to human driving forces, did they develop estimated rates of change in habitat modification and exotic species introduction in order to estimate rates of extinction, or (more likely) did they simply base their estimate upon historical trends of freshwater special extinctions? Indeed, in their paper Ricciardi and his co-investigator admit to their scientific peers that their method of estimating extinctions is "crude" (Ricciardi and Rasmussen, 1999: 1221); yet this admission is entirely absent in the ENN story.

Once examined more closely, then, a rather straightforward assertion of environmental 'fact' – such as high rates of freshwater species extinction – starts looking quite complex indeed, and it becomes apparent that those who constructed this knowledge had to make many crucial assumptions and simplifications along the way. Yet many, many environmental assertions are of this order of complexity. Imagine if the headline to the ENN daily news had read: "One freshwater species in one drainage has declined in last five years." That, certainly, is the kind of conclusion warranted by many empirical scientific studies, but it lacks a certain bang, a certain moral and political imperative to care. I would assert that the social constructivist distrust of facts-as-naive-representations-of-reality becomes more and more salient as these 'facts' take on a complex and composite nature – precisely the kinds of facts that motivate a good deal of contemporary environmental concern. Consider global warming, biodiversity loss, the ozone hole, acid rain, deforestation, desertification: these are each composite facts on an order of complexity much higher than that of the ENN story. Are they true? The social constructivist would have a hard time forgetting their human origins. Are they compelling? You bet they are, to a good number of environmental sympathizers. And thus lies the apparent threat social constructivism poses for conventional environmental ethics.

I do not wish to imply from what I have suggested above that there is necessarily some conspiracy out there in which certain powerful environmentally-leaning organizations are propagating fact and value soundbites as a way of raking in financial and political support. Indeed, there is nothing to me sinister about trying to simplify the vast complexity of environmental issues into more concise statements, such as that freshwater species are declining at a certain rate or that biodiversity is valuable. At some level this is an inherently human tendency of making meaning out of complexity. One way to think about this tendency involves the concept of narrative. As the environmental historian William Cronon has said:

> Narrative is the chief literary form that tries to find meaning in an overwhelmingly crowded and disordered chronological reality. . . . By writing stories of environmental change, we divide the causal relationships of an ecosystem with a theoretical razor that defines included and excluded, relevant and irrelevant, empowered and disempowered. . . . Narrative succeeds to the extent that it hides the discontinuities, ellipses, and contradictory experiences that would undermine the intended meaning of its story. (Cronon, 1992: 1349–50)

A narrative, in other words, is a story, not a fairytale devoid of real content but rather an intentional selection and construction of evidence to bring forth some meaning or moral.

Perhaps the moral to the ENN story is clear precisely because it *is* a story, a deliberately constructed narrative, the result of including certain facts and values and excluding countless others, of shaping the result into a notion of human–environment interaction with some profoundly disturbing moral implications.

Narrative allows us to say that the ENN story is not so much untrue as partially true, in that it is quite literally made up, that is, constructed and shaped – in this case by scientists and journalists working to form a meaningful narrative out of a very complex environmental issue. Universalism is a very important though unmentioned component of this narrative. Universalism helps us interpret the facts and values that provide its moral justification as being universally binding – that is, not just the facts and values that Dr. Ricciardi chooses to believe, but facts and values we *all* must listen to and heed.

Social constructivism's most serious charge, then, is to question – and perhaps legitimately so – the universalism underlying the ways conventional environmental ethics invokes facts and values in its defense. Yet if we discard universalism, what do environmentalists have in place of that secure basis? Constructivism seems to imply that we must replace the solid rock of universalism upon which much environmental concern is founded with the shifting sands of specific cases and multiple perspectives. This is the decidedly sub-universalist stance that facts and values are true and morally compelling only as understood in a certain context, a position we can call *particularism*.

How will environmentalists retain their distinctive voice on environmental problems if theirs is now one of many voices, each granted a measure of *de facto* legitimacy given the particularistic limitations of each claim to represent the truth? That, indeed, is a major worry among those who argue that recent theoretical perspectives on nature will wreak havoc on legitimate environmental concerns. The Pulitzer Prize-winning poet and self-avowed bioregionalist Gary Snyder recently put it this way in an article entitled "Nature as Seen From Kitkitdizze [his home] is No 'Social Construction'" (Snyder, 1996: 8):

> I must confess I'm getting a bit grumpy about the dumb arguments being put forth by high-paid intellectual types in which they are trying to knock Nature, knock the people who value Nature, and still come out smelling smart and progressive.... The current use of the "social construction" terminology ... is based in the logic of European science and the "enlight-enment" ... this socially constructed nature finally has no reality other than the quantification provided by economists and resource managers. This is indeed the ultimate commodification of Nature, done by supposedly advanced theorists, who prove to be simply the high end of the "wise use" movement. [For background on wise use, see Echeverria and Eby, 1994.]

The Perspective of Paradox

As noted above, not all of what goes under the banner of social constructivism directly contradicts conventional accounts, and so to some extent social constructivism simply enriches realist discussions of environmental ethics by including certain important social considerations. We could thus resolve differences between the two by the position of *separation*, which maintains that they do not really contradict each other so long as they keep to their own place. Let the scientist tell us about reality; let the constructivist tell us about the social conditions under which truths about reality have been produced. That way neither treads on the other's turf. This resolution assumes that the contradiction between the two positions obscures their relative independence – that, although there are points of disagreement, another look would suggest that the two actually address different concerns, and that if only they would remain in their separate domains there would be much less conflict.

Yet at another, more fundamental, level, what to many environmentalists is a truthful and compelling case of facts and values is to the constructivist just one of many possible accounts and hence not universally binding. So we are faced with a classic dilemma in which one position contradicts the other in quite fundamental ways. How are we to make sense of this conflict? I would like to discuss two common solutions, then proceed to a more paradoxical way of understanding it. The first is the position of *exclusion*: you choose the side you like best and you ignore, or work to disprove, the other. Say you believe that truth does really correspond to reality and all that social constructivist talk is beside the point. Maybe, for instance, you share the concerns expressed in the ENN story that freshwater species are disappearing at an alarming rate, and the implicit value statement that these species are worthy of our concern. You believe the account to be fully truthful and compelling, and you find any social constructivist challenge to this account to be unwarranted and possibly politically dangerous in that it may deflect the resultant call to action. The clear choice for you is to deny the legitimacy of social constructivism in this case, and maintain the purity of the conventional position. The opposite position can be maintained as well: suppose you are quite suspicious of the truth of the story in social constructivist fashion. The simplest thing to do is to deny the validity of a nonconstructivist basis for the ENN story and thus maintain the purity of your own position.

The exclusion position is what feeds many battle cries to rid the world of the enemy. It is hence enormously powerful politically, in large part due to its purity and simplicity. It is also intellectually and morally suspect, for what I hope to be obvious reasons: the realist view or and the constructivist view cannot and, I believe, should not be dispensed with so readily. This leads to a much different position of *compromise*, quite common in environmental rhetoric today. From the perspective of compromise, the conventional and social constructivist arguments should be viewed as two extremes, and as such can probably be reconciled if interpreted in less extreme ways. Somewhere nearer to the middle, the compromise position argues, lies a place where a milder version of each can meet. In the case of the ENN story, for instance, consider an account that admits that the story was constructed by scientists but emphasizes that they used facts, not made-up pseudo-evidence, to build their case.

The compromise position makes a good deal of pragmatic sense in the political arena of environmental debate, where polar opinions are more the rule than the exception. It speaks to an attempt to recognize what is worthy in two contradictory positions while trying to reconcile them nonetheless. Yet it does so in many cases by necessarily diluting each, reducing them to at best a weakened version and at worst a mere shadow of their core argument. This is one reason compromise is so hard to attain in many cases of environmental conflict.

My work on conflicts over nature has suggested another possible way to understand this contradiction: *paradox* (Proctor, 1998a). A paradox is a contradiction that is nonetheless true, i.e., a contradiction whose truth resides in the paradox and is not revealed by resolving it in some way. If the exclusion position resolves contradiction by tossing out one side and the compromise position dilutes both elements of a contradiction to the point where they meet somewhere in the middle, paradox suggests that these modes of resolution lose important truths captured best in the tension that exists in a contradiction. The paradoxical 'resolution' of the realist–constructivist contradiction thus lies not in choosing sides nor in searching for some elusive balance, but rather in admitting, in true paradoxical fashion, that both sides are basically correct as they stand yet neither is fully correct without the other. It is thus a resolution that defies resolution. Paradox suggests that many important truths have their shadow, and that they and their shadow constitute a more whole – though certainly also a more tense and twisted – truth.

Paradox may sound like so much rhetoric to the reader, but I am convinced that we live with paradox all the time; indeed, paradox is resolved not in theory or concept but in practice. Each of us can probably recite our own list: I recall, for instance, how much I struggle with understanding the ways in which joy and pain are interwoven, the contradictory virtues of discipline and abandon, my desire to connect with others yet retain my distinctive voice, and the beauty and struggle of relationships, where I and my partner seek to understand the tensions that both draw us together and send us apart. Being an academic, I try to think my way through problems, but I simply cannot in these cases; I can only live my way through them. Indeed, the Greek *paradoxos*, a compound of *para* (beyond) and *doxa* (opinion; from *dokein* (to think), roughly means 'conflicting with expectation,' and suggests the futility of conceptually resolving paradox.

Many apparent paradoxes are, however, false paradoxes, and must be labeled as such if we are to retain some dignity to the concept of paradox. Indeed, one of the earliest philosophical uses of paradox was by the fifth-century BCE philosopher Zeno as a logical strategy of proving the soundness of his master Parmenides' teachings by pointing out the absurdities – or false paradoxes – that would result from following premises contrary to those of Parmenides. Thus the Achilles paradox, for example, claimed that a slower runner will never be passed by the faster runner in a race as a means of defending Parmenides' doctrine of the unreality of motion.

We encounter false paradoxes in our lives all the time, and these too expose inconsistencies in our assumptions. Yesterday, for instance, I was sure it was going to be a cold day because the morning was cool, but I ended up sweltering in my heavy clothes as the heat rose through the afternoon. How can a cool morning end up a hot day? Well, ask any meteorologist and you will hear all about low humidity and descending air masses warming up and so forth; the bottom line – which most inhabitants of arid areas know well – is that there is no necessary contradiction at all between waking up to a cool morning and sweating through a hot day. To what extent, then, is the apparent contradiction between realist and constructivist views of nature not a contradiction at all? The separation argument noted above would maintain that contradiction can be removed if only the two views on nature would restrict themselves to their appropriate domains; but this would necessitate avoidance of the fundamental constructivist critique of universalist elements inherent in the conventional view. No, from what I see the contradiction between the two is real and volatile, as statements like that of Gary Snyder noted above and recent anticonstructivist works like *Reinventing Nature? Reponses to Postmodern Decon-struction* attest (Soulé and Lease, 1995; for discussion see Proctor, 1998b).

What light does paradox cast on the ENN story? Its perspective concerns not so much the details as the moral that arises from it. The conventional account cries out for our moral attention: North American freshwater species need our conservation efforts immediately! The constructivist critique challenges the universalistic assumptions in how facts and values were invoked to arrive at this moral. Paradox honors the truth in both of these claims, and in so doing acknowledges the necessary tension between universalism and particularism in the ways we justify our environmental concerns. Let us listen to those who tell us that we must act to save freshwater species, says the perspective of paradox; they have at some level a legitimate and universally binding claim on reality. And at the same time let us be prepared to challenge the constructedness of their claims, and the constructedness of our own counterclaims, in the spirit of particularistic limitation. The environmental ethic underlying the ENN story must be modified to embrace both universalistic confidence – the ability to speak *the* truth and willingness to trust those who claim to do so – and particularistic critique and humility – the ability to question the context of truths we hear and speak. If paradox seems to steal the thunder from the moral bang of the ENN story by validating constructivist critiques, it however refuses to honor some flip-flop from realism to constructivism, which – among more theoretical implications – may unfortunately neglect the plight of freshwater animals in so doing.

Paradox also implies that none of us can embody the 'whole truth'; each of us must admit our shadow but cannot become a shadowless being due precisely to the specificities of our lives and truths. I cannot ask Dr. Ricciardi, for instance, to take constructivism fully into consideration in his realist account of North American freshwater fauna, because to do so he may risk diluting what he has to say. But I can ask him to respect the integrity of the constructivist critique at the same time he speaks his realist truths. The tension between Dr. Ricciardi and his constructivist (indeed, constructed! I know of none so far) critics is, paradox argues, unavoidable, and not resolved by exclusion, compromise, or separation.

Paradox yields to compromise and other inclusive methods of resolving contradiction when the question turns to policy, as indeed we cannot simultaneously decide to embrace and shun corrective policy for North American freshwater fauna. Yes, some compromise is needed; no one has an inviolable claim to the truth; we must listen to each other. Yet we can and must speak also: Dr. Ricciardi has a legitimate role to play given his training and experience. And his is not the final word. At the same time environmentalists negotiate with other interests in securing adequate policy for protection of North American freshwater ecosystems, they must respect that theirs is not the full truth, that the full truth is nowhere to be found, but perhaps best represented in the paradoxical tensions that accompany struggles over what is true and right.

Larger Implications

Poet Robert Frost once said, "We dance around a ring and suppose, but the Secret sits in the middle and knows" (Frost, 1942: 46). In a recent book, Chet Raymo paints a word-picture of knowledge as an ever-increasing island in a sea of inexhaustible mystery (Raymo, 1998: 46ff.) Both speak to me of our own particularistic limitations in the search for universalism. We will never know the complete truth that sits in the middle; the island of knowledge will never fill the sea. But we must not abandon what we believe we do know; we must not stop dancing with others (I am thinking here of realists and constructivists, for instance) around that ring either. We yearn for an environmental ethics that speaks out of our own particular experiences yet has something to say beyond those particulars as well. We want to speak to what is true and morally compelling in the case of North American freshwater fauna and other forms of nonhuman nature with whom we share life. Paradox reminds us that – figuratively speaking – the Secret, the mystery, will always be with us in that quest.

To me, then, social constructivism leads not so much to an abandonment of realism in environmental ethics as an embrace of the paradox that the realist *and* the constructivist have something important to say, though their positions will never be blended. Paradox asks us to admit our shadows and look for the shadows in others while not expecting that any of can live perfectly shadowless lives in merging all positions with our own. Paradox is a hard concept to expect everyone to acknowledge, yet minimally we can ask that everyone respect each other's role in helping define what is true and right. There must, of course, be rules for these negotiations over meaning, for which different formulations of social interaction have been proposed and anyone familiar with Habermas and his critics (e.g., Habermas, 1979; Benhabib, 1996) knows what kind of theoretical excursion that would be, so I can't fully discuss this here.

Paradox thus inspires a dual spirit of confidence and humility in making moral proclamations concerning the environment, and in so doing responds to some of the major historical themes of our times. Underlying the ENN story is the modernist desire for universalism (though modernism includes many contradictions in this regard – see Berman, 1982; Habermas, 1987). This desire furthered the role of science as the preferred vehicle for obtaining truth, and partially explains the profoundly misguided assumption that Western modes of thought and practice are typical (hence universal) among the peoples of this planet. Underlying the constructivist critique of the ENN story lies something of the postmodernist distrust for universally binding grand narratives, for sweeping statements of fact and value (Lyotard, 1984; Lyotard et al., 1993; Harvey, 1989).

As modernists struggle for universals, so postmodernists struggle for particulars, and both, I feel, have their role to play, yet neither will play their role well without being held in paradoxical tension by their counterpart. Indeed, ethics finds rich soil in this tense terrain: as but one of many examples that come to mind, I think of differences between impartial conceptions of ethics such as social justice, and avowedly partial conceptions of ethics such as the feminist ethics of care (see Smith, 1998, for a geographically based discussion). To base environmental ethics on anything less than the modernist/postmodernist tension is to close the doors of environmental concern to some of the most important intellectual pulses beating in our collective hearts. Environmental concern can certainly thrive in this context; we will not lose our ability to speak our truths. Yet perhaps we will all be reminded to listen as well.

Further Reading

For a more in-depth discussion of the issues raised here see Proctor (1998a) and the essays in Proctor and Smith (1999).

References

Benhabib, S. (ed.) (1996). *Democracy and Difference.* Princeton, NJ: Princeton University Press.

Berman, M. (1982). *All That is Solid Melts into Air.* New York: Simon and Schuster.

Botzler, R. G. and Armstrong, S. J. (1998). *Environmental Ethics.* Boston: McGraw-Hill.

Cronon, W. (1992). A Place for Stories: Nature, History, and Narrative. *Journal of American History*, 78: 1347–76.

Echeverria, J. and Eby R. B. (eds.) (1994). *Let the People Judge: Wise Use and the Private Property Rights Movement.* Washington, DC: Island Press.

Frost, R. (1942). *A Witness Tree.* New York: H. Holt and Company.

Habermas, J. (1979). *Communication and the Evolution of Society.* Boston: Beacon Press.

Habermas, J. (1987). *The Philosophical Discourse of Modernity.* Cambridge, Mass.: MIT Press.

Harvey, D. (1989). *The Condition of Postmodernity.* Oxford: Blackwell.

Lyotard, J.-F. (1984). *The Postmodern Condition.* Minneapolis: University of Minnesota Press.

Lyotard, J.-F., Harvey, R., and Roberts, M. S. (1993). *Toward the Postmodern.* Atlantic Highlands, NJ: Humanities Press.

Pojman, L. P. (1998). *Environmental Ethics.* Belmont, Calif.: Wadsworth.

Proctor, J. D. (1998a). Geography, Paradox, and Environmental Ethics. *Progress in Human Geography*, 22; 234–55.

Proctor, J. D. (1998b). The Social Construction of Nature. *Annals of the Association of American Geographers*, 88: 352–76.

Proctor, J. D. (1998c). The Spotted Owl and the Moral Landscape of the Pacific Northwest. In J. Emel and J.

Wolch (eds.) *Animal Geographies.* London: Verso, 191–217.

Proctor, J. and Smith, D. M. (1999). *Geography and Ethics.* London: Routledge.

Raymo, C. (1998). *Skeptics and True Believers.* New York: Walker and Co.

Ricciardi, A. and Rasmussen, J. B. (1999). Extinction Rates of North American Freshwater Fauna. *Conservation Biology*, 13: 1220–2.

Smith, D. M. (1998). How Far Should We Care? On the Spatial Scope of Beneficence. *Progress in Human Geography*, 22: 15–38.

Snyder, G. (1996). Nature as Seen from Kitkitdizze is No "Social Construction." *Wild Earth*, 6: 8–9.

Soulé, M. E. and Lease, G. (eds.) (1995). *Reinventing Nature? Responses to Postmodern Deconstruction.* Washington, DC: Island Press.

Williams, R. (1980). Ideas of Nature. In *Problems in Materialism and Culture.* London: Verso, 67–85.

Index

NOTE: Page numbers in italic represent information in a figure.